Exploring the Nature of Law

Exploring the Nature of Law

Thomistic Juridical Realism and the Elements of Law's Ontology

Petar Popović

Foreword by Kevin C. Walsh

The Catholic University of America Press
Washington, D.C.

The paper used in this publication meets the minimum requirements of American National Standards for Information Science—Permanence of Paper for Printed Library Materials, ANSI Z39.48-1992.
∞

Cataloging-in-Publication Data is available from the Library of Congress

ISBN: 978-0-8132-4023-7
eISBN: 978-0-8132-4024-4

Contents

Foreword

KEVIN C. WALSH

To understand law more fully, one needs to become a certain kind of person, someone disposed toward reality in a certain kind of way. Our most conducive disposition for this purpose is one of openness—being open to accept that we are caught up in an ordered universe, and that this ordering we inhabit includes obligations owed in justice as an aspect of our social human nature.

This personal disposition presupposed by Thomistic juridical realism is not embraced by all. Nor is it required by the prevailing account of what is necessary for a complete understanding of law in contemporary Anglophone philosophy of law. The American legal philosopher Brian Leiter, for instance, has contended that "[t]he concept of law is the concept of an artifact, that is, something that necessarily owes its existence to human activities intended to create that artifact.... Those who might want to deny that law is an artifact concept are not my concern here; the extravagance of their metaphysical commitments would, I suspect, be a subject for psychological, not philosophical investigation."[1]

Leiter's outlook on juridical reality, too, is part of the world in which we live. This is the world for which Petar Popović has authored this formidable—and formidably titled—book, *Exploring the Nature of Law: Thomistic Juridical Realism and the Elements of Law's Ontology.* Some law is an artifact, Popović readily affirms (who

1. Brian Leiter, "The Demarcation Problem in Jurisprudence: A New Case for Scepticism." *Oxford Journal of Legal Studies* 31, no. 4 (2011): 666.

would deny it?), but he contends that not all law necessarily owes its existence to human activities intended to create that artifact.

Popović critiques and upgrades the now-dominant position that all law is humanly posited law. That places him in rare company today, but in close communion with many jurisprudential minds from the past. Popović presents the juridical realism he proposes as a retrieval of the thought of St. Thomas Aquinas. His commitment to proceeding in this way arises out of conviction that "Aquinas's theses on the ontology of law denote the most accurate understanding of the phenomenon that we call law." This is not exegesis for its own sake, though, or even for the sake of expounding Aquinas's systematic thought more generally. Popović engages in reasoned elaboration of Aquinas's jurisprudence in service of speculative truth. He disclaims "some quasi-utopian project of restoring the classical meaning of law understood as *ius* ... to the detriment of that which is valid in postclassical and contemporary legal-philosophical approaches, motivated by some kind of nostalgia for premodern scholarly and cultural contexts." His Thomism reflects, instead, the more modest authorial outlook that "a contemporary reading of Aquinas may indeed contribute to an improved understanding of our present-day legal-philosophical analyses."

What Thomistic viewpoint does Popović identify for understanding "what law is"? The answer, in a word, is "justice." Popović sets out to establish that, for Aquinas, "justice is the starting point for elucidating law, and ... all law is justice-based." He follows Aquinas in adopting the definition of justice from the Roman jurist Ulpian, who described this virtue as the constant and perpetual will to render to each person his or her *ius*. This is the definition that Popović has in mind in writing that "[w]hen we talk about 'the nature of law,' 'the concept of law,' and so forth, we are referring to a phenomenon Aquinas and other proponents of classical juridical realism called *ius*."

The focal meaning of *ius* for Thomistic juridical realism is the object of justice, the thing that is rendered from one person to another in an act of justice. If one were to translate into English the word "*ius*" from Ulpian's formulation of the virtue of justice, "law" would not be one of the top-three best choices. Better translations would be "due," or "right," or "own," probably in that order. Popović nevertheless—and for good and sufficient reasons that he justifies throughout the book—develops his exploration of the ontology of law exegetically, systematically, and speculatively by reference to the ontology of *ius*.

Where does this leave *lex*? This is the term that corresponds most closely with the dominant understanding of "law" in Anglophone legal philosophy, and "[t]he central argument of this book is that Aquinas referred to the reality that lawyers and legal officials today call 'law' by using the term *ius*, which is broader than the term *lex*." On Popović's rendering of the ontology of law, the discourse of *lex* is "englobed" by *ius*. We encounter *lex* as a cause through its effects in the juridical domain—the domain of *ius*, object of justice. To explain this relationship between *ius* and *lex* more precisely, Popović moves from Latin terminology to Greek philosophy, namely Aristotle's four causes. According to Popović's analysis of *ius* within this metaphysical framework, *lex* is understood to give rise to *ius* as an efficient cause.

All of this may seem rather philosophically laden. That's because it is. This is a work of general jurisprudence, or "the philosophy of philosophy of law." It aims at and achieves theoretical clarity and precision in telling the truth about law. By synthesizing Thomistic juridical realism and placing it in dialogue with a wide range of positions in general jurisprudence, Popović redraws the field's map and brings out the attractiveness of Aquinas's juridical realism as a live option for jurists today.

Judging this book by its cover—or maybe just by pausing over its two-part title—it is fair to estimate that at least some potential readers will find themselves daunted by the prospect of "Exploring the Nature of Law" through study of "Thomistic Juridical Realism and the Elements of Law's Ontology." But while Popović's exploration of the nature of law is not for the fainthearted, the book is inviting and abuzz with the author's inquiring energy. "Questions that continue to puzzle legal philosophers or issues on which there seems to be no permanent consensus," he writes, "may be thought of as the dynamos of legal philosophy."

On May 8, 2025, as this book was nearing publication, the College of Cardinals in conclave elected a new Pope. The man they chose, Cardinal Robert Francis Prevost, elected the regnal name Pope Leo XIV. "There are different reasons for this," he explained in a formal meeting with the College of Cardinals two days later, "but mainly because Pope Leo XIII in his historical encyclical *Rerum Novarum* addressed the social question in the context of the first great industrial revolution."[2] Pointing to technological developments in particular, Pope Leo XIV stated that "[i]n our own day, the Church offers to everyone the treasury of her social teaching in response to another industrial revolution and to developments in the field of artificial intelligence that pose new challenges for the defense of human dignity, justice and labor."[3] These challenges identified by Pope Leo XIV relate directly to how we know, how we work, and what kinds of persons we are becoming through our actions. Such matters are as urgent for those who work in the field of law as for those who play other parts in the economy, government, and culture.

In a 2024 lecture introducing Thomistic juridical realism at The Catholic University of America, Popović noted that "[w]e are used to thinking about law as something that puts the acting person, usually the self, ourselves, at the center of the legal world."[4] But Thomistic juridical realism calls for a different stance, he explained: "For Aquinas, law is something that essentially belongs to another person, something other-directed, radically altruistic, to the point where we could say that it is hard for him to understand law except by putting the other person to whom something is owed, as a matter

2. Francesca Merlo, "Pope Leo XIV to Cardinals: Church Must Respond to Digital Revolution," *Vatican News* (May 10, 2025), available at https://www.vaticannews.va/en/pope/news/2025-05/pope-leo-xiv-addresses-cardinals-10-may-2025-vatican.html

3. Leo XIV, Address to the College of Cardinals, May 10, 2025, https://www.vatican.va/content/leo-xiv/en/speeches/2025/may/documents/20250510-collegio-cardinalizio.html

4. Petar Popovic, "Thomistic Juridical Realism: An Introduction," The Catholic University of America (March 21, 2024), transcript *available at*: https://cit.catholic.edu/thomistic-juridical-realism-an-introduction-transcript/.

of justice, at the center of the juridical world."[5] This is the kind of personal disposition toward what is due in justice that we need to take on if we are to more fully understand the nature of law. It is this second-person stance that Popović refers to when he writes that "Thomistic juridical realism puts a pattern for personal agency at the very basis of the phenomenon of law, and this pattern may be referred to as virtue jurisprudence.... [T]he distinctiveness of justice for human agency, arising from its being essentially a virtue, is built into the very nature of law."

In an 1887 letter to Cardinal James Gibbons commending the proposed establishment of the Catholic University of America, Pope Leo XIII instructed that "the system of philosophy should be shaped according to the noble wisdom of the ancients, and follow with docile zeal in the footsteps of the Angelic Doctor."[6] But what's the use of studying an approach to general jurisprudence that was developed initially in the thirteenth century, one might ask, an approach that was almost entirely eclipsed in later centuries, and has only been recovered in recent decades? In answering those asking about the practical utility of Thomistic juridical realism today, one Leonine response is recourse to *Rerum Novarum*: "Nothing is more useful than to look upon the world as it really is."[7]

5. Popovic, "Thomistic Juridical Realism," March 21, 2024.

6. Letter from Pope Leo XIII to Cardinal James Gibbons (Apr. 10, 1887) (on file with the Catholic University of America).

7. Leo XIII, Enyclical Letter *Rerum novarum*, May 15, 1891, in *Acta Sanctae Sedis* 23 (1890–1891): 648; cf. F. Russell Hittinger, "Three Necessary Societies," in *On the Dignity of Society: Catholic Social Teaching and Natural Law* (The Catholic University of America Press, 2024), 98:

Leo issued no Syllabus of Errors. Instead, he asked a question that was at once more philosophical and more practical: How do we *civilize* this situation? What is our proposal for social order? What can we work with in social matters, and how do we measure what's been lost and what might be regained? He remarked: "Nothing is more useful than to look upon the world as it really is." The paradigm of Catholic social teaching formulated by Leo resisted the temptation to utopianism, so seldom resisted elsewhere in the nineteenth and twentieth centuries. The Leonine paradigm for social analysis was simple and sturdy. It was a neo-Aristotelian effort to put the "spirits" of the age into perennial wineskins.

Abbreviations

Dig.	*The Digest of Justinian*
Nic. Eth.	Aristotle, *Nicomachean Ethics*
Sent. Eth.	Thomas Aquinas, *Sententia Libri Ethicorum*
ST	Thomas Aquinas, *Summa Theologiae*

Exploring the Nature of Law

Introduction

This is a book about the nature of the reality or phenomenon referred to as "law" not only by lawyers and legal officials but also by those living under law to the extent that they conceptualize the realm of "law" in a specifically jurisprudential or lawyerly sense, that is, as something sufficiently distinguishable from other phenomena.

There are several conceptions circulating in legal theory of what law is, that is, plural comprehensive and articulate accounts of law's essential nature. This multiplicity of accounts is understandable, to some extent, since each developed legal-philosophical conception or theory of the nature of law focuses on some essential properties of this nature rather than on others, or it provides a different account of what its author(s) consider(s) to be an exhaustive list of such properties. In addition, a conception of law's nature denotes an attempt to understand the essence of the juridical phenomenon, and even the most metaphysically ambitious theory of what law is should be able to admit that, in the words of the legal philosopher Brian Bix, it is, at least to some degree, "a poor substitute for the real thing, or (to change the metaphor) a smoky glass through which to view our real object of interest."[1] In other words, a conception of the essential features of law is often to some extent different from its object, the nature of law, and it is highly likely that however close it may come to elucidating law's actual nature, it is in at least some of its aspects insufficient or approximate.

There is something promising about the multiplicity of legal-philosophical conceptions of law's nature, even if individual

1. Brian H. Bix, "Joseph Raz and Conceptual Analysis," *APA Newsletter on Philosophy of Law* 6, no. 2 (2007): 2.

conceptions of law are, indeed, sometimes mutually irreconcilable. Perhaps the difference in emphases of these divergent conceptions may assist authors of competing accounts of law's nature, for example, by inviting them to verify whether they have sufficiently considered and addressed the reasons for why some alternative theory of law opts for different emphases deemed central regarding the properties of law. In this sense, I agree with Julie Dickson that law is a "multi-faceted and complex phenomenon, different aspects of which can be illuminated from different theoretical directions, at different times, and for different reasons."[2] And I also share Dickson's forward-looking and optimistic view about the plurality of lines of inquiry concerning law's nature, which is in principle open to "exploring mutual complementarities between such lines of inquiry."[3]

Regardless of the circumstance that, in my opinion, some or even most alternative conceptions of law's nature do not adequately capture that nature, on account of either excessive or insufficient emphases on certain essential features of law, I think that most explanatory conceptions of law correctly grasp that some of these emphases are important and necessary (or that they are not so central so as to exclude other relevant emphases) for understanding law's essence.

This book approaches law as, indeed, a complex phenomenon, but I cannot claim to have offered here a definitive conception of law's nature, to which nothing could be added, or which would not profit from some other emphases or explanatory directions. For example, given the widespread allure of both the positivist and the natural-law emphasis on the importance of humanly posited law for conceptualizing the juridical phenomenon, there must be something that such legal-philosophical emphasis correctly captures about the nature of law and the significance of the positivity of law for grasping

2. Julie Dickson, *Elucidating Law* (Oxford University Press, 2022), 2. For another description of the plurality of legal-philosophical conceptions of law, see Natalie Stoljar, "What Do We Want Law to Be? Philosophical Analysis and the Concept of Law," in *Philosophical Foundations of the Nature of Law*, ed. Wil Waluchow and Stefan Sciaraffa (Oxford University Press, 2013), 230–53.

3. Dickson, *Elucidating Law*, 58.

that nature. I disagree with the level of intensity of a positivistic emphasis on law's positivity and social facticity, and in this sense, I think that there is also much to be learned from the shortcomings of legal positivism as a theory about the nature of law. But I certainly think that failing to give due weight to the emphasis on the importance of law's positivity would be counterproductive for any legal-philosophical conception of law.[4]

Despite the fact of plurality of legal-philosophical conceptions of law in legal theory, I am optimistic about the very prospect of exploring the nature of law. That is, I maintain that law has a nature and that it is possible to explore and describe this unique nature in an intelligible and even reasonably detailed fashion. Hence, I side with those legal philosophers who argue that the study of law's nature is promising, achievable, and rewarding—perhaps even central—for both theorizing about law and for its everyday practice,[5] rather than with those who deem the enterprise of exploring law's nature pointless or, at best, distracting.[6]

4. Throughout the introduction, I refer to "legal-philosophical conceptions of law" rather than to "concepts of law" to highlight that my focus is primarily on well-developed accounts of the individuating features of law's nature (i.e., legal-philosophical conceptions) and on the ways in which these accounts influence potentially less developed or even (to various degrees) defective "concepts of law" shared by legal officials or members of a community under law. For the general difference between "conceptions" and "concepts" in philosophical analysis, see Maite Ezcurdia, "The Concept—Content Distinction," *Philosophical Issues* 9 (1998): 187–92. For the claim that "having a concept" of something—for example, of law—is "compatible with a shallow and defective understanding of its essential features, and of the nature of what it is a concept of," while a philosophical explanation "aims at improving the understanding of the concept" for people who use that concept, see Joseph Raz, "Two Views of the Nature of the Theory of Law: A Partial Comparison," in *Between Authority and Interpretation: On the Theory of Law and Practical Reason* (Oxford University Press, 2009), 55–56.

5. Regardless of different emphases in their respective conceptions of what law is, such optimism is shared and professed, for example, by following authors: Joseph Raz, "Can There Be a Theory of Law?" in *Between Authority and Interpretation*, 17–46; Michael Giudice, *Understanding the Nature of Law: A Case for Constructive Conceptual Explanation* (Edward Elgar, 2015), 49–55, 106–9; Dickson, *Elucidating Law*, 15–24, 52–53.

6. See, for example, Brian Leiter, "The Demarcation Problem in Jurisprudence: A New Case for Scepticism," *Oxford Journal of Legal Studies* 31, no. 4 (2011): 669–70; Frederick Schauer, "On the Nature of the Nature of Law," *Archiv für Rechts- und Sozialphilosophie* 98, no. 4 (2012): 458, 462, 467; Dan Priel, "The Misguided Search for the Nature of Law,"

This book thus belongs to the legal-philosophical field dedicated to the study of the nature of law, that is, to the most basic or abstract part of the philosophy of law, which is sometimes referred to as "the philosophy of philosophy of law"[7] or "general jurisprudence."[8] However, the aim of the book is not to explore and defend the general claim that law has a nature, and that this nature can be grasped by legal philosophers, legal officials, or members of a community who live under law. I take these claims for granted. Rather, the scope of the present research is to explore the essential features of law's nature, that is, all those realities that pertain to law's essence, the properties that make law into what it is.

The field of research dedicated to the identification and description of the essential properties of the reality or of the phenomenon of law is sometimes labeled "the ontology of law." Ontology, in general, is the study of "being *qua* being, i.e., of the most general and necessary characteristics that anything must have in order to count as a being, an entity (*ens*)."[9] The ontological problem in legal philosophy concerns the question "what is law?" and, according to Corrado Roversi, this question is ambiguous since it regards two distinct but interrelated problems. The first way to understand the "what is law" question is to see it pointing to the problem of what encompasses the domain of law: "the problem of what sorts of things or facts ought to be considered law and what their makeup or structure is." Roversi immediately adds that the second problem revolves

---

Osgoode Legal Studies Research Paper No. 34, August 13, 2015, accessed October 29, 2024, https://dx.doi.org/10.2139/ssrn.2642461; and Imer B. Flores, "The Problem about the Nature of Law vis-à-vis Legal Rationality Revisited: Towards an Integrative Jurisprudence," in *Philosophical Foundations of the Nature of Law*, 103.

7. For example, Leslie Green gave the subtitle "A Philosophy of Legal Philosophy" to the introductory chapter of his collection of essays on general jurisprudence. See Leslie Green, introduction, in *The Germ of Justice: Essays in General Jurisprudence* (Oxford University Press, 2023), 1–27.

8. See, for example, Leslie Green, "General Jurisprudence: A 25th Anniversary Essay," *Oxford Journal of Legal Studies* 25, no. 4 (2005): 565–80; Brian Tamanaha, "What Is 'General' Jurisprudence? A Critique of Universalistic Claims by Philosophical Concepts of Law," *Transnational Legal Theory* 2, no. 3 (2011): 287–308.

9. Panayot Butchvarov, "Metaphysics," in *The Cambridge Dictionary of Philosophy*, ed. Robert Audi, 3rd ed. (Cambridge University Press, 2015), 662.

around the issue of "what is distinctive about law, or what marks it out as specifically legal."[10]

In this book, I seek to provide answers to both of these ontological problems of the phenomenon of law. I start with the second ontological problem, that is, with the question of what is distinctive about law, which individuating features enable us to distinguish the juridical domain and the phenomenon of law from other domains and phenomena. In other words, I explore the following question: which properties may be seen to be characteristic of law, at the level of its essential nature? With the criteria reached by answering that question, I then proceed to resolve the first ontological problem: identifying the sorts of things or realities to be considered law. Neil MacCormick referred to this ontological problem of general jurisprudence in terms of the following question: "Where in the world does law belong?"[11] Throughout the book, this procedure of law-identification is presented as an answer to another formulation of the same question: "What is law in?" Said differently, in which things or realities can we find law, or which things or realities may be considered to instantiate the phenomenon of law, under the relevant conditions or circumstances?

As I will show, the approach to understanding law's nature that can be labeled "Thomistic juridical realism"—and which is basically a development of Thomas Aquinas's ideas of what law is, adapted for contemporary purposes and contexts—may be categorized as a version of a natural-law theory of law. It is important to highlight that a plurality of explanatory conceptions of the nature of law can also be found in the "extended" family of natural-law theories of law, as well as in the "nuclear" family of Thomist versions of natural-law theories of law. The theory of law's nature advanced by Thomistic juridical realism is somewhat different from comparable accounts

10. See Corrado Roversi, "Ontology of Law," in *Encyclopedia of the Philosophy of Law and Social Philosophy*, ed. Mortimer Sellers and Stephan Kirste (Springer, 2018), accessed April 16, 2024, https://doi.org/10.1007/978-94-007-6730-0_59-1.

11. Neil MacCormick, foreword, in *Controversies about Law's Ontology*, ed. Neil MacCormick and Paul Amselek (Edinburgh University Press, 1991), vii.

of what law is in the various branches of the family tree of a natural-law theory of law. This does not mean that the arguments in this book are irreconcilable to these natural law accounts of law's nature. Quite the contrary. But the reader should be aware that what I think is Aquinas's position on the nature of law is to some extent different—more precisely, *broader*—than what other comparable natural law approaches consider to be the nature of law, or what they believe is Aquinas's actual position regarding law's nature.

The default natural law position regarding law's nature is that the ontology of law is dual: law is necessarily both humanly posited and evaluative (or normative) according to some standards of what constitutes human individual and common good.[12] More will be said about this default position throughout the book. Thomistic juridical realism welcomes and accommodates this position, but it also furthers and broadens it into an even more complex account of the nature of law. While the default natural law position argues that whatever else law is, it is always and necessarily a humanly posited *lex* (to use Aquinas's Latin word for a legal norm), in my reading of Aquinas's stance on the nature of the juridical phenomenon, what lawyers refer to as law is conveyed by a broader term, *ius*, which includes the entire legally relevant conceptual range of the term *lex*, wrapping it in a wider framework. To put this in the simplest possible way, I hold that law indeed has a unique nature, which can be grasped and explored, and that according to that nature, law is not just one thing (e.g., only humanly posited law or only natural law), or even only two things (as the supporters of law's dual nature advocate) but rather a complex whole that includes these two things—humanly posited legal norms and the relevant evaluative arguments

12. See, for example, Jonathan Crowe, *Natural Law and the Nature of Law* (Cambridge University Press, 2019), vii, 8, 138, 146, 156, 180–81; John Finnis, "The Nature of Law," in *The Cambridge Companion to the Philosophy of Law*, ed. John Tasioulas (Cambridge University Press, 2020), 38–58; and Daniel Mark, *The Nature of Law: Authority, Obligation, and the Common Good* (University of Notre Dame Press, 2024), 1–41, 185–278. For the claim that the "dual nature of law" thesis can be shown to be neutral with respect to the dispute between legal positivism and nonpositivism, and thus endorsed by both approaches to understanding law's nature, see Stefano Bertea, "The Dual Nature Thesis as a Cornerstone of Jurisprudence," *The American Journal of Jurisprudence* 67, no. 1 (2022): 57–82.

somehow grounded in human individual and common good—together with some other relevant things, realities, and perspectives.

Hence, the main arguments of this book may be to some degree surprising and novel even to Thomist legal philosophers. And these arguments will probably be challenging to the supporters of other versions of nonpositivism, as well as to legal positivists. But, again, even if readers will remain unconvinced that the conception of law's ontology presented in this book corresponds to the actual nature of law (if they think that such a nature exists at all), they may still find that some emphases advanced in these pages are worth pursuing in legal philosophy and legal practice.

Chapter 1

Identifying an Alternative Persistent Question for Understanding the Ontology of Law

The "Old" Persistent Question: Morality in Law

Questions that continue to puzzle legal philosophers or issues on which there seems to be no permanent consensus among these scholars may be thought of as the dynamos of legal philosophy, the catalysts of a better and more profound understanding of the principal object of this discipline, namely, the nature or the essence of law. In his 1961 seminal book *The Concept of Law*, which is usually considered as marking a new starting point in contemporary legal-philosophical analysis, H. L. A. Hart identified some of these persistent questions and then dedicated the rest of the book to elucidating answers to them. Each persistent question in that book, or in the works of other legal philosophers, presents an opportunity to better understand what law is. Even the most basic question regarding the ontology of law—namely, the question "What is law?"—continues to be a persistent question in legal theory, since we still do not seem to have a complete, definitive answer to that question apt to generate a broad consensus among legal scholars and practicing lawyers.

Perhaps the most intriguing and debated persistent question regarding law's ontology concerns the relationship between law and morality, and at least part of its allure consists in the conviction that different answers to this question allow us to successfully categorize their authors as either legal positivists or as proponents of a natural-law theory of law. However, it seems that this "promising" feature of this persistent question ultimately fails to establish a clear divide between positivists and natural-law proponents. It is important to understand the causes of this failure, since legal scholars and practitioners of law are used to approaching the question of "What is law?" by assuming the existence of some essential discord between legal positivism and a natural-law theory of law.

In recent decades, it has become increasingly difficult to grasp the central tenets of legal positivism as well as the essential features of a natural-law theory of law with sufficient precision if one takes the quality of the connection between law and morality as the starting point.

In the positivist camp, even the most radical or exclusive legal positivists seem to maintain that there are some conceptual or necessary connections between law and morality, or broadly accept that there are certain evaluative features of law that make it possible for us to grasp law's nature. To give one example, Joseph Raz holds that the very institution of law has an essential moral task: "The law's task, put abstractly, is to secure a situation whereby moral goals which, given the current situation in the country whose law it is, would be unlikely to be achieved without it, and whose achievement by the law is not counter-productive, are realized."[1] Of course, Raz does not thereby argue that certain substantive moral values, such

1. Joseph Raz, "About Morality and the Nature of Law," in *Between Authority and Interpretation*, 178. See also the following claims advanced by legal positivists: "necessarily, law makes moral claims of its subjects" (Julie Dickson, "Legal Positivism: Contemporary Debates," in *The Routledge Companion to Philosophy of Law*, ed. Andrei Marmor (Routledge 2012), 49); "[necessarily,] law is the kind of thing that can be judged by moral standards" (John Gardner, "Hart on Legality, Justice, and Morality," in *Law as a Leap of Faith* (Oxford University Press, 2012), 222); "necessarily, law regulates objects of morality," "necessarily, law is justice-apt," "necessarily, law is morally risky" (these last three claims are

as, say, the inherent telic goods and essential properties of marriage, are immediately juridical on account of their moral correctness and that these values thus pertain to the legal world regardless of their proper inclusion in the content of valid norms of the relevant legal system. He still maintains that such moral goods become "juridicized" exclusively by reference to social facts, namely, by their inclusion in the content of valid posited legal norms, without the necessity of consulting substantive moral standards or verifying the moral merit of these norms for their juridical relevance. He cannot, however, be said to unqualifiedly belong to the camp of the so-called "legal descriptivists," namely, those who advocate that the essential properties of law must be elucidated in a purely descriptive way, by reference solely to social facts. This is because he identifies at least some necessary or essential evaluative features or purposes of law, even if those features or purposes are merely systemic and never postulated in terms of nonposited substantive human goods that would somehow already be necessarily juridically relevant.

Furthermore, in some parts of the legal-philosophical universe over the last few decades, the term "natural law" underwent a thorough reconstruction and, at times, began to denote virtually any legal theory that made the necessary inclusion of certain evaluative features—even those that are purely systemic, procedural, or methodological—somehow central to the project of answering the question "What is law?"[2] Thus, on the conceptual map of the main legal-philosophical accounts of law's ontology, which references this reconstructed notion of natural law, even Raz's account of the legal phenomenon and its essential moral task could now easily be seen as partially overlapping with a natural-law theory of law. The same could be said of Hart's more inclusive version of a positivistic account of the nature of law, which seems to necessarily

taken from Leslie Green, "The Inseparability of Law and Morals," in *The Germ of Justice: Essays in General Jurisprudence*, 186–93).

2. For an assessment of the reconstruction of the term "natural law" in legal and moral philosophy, see Russell Hittinger, "Varieties of Minimalist Natural Law Theory," *The American Journal of Jurisprudence* 34, no. 1 (1989): 133–70; Russell Hittinger, "Liberalism and the American Natural Law Tradition," *Wake Forest Law Review* 25 (1990): 429–99.

or conceptually allow for the possibility or openness (rejected by exclusive legal positivists, such as Raz) that moral standards, even substantive moral values, be included among the criteria for the identification of valid law, provided that this inclusion is grounded in (or invoked by) posited sources of law, and thus ultimately in social facts.[3]

The frequent understanding of the term "natural law" according to its reconstructed features made it possible for the category of "natural lawyers" to be extended to include an antipositivist author such as Ronald Dworkin, who sees no problem in supporting a set of necessary connections between law and at least some elements of substantive morality. However, Dworkin's vision of legally relevant substantive morality is limited only to a minimalist set of moral values—or even to only one central moral good—which he deems architectonic for all the other manifestations of law: the natural right to equal concern and respect. He promotes this right as the political-moral core value that (1) models all other relevant moral and legal rights in a legal system and (2) provides the key for interpretation of all positive legal norms.[4] Interestingly enough, Dworkin is quite clear in his insistence that his architectonic natural right to equal

3. For an example of Hart's explicit commitment to what he called "soft positivism" (and what is now also called "inclusive legal positivism"), see H. L. A. Hart, *The Concept of Law*, 3rd ed. (Oxford University Press, 2012), 250–54. The disagreement between inclusive and exclusive positivism regards those situations when a posited legal norm, or a society's rule of recognition of valid law, affirms that a social norm that passes a certain moral test or possesses some sufficiently determinate moral merit has juridical status and is to be considered law in that society, or a part of that society's legal system. For example, imagine the following formulation of an article of the constitution of some legal system: "The evaluative content that pertains to the primary precepts of natural law, as understood in Thomas Aquinas's teaching on *ius naturale*, is to be considered law in this legal system." Soft positivism and hard (or exclusive) positivism have different assessments of the impact of such social-factual, source-based incorporation of moral standards on the nature of law. The main point of their disagreement is the question of whether such moral standards—broadly incorporated by legal sources or rules of recognition of valid law but still in need of passing some moral test—become law upon passing that moral test (soft positivism) or require some further, formal social-factual recognition of passing that moral test, whether through additional legal norms or the practice of legal officials, to be fully incorporated in law (hard positivism).

4. See Ronald Dworkin, *Taking Rights Seriously*, 2nd ed. (Harvard University Press, 1978), xii, xv, 179–83.

concern and respect is fully juridical even in the absence of the exhaustive regulation of all its aspects in posited legal norms. His entire legal-philosophical project rests on the idea of the existence of nonposited or prepositive elements of true juridicity outside of the "collection" of all posited legal rules that are identified as valid in a legal system.[5] Given this legal-philosophical framework, Dworkin sees no problem in acknowledging that his antipositivist theoretical project possesses remarkable similarities to most of the key features of a natural-law theory of law,[6] if we disregard for a moment his reluctance to subscribe to a metaphysically richer range of the legally relevant aspects of the human good beyond the central value of equal concern and respect.

Perhaps even more interesting developments occurred, roughly during the same timeframe, in the camp of what is known as the restatement of a classical natural-law theory of law. It is usually thought that this camp is at least in principle immune to the aforementioned reconstruction of the term "natural law." John Finnis, certainly the most prominent contemporary proponent of a new classical natural-law theory of law, builds his account of the nature of law on the premise that understanding what law is necessarily

5. Already in his first book, *Taking Rights Seriously*, Dworkin argues that "legal positivism ... is that theory that individuals have legal rights only insofar as these have been created by explicit political decisions or explicit social practice," while he instead suggests "an alternative conceptual theory which shows how individuals may have legal rights other than those created by explicit decision or practice" (Dworkin, *Taking Rights Seriously*, xii). This line of reasoning represents a longstanding argument in his legal theory. Dworkin reaffirms it in his last published book that deals with this argument: "Interpretivism ... argues that law includes not only the specific rules enacted in accordance with the community's accepted principles but also the principles that provide the best moral justification for those enacted rules. The law then also includes the rules that follow from those justifying principles, even though those further rules were never enacted.... Legal positivism argues that ... historical acts or conduct is exclusively decisive in deciding what legal rights people have. Interpretivism offers a different answer, in which principles of political morality also have a part to play." See Ronald Dworkin, *Justice for Hedgehogs* (The Belknap Press of Harvard University Press, 2011), 402, 407.

6. See his following remark: "If the crude description of natural law I just gave is correct, that any theory which makes the content of law sometimes depend on the correct answer to some moral question is a natural law theory, then I am guilty of natural law." See Ronald Dworkin, "'Natural Law' Revisited," *University of Florida Law Review* 34, no. 2 (1982): 165.

includes the work of evaluation, of understanding the reasons for action that are apt to explain why we should have something like law at all, and why such an institution or social practice is an inherent good to be pursued in the social context of a political community. Faithful to his maximalist natural-law subscription to a full-range vision of the aspects of authentic human good, a significant part of Finnis's theoretical project is dedicated to showing why and how substantive moral goods, especially the so-called "basic human goods" (such as life and health, marital/procreative union, knowledge, etc.),[7] are inherently relevant for the juridical realm and necessarily connected to it.

The somewhat surprising aspect of Finnis's theory is his insistence that the evaluative features and purposes of law as reasons for action, together with the basic human goods as the core content of those reasons, exist as something that is fully juridical—fully law—only when they are articulated according to descriptive social-factual features, that is, when they are *posited* as valid human law. Human law, including those parts of it that pertain to the protection and determination of basic human goods, is essentially and exclusively manifested as such—as law—based on the social fact of its positivity, so that basic human goods are not law before or outside of the hypothesis of their being somehow posited in valid legal norms. Indeed, they are non-law prior to their being posited. According to Finnis, the legal status of these substantive moral values can never depend solely on their merits, their conformity with some objective moral truth, or with some other moral test not posited or invoked by valid law for the purposes of law-identification. Rather, the legal status of substantive (or other) moral values necessarily depends also on the social fact of their positivity, which satisfies the criteria of legal validity and other relevant conditions of law-identification established by the society's rule of recognition of valid law. As Finnis

7. An "open-ended" list of basic human goods may be consulted in John Finnis, "Aquinas and Natural Law Jurisprudence," in *The Cambridge Companion to Natural Law Jurisprudence*, ed. George Duke and Robert P. George (Cambridge University Press, 2017), 18–19.

says, "law is all made—posited, even those parts of it that are made by adopting moral principles whose truth and applicability is not made but discerned."[8]

The nature of law is best explained, argues Finnis, by taking into consideration the reality that it has not one but two aspects or "lives," its descriptive or social-factual "life" and its evaluative or moral "life," both of which must necessarily be actualized for us to be able to say that an instance of the phenomenon of law exists, that it became manifest in human social reality. In sum, according to Finnis, morality must necessarily be "in" law, but there is no way to envision how law could be "in" morality, or really anywhere else, outside of the setting fixed by the positivized social-factual features characteristic of law's descriptive "life." Morality *and* legal positivity, taken together and only under that condition, make law what it is.[9]

The emphasis on the social-factual character of law in Finnis's theoretical enterprise is particularly intriguing, because of its shared premise with legal positivism's commitment to positivity as the decisive feature of law's nature. Robert Alexy, a legal philosopher who describes his theory as nonpositivism disconnected from the natural-law premises, makes roughly the same theoretical move. In Alexy's estimation, law is necessarily both "real" and "ideal." All that law ideally should be, namely, its evaluative features and especially moral values, must be expressed through its "real" or properly positivized social-factual features in order to be considered as law in the true sense of that term.[10]

8. John Finnis, "Reflections and Responses," in *Reason, Morality and Law: The Philosophy of John Finnis*, ed. John Keown and Robert P. George (Oxford University Press, 2013), 551.

9. For Finnis's thesis on the dual nature of law, see, for example, Finnis, "Reflections and Responses," 547–53. See also John Finnis, "A Grand Tour of Legal Theory," in *Collected Essays*, vol. 4, *Philosophy of Law* (Oxford University Press, 2011), 101–2, 107; John Finnis, "Law as Fact and as Reason for Action: A Response to Robert Alexy on Law's Ideal Dimension," *The American Journal of Jurisprudence* 59, no. 1 (2014): 95–96; and Finnis, "Aquinas and Natural Law Jurisprudence," 47–48.

10. See Robert Alexy, "The Dual Nature of Law," in *Law's Ideal Dimension* (Oxford University Press, 2021), 36–50. For a detailed assessment of Alexy's account of the nature of law from the viewpoint of his approach to the question of the connection between law and morality, see Petar Popović, "Are There Any Elements of Juridicity beyond Positive Law in

Of course, the remaining differences between the approaches of authors such as the natural lawyer Finnis and the hard positivist Raz, are still quite easily perceivable, particularly the commitment of the former (and the refusal of the latter) to establish certain necessary connections between substantive moral values, such as certain basic human goods, and law. But at the same time, it has become increasingly difficult to grasp these differences when one takes as the starting point the positions of present-day positivists and natural lawyers with regard to the problem of the existence or nonexistence of any necessary connections between law and morality.

The important legal-philosophical work of Julie Dickson further testifies to that increasing difficulty. Dickson sees no problem in simultaneously (1) explicitly expressing her affinities to the central tenets of legal positivism and (2) advocating that a successful theory of law's nature should take into account its "key duality," namely, that law "exists both as institutional practice and social fact, and as a normative, reason-giving, and value-aspiring phenomenon."[11] In constructing accounts of the law's dual nature, she says, "legal philosophers must make evaluative judgments in selecting features of law which are important and significant to explain," but "without yet taking a view on whether those features of law render law morally bad or good."[12] According to Dickson, it is practically impossible to explain law's essence without recourse to certain evaluative standards from the outset of the project of explaining what law is, but those standards do not necessarily or otherwise conceptually entail an evaluative viewpoint that resorts to substantive moral goods.

Thus, positivists, nonpositivists (such as Alexy), and some natural lawyers (such as Finnis), seem to take the reality of law's dual nature as their starting point. The main difference between their approaches to explaining the ontology of law, according to the line of

Robert Alexy's Non-Positivism?" *Revus: Journal for Constitutional Theory and Philosophy of Law* 49, no. 1 (2023): 87–105.

11. Dickson, *Elucidating Law*, 87. For Dickson's acknowledgement of her affinities with the tradition of legal positivism, see Dickson, *Elucidating Law*, 101.

12. Dickson, *Elucidating Law*, 102.

reasoning presented so far, seems to be located at the level of the importance or even necessity (or lack thereof) that they assign to certain moral, or substantively moral, elements pertaining to the evaluative aspect of law's nature in their efforts to adequately explain that nature. Simply said, the primary mode of establishing the difference between legal positivism and a natural-law theory of law (or, broadly speaking, nonpositivism) seems to be organized around the question of how much morality should we fit "in" law to adequately explain its nature. If we understand morality to denote a Finnisian natural-law maximalist (hence, not a Dworkinian, or similarly minimalist) account of the legally relevant range of substantive basic human goods, then the standard versions of the law-morality separability thesis still maintain their intelligibility and still succeed in determining the limit between legal positivism and a natural-law theory of law. Instances of this standard formulation of the separability thesis may be found in the Hartian insistence on the "merely contingent" and never necessary or conceptual connections "between law as it is and law as it morally ought to be,"[13] as well as in the Razian argument that "determining what the law is does not necessarily, or conceptually, depend on moral or other evaluative considerations about what the law ought to be."[14] If the evaluative features necessary for both identifying law and for understanding its nature are so value-laden as to include an indispensable reference to substantive moral standards akin to Finnis's basic human goods, then positivists and natural lawyers are still quite easily identifiable and distinguishable. The more one envisions the evaluative features inherent to law's nature in broader, less-than-substantive, and minimalist terms, the more the divide between positivists and natural lawyers becomes progressively blurrier.

13. H. L. A. Hart, introduction, in *Essays in Jurisprudence and Philosophy* (Oxford University Press, 1983), 8.

14. Joseph Raz, "The Argument from Justice, or How Not to Reply to Legal Positivism," in *The Authority of Law*, 2nd ed. (Oxford University Press, 2011), 319.

The Emergence of Another Persistent Question

But there is another, more successful way of distinguishing and categorizing the various approaches to understanding the nature or the essence of law. This alternative strategy does not take as its staring point the query of how much morality should we fit "in" law to adequately describe its essential nature. Instead, it relies on a different persistent question that does not entirely overlap with the question regarding the separability thesis or the correct relationship between law and morality. And in my opinion, this persistent question contributes to a better grasp not only of the differences but also of the shared elements between legal positivism and a natural-law theory of law (or at least some versions of it).

The analysis of this different persistent question is the starting point for this book. I deem it highly important and perhaps even decisive for approaching the query "What is law?" I propose that instead of beginning with the question of "which kind of" or "how much," morality must necessarily or contingently be implemented in law in order to correctly describe its essential nature, due attention should be given to a different, though not entirely separate, question: *What is law "in?"* In other words, where can law be found? What are the criteria for determining the precise differences between law and non-law? What are the exact boundaries or limits of law, beyond which law is no more, and where we enter into the field of other nonlegal domains, like nonjuridical morality or some other evaluative field that is in some sense usually thought to be emptied of any necessary reference to juridicity?

Of course, if we assume that law has a dual nature, and that each manifestation of law must necessarily be somehow humanly posited, then the task of identifying of the nature of law, or of the boundaries of law, may be approached by inquiring into how much morality should be included in law.

My intention, instead, is to question the boundaries or limits of law by asking whether law may be found "in" domains, realities, things, states of affairs, or norms beyond the instantiations of humanly posited law, that is, beyond the convention-based or purely artifactual conditions for recognizing what counts as valid humanly posited law. In sum, are there any elements of juridicity to be found beyond, or in abstraction from, the domain of humanly posited valid law? Is there some intelligible and philosophically sound way of maintaining that it is possible and reasonable to claim that law may somehow be found "in" morality? Or, more precisely, are there some evaluative or moral features that are already somehow fully juridical prior to or in abstraction from law's descriptive, social-factual, posited features? Can we detach law's evaluative, ideal, or moral "life" from its descriptive social-factual "life" and still claim that at least some of the detached evaluative features are fully law? Does morality contain instances of nonposited law, and if so, according to which conditions can we identify such instances of juridically relevant morality?

I find it remarkable that a version of this alternative persistent question concerning the existence of the elements of juridicity beyond humanly posited valid law was formulated (and answered in the negative) within legal positivism. In a recently published *Cambridge Companion to Legal Positivism*, the positivist Leslie Green notes, in continuity with the line of argument presented in the preceding section, that "it is hard to find contemporary positivists who still hold that ... there are no necessary connections between law and morality"—a claim "*once associated* with legal positivism."[15] Green then claims to have found one distinctive feature of legal positivism on which there is no disagreement in the positivist tradition: "Any theory of law that a positivist would be willing to call 'positivist' endorses a version of the following claim: *All law is positive law*."[16] In other words, there are no necessary elements of juridicity

15. Leslie Green, "Positivism, Realism and Sources of Law," in *The Cambridge Companion to Legal Positivism*, ed. Torben Spaak and Patricia Mindus (Cambridge University Press, 2021), 39 (emphasis added).

16. Green, "Positivism, Realism and Sources of Law," 40–41. Green reiterates this argument in his introduction to *The Germ of Justice*, 10. John L. Mackie previously highlighted this formulation of a central tenet of legal positivism, perhaps with even more precision: "Law is, as I have maintained that morality also is, a human product.... This amounts to

outside the scope of humanly posited valid law that could alter the basic ontological fabric of law, namely, its impossibility to exist as something different than a posited source-based social fact.

It is quite surprising that Alexy, a nonpositivist, and Finnis, a proponent of a natural-law theory of law, fully agree with this central tenet of legal positivism that all law is positive law. As previously mentioned, both authors are firmly convinced that within law's dual nature an essential aspect or "life" of law is manifested through its positivity. Positivity is a "necessary" property of law, claims Alexy.[17] Finnis holds that "the *whole* of community's existing law, however completely just and decent, is *posited, somehow humanly posited*."[18] Elsewhere, Finnis even attributes this account of the nature of law, namely, that all law is positive law, to Thomas Aquinas: "In Aquinas's clarification and adjustment of the Aristotelian and Roman juristic categories and nomenclature, *all human law is positive law*."[19]

This rather wide consensus regarding the thesis that all law is positive law, between legal positivists, nonpositivists, and natural lawyers, is quite telling. It suggests that the map of legal-philosophical

---

saying that *all law is positive law*: it is law wholly in and by being 'posited' by some society or institution." See John L. Mackie, *Ethics: Inventing Right and Wrong* (Penguin Books, 1977), 232–33 (emphasis added).

17. Alexy, "The Dual Nature of Law," 36.

18. John Finnis, "The Truth in Legal Positivism," in *Collected Essays*, vol. 4, *Philosophy of Law*, 185 (emphasis added).

19. John Finnis, *Aquinas: Moral, Political, and Legal Theory* (Oxford University Press, 1998), 266 (emphasis added). This is not the only example of Finnis's claim that for Aquinas all law is necessarily humanly posited. See also the following claims: "Aquinas, in his later work, describes the whole of the law administered by a state's courts as 'law humanly posited' or 'positive law,' even though part of it ... is wholly or substantially part of, or a deduced conclusion from, the permanent principles and precepts of natural law" (Finnis, *Aquinas: Moral, Political, and Legal Theory*, 268); "Indeed, the very term 'positive law' is one imported into philosophy by Aquinas, who was also the first to propose that the whole law of a political community may be considered philosophically as *positive* law" (Finnis, "A Grand Tour of Legal Theory," 100); "Law, as Aquinas speaks of it, in its central case [is] human positive law" (Finnis, "Aquinas and Natural Law Jurisprudence," 45); and "Aquinas treats all human law as 'posited' and (synonymously) 'positive,' even those of its rules that are restatements of, or authoritatively promulgated deductions (*conclusiones*) from, general moral principles or norms" (John Finnis, "Aquinas's Moral, Political, and Legal Philosophy," in *The Stanford Encyclopedia of Philosophy* (Spring 2021 ed.), ed. Edward N. Zalta, accessed October 31, 2024, https://plato.stanford.edu/entries/aquinas-moral-political/).

approaches to explaining law's nature is radically rearranged when we focus on the question of the existence of elements of juridicity beyond humanly posited valid law instead of concentrating on the question regarding the quality of the law-morality connection. If we focus on the question of the so-called separability thesis between law and morality, we end up with the following results: legal positivists could be placed on one side of the divide and nonpositivists together with natural lawyers on the other, even if that divide is occasionally blurry, as shown above. However, when the question of the presence of morality "in" law is substituted with the question regarding the conditions for the presence of law "in" morality (or completely outside of the realm of positive law), some nonpositivists and natural lawyers will be categorized together with the legal positivists and adhere to what these latter theorists consider to be the core positivistic "all law is positive law" thesis, thereby forming a single, united camp.

One would normally expect a more or less elaborate justification of the grounds for the metapositive existence of law from a natural-law theory of law (perhaps even from nonpositivistic accounts of law's nature), that is, a full-fledged account of the elements of juridicity existing beyond the realm of humanly posited valid law. Even authors who are not natural lawyers are on record as saying that they expect such arguments from natural-law theorists. Thus, for example, Jeremy Waldron, certainly not an exponent of the natural-law theory of law, argues:

> We should expect natural law to be law-like. It should be *like law*.... Natural law should manifest itself as something capable of ordering our actions and interactions in something like the way that positive law orders our actions and interactions. Otherwise we would not call it "law." ... The experience of being governed, ruled, and ordered by natural law should add to our repertoire of being governed, ruled, and ordered by law.[20]

20. Jeremy Waldron, "What Is Natural Law Like?" in *Reason, Morality and Law*, 73.

Now, if legal positivists, leading nonpositivists, and prominent natural lawyers maintain that all law is positive law, that all that law is must necessarily and essentially be posited, the question that must be addressed now is: does anybody remain on the other side of the divide, established by the persistent question of the existence of metapositive law? Is there a divide at all? To what degree is this question even persistent? Do all legal philosophers generally agree that all law is necessarily posited, whichever position each holds regarding the necessary connections between law and morality?

The Other Side of the Divide

The answer to the aforementioned question is, yes, there are some approaches to explaining law's nature that maintain that certain elements of juridicity exist beyond humanly posited valid law.

Ronald Dworkin is one such author. We already had the chance to present the foundational idea in his legal philosophy, according to which law includes not only the sum of all posited valid rules but also certain principles or standards of political morality that point to fully legal rights (e.g., Dworkin's architectonic right to equal concern and respect) that persons have and should be able to claim and enjoy, even in the absence of their posited recognition or determination. Thus, such metapositive evaluative or moral principles, values, or standards may constitute authentic legal rights—they are already fully law or a source of law—before their positivization. The task of a legal official, perhaps more often a judge in a supreme court or in a constitutional court (e.g., Dworkin's Hercules), is to declaratively (hence, not constitutively) identify these metapositive principles, values, or standards as existing law in cases where such identification is difficult, as well as to be attentive to their pertinence in all cases, whether easy or hard.[21]

21. Ronald Dworkin, *Law's Empire* (The Belknap Press of Harvard University Press, 1986), 265–66. See also Ronald Dworkin, *Justice in Robes* (The Belknap Press of Harvard University Press, 2006), 54–55, 68.

In sum, to argue in favor of the existence of law as a nonposited entity, Dworkin had to inquire into the issue of the boundaries of law[22] by addressing both issues of (1) what law is "in" and (2) under which condition(s) law may be thought to be "in" morality.

There is good evidence for holding that the core issue in Dworkin's long-term famous debate with Hart—arguably the most important legal-philosophical debate on crucial persistent questions in this scholarly field—was their radical divergence regarding the question of the existence of the elements of juridicity beyond humanly posited valid law, or beyond the standards for identification of such law. If we asked Hart to briefly explain to us what law is "in," he would say that law is essentially and exclusively "in" positive law. He would probably add that law is thus "in" all those rules or standards for conduct—indeed, in all those "things," broadly speaking—that are picked out and thereby juridicized or rendered legal by the law-identifying conditions contained in the rule of recognition of valid law. He would quite likely also tell us that principles of substantive morality or justice may be a source of law only if they are explicitly identified as included either (1) in the content of valid law or (2) among the relevant conditions for identifying valid law by the rule of recognition.[23] According to Hart, then, law is only and necessarily "in" descriptively ascertainable social facts: from the fact of the existence of a posited social source containing a rule or standard for conduct, to the fact that this rule satisfies determinate criteria of legal validity accepted and followed in the unified practice of legal officials. If we then asked Dworkin the same question, he would respond that law is not only to be found "in" those rules and moral (or otherwise evaluative) principles that Hart envisions to be identified and rendered juridical by a rule of recognition but that law or elements of juridicity may be found also "in" certain

22. Some authors acknowledge Dworkin's theoretical account as his inquiry into law's boundaries. See Nicos Stavropoulos, "The Debate That Never Was," *Harvard Law Review* 130, no. 8 (2017): 2091; Frederick Schauer, "Law's Boundaries," *Harvard Law Review* 130, no. 9 (2017): 2455–56.

23. Hart, *The Concept of Law*, 250–54.

evaluative standards that are not identifiable by a Hartian rule of recognition. Whatever else the Hart-Dworkin debate may be about, it is at least about starting to make sense of this important difference in approaching the nature of law.[24]

One way to start making sense of this fundamental difference is to view it as not only a characteristic of a debate between two legal philosophers, namely, Hart and Dworkin but also as a divide that pervades the entire segment of legal philosophy dedicated to the analysis of the question "What is law?" Each legal-philosophical approach to understanding and describing the nature of law may be categorized (among different, equally effective standards for categorization) according to a position taken by that approach regarding the existence of the elements of juridicity beyond humanly posited valid law, or, conversely, regarding the thesis that all law is positive law.

Are there other authors, besides Dworkin, who stand on his side of the divide and hold that all law is not posited, and that law may, indeed, be found under certain conditions "in" morality? In this book, I will argue that there is at least one other author who stands on Dworkin's side of the divide, namely, Thomas Aquinas. I will present Aquinas's legal-philosophical line of reasoning, according to which, to introduce only a few central claims of the book, (1) not all law is positive law, (2) political communities genuinely need positive law for justice to be fully secured, and thus the existence of humanly posited valid law constitutes a form of human good, (3) positive law may, indeed, be, and usually is, law, (4) there are humanly posited and valid norms that are not law (i.e., they are non-law), on account of the injustice of their content, and (5) there are elements of juridicity beyond humanly posited valid law.

These and other claims, which will be further elaborated in

24. For a detailed analysis of the Hart-Dworkin debate seen through the prism of their major difference regarding the existence of nonposited law, that is, of the elements of juridicity beyond humanly posited valid law, see Petar Popović, "And Then There Were Two: Further Remarks on Identifying the Core Question in the Hart-Dworkin Debate," *Rivista di filosofia del diritto* 11, no. 2 (2022): 415–34.

various chapters of the book, originate in an approach to analyzing the essence of law or the juridical phenomenon that is most adequately referred to as Thomistic juridical realism. This approach thus stands on the other side of the divide when compared to legal-philosophical accounts that fully endorse the thesis that all law is positive law. However, I am highlighting the terms "divide" and "division" with the sole intention of pointing to a somewhat neglected standard of categorization of accounts of law's nature, which originates in the persistent questions of "What is law in?" and of whether there are certain elements of juridicity beyond humanly posited valid law. Everything in this book related to highlighting the differences between diverse accounts of the nature of law is an attempt to make more sense of the situation that Julie Dickson describes in the following way: "each of those properties which make law into what it is can be examined from different angles, in response to different puzzles and questions which strike us as interesting at any given time."[25]

Of course, it would be absurd and dishonest to suggest that Thomistic juridical realism and, say, legal positivism, may be seen to fully overlap. Quite the contrary, it is important to identify the crucial differences between them as clearly as possible to avoid superficial misconceptions. But at the same time, I firmly hold that the legal-philosophical landscape should not be thought of as a world of perennial irreconcilable divides, with walls of separation and entirely parallel scholarly approaches without any places of contact, which at some point simply stop the conversation. I personally prefer Anthony Honoré's metaphor of perennial finals of the "World Cup" of legal theory,[26] where legal positivism and the natural-law theory of law continuously play against each other. Given their emphases on different features of law's nature, they know that, in a way, they cannot play this "game" by themselves, and they can acknowledge and even applaud brilliant moves made by the other team, helping the

25. Dickson, *Elucidating Law*, 58.

26. Anthony M. Honoré, *Making Law Bind: Essays Legal and Philosophical* (Oxford University Press, 1987), 32.

opponents to get back on their feet if they fall, instead of seeking to annihilate their agency entirely.

Hence, even if the casual reader, a practicing lawyer, or a legal scholar and philosopher of law will not be able to fully support or identify with all the theses of Thomistic juridical realism presented in this book, I believe they may profit from engaging, even critically, with Aquinas's legal theory and its peculiar way of conceptualizing law. One of the reasons why I thought it appropriate to write this book on Thomistic juridical realism is my conviction that the main features of this legal-philosophical approach are largely unknown in present-day legal philosophy, especially in the Anglophone world. In addition, just as legal positivism has its internal tensions between various fractions of a positivistic way of conceptualizing law, there seems to be more than one account of law's nature that invokes Aquinas as the leading source of inspiration. I believe that the Thomist legal theory presented in this book is faithful to Aquinas's original insights, but, as will become evident throughout the book, it significantly differs in various aspects from other versions of a Thomist natural-law theory of law.

Since it is possible that each word in the label "Thomistic juridical realism" may already sound quite unusual to some readers, let me briefly explain what each component of that label exactly means.

"Thomistic"

The adjective "Thomistic" reveals my commitment to the legal philosophy of Thomas Aquinas, a thirteenth-century philosopher and theologian (1225–1274) who dedicated numerous texts, the most important of which will be presented in this book, to describing the nature of law. There are several contemporary natural-law theorists who significantly rely on Aquinas's positions on what law is, John Finnis being arguably the most famous among them. I identify myself as a Thomistic legal philosopher because I hold that Aquinas's theses on the ontology of law denote the most accurate understanding of the phenomenon that we call law.

However, my admiration for Aquinas's legal philosophy certainly does not amount to some quasi-utopian project of restoring the classical meaning of law understood as *ius*—or, as Finnis correctly notes, of "wanting to put the clock back"[27]—to the detriment of that which is valid in postclassical and contemporary legal-philosophical approaches, motivated by some kind of nostalgia for premodern scholarly and cultural contexts. Instead, I claim that a contemporary reading of Aquinas may indeed contribute to an improved understanding of our present-day legal-philosophical analyses. Thus, just as my interest in presenting Aquinas's legal theory in this book is not archaeological, neither is it merely exegetical. I am not trying to understand what Aquinas advocated only for the purposes and within the limits of his particular historical context. Rather, I am primarily interested in exploring the extent to which his insights into law's nature may be of considerable interest to us today, even if these insights will satisfy, for some readers who are less sympathetic to his ideas on law, only a curiosity to better grasp a legal-philosophical proposal that is entirely parallel or even at times contrary to their own.

Furthermore, I do not consider Aquinas's legal theory to represent a doctrinal "divinity" that is meant to be taken as "descending from heaven" with unquestionable authority in matters of legal philosophy. As always, it is the force of the arguments themselves, together with their capacity to incorporate and dialogue with the valid insights of others, that makes an author and his theory appealing. As I will show throughout the book, I hold that Aquinas did not say everything there is to be said regarding the nature of law—really, what author can claim to have done that? Many of Aquinas's fascinating arguments have been revisited and elaborated by other authors, and I will offer some of my own interpretations and further developments of his account of the nature of law. At the same time, I would like to remain open to being illuminated by arguments made

27. John Finnis, *Natural Law and Natural Rights*, 2nd ed. (Oxford University Press, 2011), 209.

by other authors—including those who are not Thomistic philosophers or natural-law theorists—when they put forward ideas that take us a step further in a deeper understanding the nature of law.

"Juridical"

Throughout the book I will use the term "juridicity" (or the adjective "juridical") to denote the specific field that pertains to law and thus not to other, possibly overlapping fields, such as morality. I take juridicity to mean, at the highest level of analysis, a specific quality of a given reality—whether a norm, a "thing" (broadly speaking), aspects of human agency, a state of affairs, and so forth—that arises from a fixed set of constitutive properties that render that determinate reality somehow suitable for being considered to pertain to the domain of law, while other realities that do not possess the aforementioned quality are deemed non-law. In short, the idea of juridicity is developed for exploring the conditions for grasping the "whatness" of law.

At this general level of analysis, the term "juridicity" does not rely on a certain concrete set of such properties but is presented instead as a structural vehicle for the subsequent implementations of such properties in a particular theory of what is to count as law, presented at the level of general jurisprudence. Thus, for example, Hart's idea of a rule of recognition represents a particular theory of the constitutive properties of juridicity that yields the conclusion that all law is positive law. Another example of the set of standards for envisioning juridicity may be found in Dworkin's idea that law consists not only of posited legal rules but also of rights drawn from the principles of political morality inherent in a political community's moral traditions that most successfully control, support, and justify those posited legal rules. These two sets of properties of juridicity are, as we said before, irreconcilable and irreducible to one another, but both seek to provide us with an understanding of what constitutes the domain of law, what the boundaries and limits of that domain are, and what ought to be deemed non-law.

The idea or the concept of juridicity was predominantly developed in French legal philosophy. In his brief overview of that development, Neil Duxbury argues that this concept is predominantly used as "a convenient rubric under which purely speculative pronouncements about what are taken to be the essential foundations of law can be made."[28] André-Jean Arnaud claims that this concept of juridicity (*juridicité*) was first systematically elaborated by French legal theorists in the 1960s, and that it was used prior to that period in a more general sense as pertaining to the domain of law, but without the need to better elucidate the concept. In Arnaud's view, this concept finds its *raison d'être* in relation to the "problem of knowing where the law, the juridical sphere, starts"; it is, indeed, this problem that "justifies the emergence of an independent concept of juridicity."[29] The same author emphasizes that the concept of juridicity aims to "specify the domain of law" precisely by distinguishing it from the field of nonjuridical social reality.[30]

According to Arnaud, the French word *juridicité* could be translated into English as "legality,"[31] and we can easily find examples of the usage of the term "legality" that could be said to imply, though without much further explanation, a meaning related to the aforementioned sense of juridicity.[32] Although the term "legality" seems to be more connatural to the English language, I will use the term "juridicity" and the adjective "juridical," for two reasons. First, given the relative prevalence of legal positivism in present-day philosophy of law, and taking into consideration the abundance of nonpositivist authors who subscribe to the thesis that all law is positive law, the term "legality" is usually used to denote a determinate set of

28. Neil Duxbury, "Juridicity as a Theme in French Legal Philosophy," *International Journal for the Semiotics of Law* 2, no. 1 (1989): 89.

29. André-Jean Arnaud, "Fact as Law," in *Semiotics, Law and Social Science*, ed. Domenico Cardozo and Bernard S. Jackson (Gangemi Editore 1985), 130, 138.

30. André-Jean Arnaud, "Juridicité," in *Dictionnaire encyclopédique de théorie et de sociologie du droit*, ed. André-Jean Arnaud (Librairie Générale de Droit et de Jurisprudence, 1993), 322–23.

31. Arnaud, "Fact as Law," 131–32.

32. For instance, see Dworkin, *Justice in Robes*, 168–86.

properties of pertaining to the domain of law, tailored according to this central tenet of legal positivism widely shared by other authors. In other words, legality is normally considered to denote law's essential positivity, whatever else may be also included among the properties of a reality pertaining to the domain of law. Conversely, the meaning of the term "juridicity" carries the conceptual possibility of positing any conceivable set of properties—whether positivist, nonpositivist, natural-law related, or other—that enable us to understand what pertains to the domain of law.

This leads us to the second reason: the term "legality" is predominantly associated with a legal-philosophical framework that supports the thesis that "all law is positive law" because the term is derived from the words "law," "legal," or *lex* in Latin, which seem to be principally understood to denote posited or enacted law. The word "juridicity," on the other hand, is terminologically associated with another Latin term, *ius*, which denotes "law" on a level of analysis that is higher than and not necessarily connected only to positive law, or to *lex*. While a number of languages provide different terms to denote *ius* (*droit* in French, *diritto* in Italian, *derecho* in Spanish, *Recht* in German, and so forth) and *lex* (*loi* in French, *legge* in Italian, *ley* in Spanish, *Gesetz* in German, and so forth), the English language has only one word, "law," which is meant to capture the essence of both *ius* and *lex*. True, the English word "right" is frequently used to translate the Latin word *ius* when the latter word is employed in the senses that refer to subjective claims, liberties, powers, or immunities in the juridical realm (i.e., the so-called "subjective rights"), but these senses certainly do not exhaust the meaning of the term *ius*.

The term *ius* denotes the phenomenon of law at the highest level of analysis—the level we mean when we say "law" even prior to having a clear idea that all law is (or is not) positive law. And since the term juridicity corresponds to this level of analysis and can convey all possible answers to the question of what law is "in" (and what law is not "in"), I will use this term throughout the book. It seems to me that the English word "law" may be used, and is in fact used to denote, among other meanings, the meaning that refers to its "whatness" at the highest level of analysis. At this level, we inquire into the conditions under which the phenomenon we call law has, so to speak, appeared, under which it has become sufficiently perceptible for our grasp of it, as well as sufficiently distinct from neighboring fields such as morality. It is possible and fitting to explore this level of analysis even before we decide on all the concrete conditions under which something (a rule or a thing) counts as law, that is, even prior to determining all the exact properties that award membership to the legal domain, and certainly prior to answering the question of whether all law is ultimately positive law. When we talk about "the nature of *law*," "the concept of *law*," and so forth, we are referring to a phenomenon Aquinas and other proponents of classical juridical realism called *ius*.

Thus, Thomistic juridical realism is a legal-philosophical approach that seeks to provide the criteria for establishing what law is "in" and what constitutes non-law, that is, which realities or domains are devoid of law. Said differently, it proposes its own set of criteria of juridicity that enable us to grasp that something—some *thing*, reality, state of affairs, and so forth—is "law" or *ius*.

"Realism"

The central meaning of the term "realism" corresponds to a position regarding the essence of law that may sound a bit shocking to contemporary legal-philosophical ears used to thinking about law in terms of posited legal norms and subjective legal rights. This is the position: according to Aquinas and the authors subscribing to Thomistic juridical realism, whatever else is necessarily included in envisioning law, or *ius*—whether social facts of humanly posited law or the different evaluative features that model law's essence—the juridical phenomenon always "appears" at the level of the things themselves (*res ipsa*, "realism" comes from the Latin term *res*). When I say that law, or *ius*, always falls at the level of concrete "things" (*res*), or that law, or *ius*, is always describable as a "thing," by "thing" I mean material or immaterial objects, realities, entities, states of affairs, and so forth that are apt to be constituted as *ius*, or law. I will dedicate an entire chapter of this book to further explain how exactly law may be considered a "thing," and what it means to say that some "things," or *res* (and not other "things"), are apt to be constituted as law.

For now, suffice it to say that according to Thomistic juridical realism, it is precisely things (*res*) that are rendered juridical, not primarily rules that concern these things or our subjective powers or faculties over them. Said differently, things, which are the object of both legal rules and the subjective legally relevant faculties and powers, are not thought to be entirely outside the necessary features of law's nature. Rather, they form part of the ontological fabric of law, together with some other necessary considerations, which I will begin to present in the next chapter. For Aquinas and those who follow him in this argument, law is essentially thing-based, and according to Thomistic juridical realism, the thingness of law cannot be overlooked in our reflections of its nature.

As will be shown in more detail in chapter 4, the emphasis of Thomistic juridical realism on the thing-centered content of the term *ius* does not amount to neglecting a necessary reference to the phenomenon of a legal rule, or *lex*, for grasping the nature of law. However, Aquinas's account of law is broader than the sole reference to the phenomena of humanly posited laws and corresponding legal practices. He incorporates these phenomena into a more complex notion of law, which is identifiable with things or realities (*res*), more than with norms, regardless of the importance of these latter for conceptualizing law.

Besides denoting law's necessary reference to things (*res*), the term "realism" also echoes one of the basic premises of Aquinas's philosophical approach, namely, his epistemological optimism regarding the possibility that the human persons cognize "things" themselves as they really are (epistemological realism), and that they are also able to understand that certain things are good and others evil, and perform their actions in accordance with that understanding (moral realism). Given that "juridical realism" accepts as its fundamental premise that law is essentially thing-based, it is certainly important to know that this legal-philosophical approach is grounded in an epistemological framework that supports the claim that things—in the broadest possible sense of the term *res* that is relevant for the juridical domain—are indeed knowable or graspable as they really are. And given that "juridical realism" considers the very essence of law, or *ius*, to possess a fundamental orientation toward the attainment of a specific form of good, namely, juridical good (I will explain what this means later in the book), it is equally important to know that this jurisprudential line of reasoning relies on the capacity of persons to grasp particular aspects, including juridically relevant aspects, of the whole human good and orient their actions accordingly.[33] Regardless, I think that most of the arguments in this book are intelligible, and at least some of them are perfectly acceptable, even if the reader does not fully subscribe to Aquinas's account of moral realism or to his epistemological realism.

The arguments presented above are, in my opinion, sufficient to distinguish Thomistic juridical realism with other legal-philosophical approaches whose names include a reference "realism," such as the American and the Scandinavian versions of legal realism. The term "realism" is employed in a different way in Thomistic juridical realism, as described above, and the difference between the adjectives "juridical" and "legal" further highlights the distinction from these other "realisms," for reasons that are presented in the previous section of this chapter.

33. I explain Aquinas's epistemological realism and its relevance for his juridical realism in greater detail in Petar Popović, *Natural Law & Thomistic Juridical Realism* (The Catholic University of America Press, 2022), 95–98. For an assessment of the interconnectedness between Aquinas's moral realism and his juridical realism, see Petar Popović, "Natural Juridical Goods: The Juridical Status of Basic Human Goods in Aquinas's Jusnaturalist Philosophy," in *The Goodness of Rights and the Juridical Domain of the Good: Essays in Thomistic Juridical Realism* (EDUSC, 2021), 71–94.

Chapter 2

Justice and Law: All Law Is Justice-Based

Exploring Law's Nature: Where Should We Start?

It is almost standard practice today to start an inquiry into the nature of law with the methodological conviction that the answer to the question "What is law?" can be reached only at the very end of an analysis, after gathering necessary insights by exploring certain prior, more basic questions. In an article in which he surveys the trends and outlines the elements of this staged inquiry, Grégoire Webber argues that for a full understanding of the phenomenon of law, it is crucial that one select the adequate prior questions and then proceed by answering them in the right order.[1] In this enterprise, it is especially important to pick out the most basic question that is apt to represent an optimal entry point for understanding law's nature. The questions presented in the previous chapter are certainly not suitable to denote a starting point in the analysis of the juridical phenomenon, since inquiring into the relationship between law and morality, or into the existence of the elements of juridicity beyond humanly posited valid law, presupposes that one has already formed, perhaps not a complete, but at least a viable idea of what law is. This is why the questions raised in the previous chapter served only to

1. Grégoire Webber, "Asking Why in the Study of Human Affairs," *The American Journal of Jurisprudence* 60, no. 1 (2015): 53.

outline the general direction for the analysis and development of the main ideas of this book.

But prior to understanding what law is and what law is "in" from the viewpoint of Thomistic juridical realism, just like in any other endeavor into understanding the essence of law, it is necessary to select a suitable starting place, an entry point that enables one to gradually elucidate law and arrive at a sufficiently comprehensive grasp of the juridical phenomenon at the very end of the analysis.

There seem to be two main candidates for this entry point offered by present-day legal philosophers. In addition, prominent authors who explore the specific question of "where should we start" in elucidating law largely agree that there is certainly more than one answer to that question and that no candidate for the starting point constitutes the most accurate option, almost to the exclusion of others. Indeed, maintaining the plurality of prospective starting points, which are not explored as necessarily mutually exclusive, may be a welcome strategy for covering more ground in investigating the essential features of the juridical phenomenon.

Each of the two main candidates, as well as the candidate that I will present later in this chapter (and which is, as we shall see, a subcategory of one of the two candidates), is meant to epitomize a phenomenon or a set of features that appears to us as most striking, peculiar, and unique when we think about law. What is the most compelling thing about law that captures the attention of our reasoning so much that we immediately know that we are encountering a phenomenon unlike any other? Which feature of the phenomenon of law "appears" before our mind in a most striking way, even while we acknowledge that there are also other similar features, perhaps less captivating but also to a degree revelatory of law's nature?

Julie Dickson advocates what is arguably the most developed or focused account of the first candidate for the answer to the question "Where should we start?" in elucidating law. Although, as shown before, she understands law's nature to be dual, that is, both descriptive and evaluative, and although she concedes that certain evaluative features are essential to grasping what law is, she holds that what first strikes us about law is its existence as a social fact. The phenomenon of law "appears" to us, above all, through the existence of posited legal rules, which are not valid on account of their moral merit but rather because of their social-factual source, and through the fact that legal officials practice their profession by authoritatively applying those rules, even coercively, if necessary.[2] As she says: "law's social facticity—the fact that it is 'out there' and has a profound effect upon the social reality of people's lives irrespective of whether it fulfils any moral task it may have—is something significant about law which it is important to foreground and adequately explain in our legal theories."[3] Accordingly, it is this feature that should have, to use her words, "explanatory priority"[4] in a "staged inquiry"[5] of understanding law's nature, an inquiry that includes, and essentially so, certain evaluative, though not necessarily moral, features.

In John Finnis's view, it does not matter where one starts in elucidating law, whether with social facts or with evaluative considerations. Even if one starts with law's posited social-factual existence—which denotes one of law's two necessary "lives," according to Finnis—one will not go far without perceiving and having to account for the reality that law is essentially a matter of evaluation and reasons for action, which include moral (even substantive moral) reasons. This is why Finnis, throughout his texts, chooses to describe law by giving a certain explanatory (though not conceptual or epistemological) priority to positive law's evaluative moral "life" as a determinate set of reasons for action. As he admits, he prefers to describe law evaluatively, by going "directly to the *needs* to which law is the generically most satisfactory kind of response, and trace out that complex of ends and means."[6] Although it may be true

2. See Julie Dickson, "Law and Its Theory: A Question of Priorities," in *Reason, Morality and Law*, 362, 372–73. For another presentation of the descriptive or "social reality of law," see also Dickson, *Elucidating Law*, 85.

3. Julie Dickson, "Legal Positivism: Contemporary Debates," 57.

4. Dickson, "Law and Its Theory: A Question of Priorities," 365.

5. Dickson, *Elucidating Law*, 135.

6. Finnis, "Reflections and Responses," 551 (emphasis added).

that people encounter or experience the phenomenon of law for the first time through the social-factual out-thereness of its posited rules and the institutional practice arising from them, in Finnis's view, the most important or decisive thing that strikes us about law is its evaluative moral claim on people's deliberations "about what to decide": "This mode of our positive law's existence—as a morally legitimate and compelling, albeit conditionally and only defeasibly compelling, *claim on my action when I am thinking what to do* as a plain citizen (child or adult), a judge, a police officer ... and so forth—is the primary reality of *law*."[7] Consequently, the "starting point"[8] for explaining law's nature is to be found in contextualizing all social-factual manifestations of the phenomenon of law in a deliberation on their evaluative features understood as a set of reasons for action: "the assumption that in relation to human things constituted by human choices, like law, you can answer the question 'What it is?' before you tackle the question 'Why choose to have it, create it, maintain it, and comply with it?' ... is a philosophical mistake."[9]

Reasons for Starting with Justice

There is, however, another phenomenon that may represent a suitable entry point for our reflection on law's nature, another set of experiential facets that strike us as constitutive of what law is and at the same time of what it, evaluatively speaking, ought to be. This starting point does not rely upon a prior premise that law is essentially a social-factual posited entity, a premise that both Dickson and Finnis endorse, albeit in different ways. Instead of starting by elucidating law's social-factual out-thereness or by inquiring into the general reasons for having an institution such as positive law that makes certain claims on the modelling of our choices and actions,

7. John Finnis, "Describing Law Normatively," in *Collected Essays*, vol. 4, *Philosophy of Law*, 29 (emphasis in original).

8. Finnis, "Describing Law Normatively," 31–32.

9. Finnis, "Describing Law Normatively," 45. See also "Evaluation and the Description of Law," in Finnis, *Natural Law and Natural Rights*, chap. 1, 3–22.

I propose that we should seek the entry point to understanding law's nature elsewhere—in a more specific set of reasons for action—without disregarding the starting points proposed by authors such as Dickson and Finnis.

Here is where I think we should start. Things are attributed, that is, not everything belongs to everyone. Rather, things belong to determinate persons in fixed ways. The attribution of things usually puts us in a position of having to respect that attribution, of owing that respect, just as other persons owe the same respect regarding things that are attributed to us in some way. If we look around wherever we are right now—a room, a hall, a vehicle of public or private transport, a road, a meadow, anywhere we are at this moment (or any other moment), or any realistic place where we could imagine ourselves to be—or if we check our pockets, briefcases, or handbags, we will notice the variety of things that are found there. Even the book that you are perhaps currently holding in your hand or reading from your tablet or e-book reader belongs to someone (to you or to somebody else). A large quantity of things that we can see in our immediate surroundings at any given moment belong to, are attributed to, somebody. This includes our psycho-corporal existence, the bodily and spiritual aspects of which—and the whole of which—may also be said to belong to somebody or to be attributed to someone, namely, to each of us, and in a way that should be respected by persons other than ourselves. If we look at our relationships (familial, educational, work-based, political, religious, etc.) and our actions, we can also find that many of these relationships and actions ought to be attained or lived out in certain ways, rather than in other ways that deform or denature something about them. In other words, "things"—in the broadest possible sense of the term, which includes practically all (and not only) the realities, entities, actions, and relational states of affairs mentioned in this paragraph—*are attributed.*

Under what conditions can the fact that things are attributed be true? What is it that makes the book that I bought in a bookshop, and that I am currently holding in my hands, truly mine and not anyone (or everyone) else's? Or what is it that makes the psycho-corporal and spiritual aspects of the "thing" that is referred to as "life" and instantiated in my concrete existence truly mine, as opposed to anyone else's? It seems that the first thing we need to establish to verify the fact that things are attributed is whether "things" are really attributed to a determinate person (or to a group of persons or to a community). Thus, we arrive at the category of a "title," something that can intelligibly be presented as a solid basis of the things attribution to a determinate person, whether an individual or group. For instance, I can present the receipt that shows that I bought the book that I am currently reading from a bookshop that was legitimately entitled to sell it, and I can further point to the relevant legislation or other valid positive-law sources that describe the transfer of ownership through an appropriate contract stipulated between a buyer and a seller. I can also invoke my human or even natural right that things such as this book may, indeed, potentially belong to me as their owner, that is, that I am capable of ownership, together with all the specificities that ownership implies. In a similar fashion, with regard to my life, I can point to the relevant valid positive-law sources that safeguard the value of "life" precisely as attributed to myself and that protect me from the intrusion or violation of that "thing" or reality by other persons, and I can further invoke my human or even natural right to life, with all that this implies. In sum, we can understand that certain things belong to determinate persons by inquiring into the existence of an appropriate title for that attribution. We will find that a large quantity of things that we can perceive in our surroundings belong to determinate persons according to certain titles. Again, it seems that things are attributed in an intelligible and verifiable way.

Besides being quite fascinating, the experience of this phenomenon—that things are attributed—may be seen to be even more striking than the certainly captivating phenomenon of law's social-factual existence and its claim on our practical deliberation and concrete action. A case could be made that the phenomenon of the attribution of things structurally precedes these latter starting points for analyzing law's nature (i.e., that the former phenomenon is even closer to our immediate experience than these latter phenomena). Of course, we still have to establish what this former starting point has to do with law, and why a reflection on law's nature can or should, and rewardingly so, start with this simple perception: things are attributed.[10]

My proposal for the selection of the evaluative feature to which we should give explanatory priority in elucidating law is highly congenial to Finnis's proposal. This is because the evaluative feature that I deem central in this endeavor also constitutes a particular set of reasons for action. I will first present this evaluative feature and then, later in this chapter, I will elaborate on where my account partially differs from Finnis's.

The state of affairs wherein things are verifiably attributed to determinable titleholders does not yet complete the picture of what we should do or not do as acting persons. The following evaluative consideration may be said to complete that picture: to the extent that I find myself in a position to at least potentially interfere with the ways in which a thing belongs to a determinate titleholder according to all the relevant ways this "belonging" is established by the title of attribution,[11] I can perceive that the ordering of my actions that

10. When highlighting the importance of reflecting upon law's nature by taking this simple perception as a starting point, I am largely indebted to the legal-philosophical work of Javier Hervada, who while pondering on Aristotle's, the Roman jurists,' and Thomas Aquinas's account of the essence of law, arrived at the conclusion that according to the jurisprudential tradition of these authors, it is fitting to start the reflection on what law is precisely here. Regardless of its importance to the arguments of these classical authors, this starting point remained largely implicit in their writings, and Hervada made it fully explicit. Although his analysis of this point of departure is outlined in a different scholarly context (not in comparison to arguments made by authors such as Dickson and Finnis), and with somewhat different emphases within the broader project of understanding law's nature than my present effort, Hervada remains a valuable source for this and some other ideas presented in this book. See Javier Hervada, *Critical Introduction to Natural Right*, trans. Mindy Emmons (Wilson & Lafleur Ltée, 2020), 7–12.

11. Here, I am again following Hervada's insightful remarks; see Hervada, *Critical Introduction to Natural Right*, 12–13.

respects said attribution constitutes a desirable end of my personal agency, indeed, a specific form of good. For instance, interfering with the way that a book belongs to you as its owner, by destroying or damaging it, by stealing it, by using it as my own without your approval, or by any number of actions that violate the purposes included in the attribution of the book to you, creates certain reasons for actions. These reasons may be articulated according to (1) their negative aspect, in terms of my obligation or duty to respect said attribution and abstain from interfering with it, and (2) their positive aspect, wherein my respecting of said attribution, whether by abstaining or by proactive actions, corresponds to a specific form of good, that is, to a desirable end or outcome. Of course, the book in question may legitimately be in the possession of another person, on the basis of her agreement with the owner of the book, and in that case, the relevant obligation consists of respecting the modality according to which, as agreed upon, another person may keep the book in her possession, use it in a certain way for determinate purposes, and then give it back to the owner.

Taken together, these two moments, (1) the moment of verifiable attribution of a thing to a determinable titleholder and (2) the moment of obligatoriness arising from the possibility of another person's illicit interference with said attribution, complete the basic structure of a specific evaluative feature: *justice*. The claim that it is precisely the evaluative standard of justice, understood according to its two foundational moments, that makes law what it is (and hence not only that what law should be), is one of the central ideas of this book. What I mean by this idea is the following thesis: "things" become juridicized—they become "law"—on account of their structural involvement in the evaluative standard of justice. Said differently, justice juridicizes—that is, renders law—everything that stands within its reach as its direct object. Another way of putting this would be to say that justice infuses everything within its reach with the idea of juridicity. For instance, a book is introduced into the domain of law not only because it became an object of a contract between two parties on the basis of valid positive rules that prescribe the necessary elements of that contract. Rather, it became juridicized on account of its involvement in the evaluative relationship of justice. This involvement of the thing in (or its standing within the reach of) justice rests on a series of juridical titles of attribution and corresponding debt: a contract as the most proximate among these titles, across the reference to the applicable content of valid positive law, straight up to the human-rights or natural-rights foundations of ownership. The relevant reasons for action regarding the book that is the object of a contract correspond to the imperative to give to each person that thing which is her own *ius*, that is, to the actualization of the two constitutive moments of justice: attribution and obligatoriness. More will be said about the structural place of both justice and juridical titles in the phenomenon of law when I present the four causes of *ius* in the next chapter. For this chapter, it is sufficient to establish that justice is the starting point for elucidating law, and that all law is justice-based.

To advance and explore the claim that justice constitutes a suitable entry point for understanding the nature of law, does not mean that other starting points should be excluded or cast aside as irrelevant in comparison. Rather, this book intends to show what it means to take justice as a starting point in elucidating law, while keeping in mind the viability of approaching law's ontology by studying its social-factual properties and its practical reasonableness.

A Brief Historical Excursus #1: The Interconnectedness between Law and Justice

Throughout the book, I will occasionally pause the development of my line of argument to present certain insights from the history of legal philosophy, which I deem revealing for the topic that is currently being analyzed. In the first excursus of this kind, and without the pretense of providing a comprehensive survey of the historical interconnectedness between the ideas of law and justice, I will limit myself to briefly presenting the historical instances that testify to defining law almost entirely from the viewpoint of justice, and I will then proceed to identify the historical moment in which the idea of law was almost entirely disconnected from justice. The authoritativeness of historical sources for the thesis on the comprehensive interconnectedness between law and justice is quite compelling, although, as I said before, the arguments of this book do not primarily rely on the authority of their sources but rather on the solidity of their scholarly allure and merit.

The very idea of law, embracing all its essential features, began its distinctive historical development precisely as a concept modelled by the evaluative standard of justice. Aristotle is usually thought to be the first author to distinguish the particular domain of a justice-based concept of law within the broader sphere of morality, and he does so precisely by insisting on specifying the object of justice—*to dikaion*, that which is just—as something that is already terminologically, but also and more importantly conceptually, distinguishable from the subjective moral efforts of a man to become a just person—*dikaios*.[12] That which is just is an objectively measurable, outwardly ascertainable reality that ought to be attained through interpersonal agency (i.e., by performing the acts of justice, *dikaiosunê*) in a way that is not confined merely to a person's subjective internal moral aspirations.

Aristotle thus distances himself from the preceding line of reasoning, which reached its peak with his immediate precursor, Plato, for whom the realm of justice and law virtually overlaps with the entire domain of morality. For Plato, justice is the right ordering or harmony of the elements within the soul of the individual person: it "is not concerned with someone's doing his job on the outside, on the contrary, it is concerned with what is inside; with himself, really, and the things that are his own."[13] By contrast, in Aristotle's

12. See *Nic. Eth.* V.1, 1129a5–1129a10. For the English translation of Aristotle's *Nicomachean Ethics*, I will use the following edition: Aristotle, *Nicomachean Ethics*, 2nd ed., trans. Terence Irvin (Hackett Publishing Company, 1999).

13. See Plato, *Republic*, IV, 443c-e. For the English translation of Plato's *Republic*, I

understanding, although justice and law are necessarily contextualized in the domain of moral goods, they are not coextensive with that domain but pertain instead to a specific realm—essentially outward and intersubjective—that is more specific than the full range of the moral domain.

That the conception of law is entirely controlled by the idea of justice at this point and in the subsequent stages of historical development is further confirmed by the terminological and, more importantly, conceptual choice of the Roman jurists[14] to define *ius* as the object of justice: "A law student at the outset of his studies ought first to know the derivation of the word *ius*. Its derivation is from *iustitia*.... Justice is the steady and enduring will to render unto everybody his *ius*."[15] These remarks are gathered from the opening book of *The Digest of Justinian*, entitled "Justice and Law" ("*De iustitia et iure*").

Thomas Aquinas begins his reflections on justice in his *Summa Theologiae* by analyzing its object, *ius*. He cites the Roman jurist Ulpian's definition of justice verbatim, which he then proceeds to analyze as "fitting": "Justice is the perpetual and constant will to render to each his own *ius* [*ius suum cuique tribuendi*]."[16] In continuity with Aristotle and the Roman jurists, he primarily and paradigmatically refers to *ius* as an objective reality that becomes intelligible

---

will use the following edition: Plato, *Republic*, trans. C. D. C. Reeve (Hackett Publishing Company, Inc., 2004).

14. Thomas Aquinas holds that the Roman jurists embraced the meaning of the Aristotelian term *to dikaion* by translating it as *ius*: "They [the Roman jurists—*iuristae*] call *ius* the very thing that Aristotle calls the just object [*iustum*]" (*Sent. Eth.* V, lect. 12, n. 1016). For the English translation of the texts from this Aquinas's work, I will use the following edition: Thomas Aquinas, *Commentary on Aristotle's Nicomachean Ethics*, trans. C. I. Litzinger, OP (Dumb Ox Books, 1993).

15. *Dig.* 1, 1, 1–2 and 10. For the English translation of the texts from *The Digest of Justinian*, I will use the following edition (with some modifications to better convey the sense of the Latin original): *The Digest of Justinian*, vols. 1–4, ed. Alan Watson (University of Pennsylvania Press, 1998).

16. *ST* II-II, q. 58, a. 1, arg. 1. For the English translation of texts from Aquinas's *Summa Theologiae*, I will use the following edition (with some modifications to better convey the sense of the Latin original): Thomas Aquinas, *Summa Theologiae: First Complete American Edition in Three Volumes*, trans. Fathers of the English Dominican Province (Benziger Brothers, 1947–1948).

only within the framework of justice. In his view, *ius* may be referred to simply as "the just," "that which is just" (*iustum*), or, with even more precision, "the just thing itself" (*ipsa res iusta*).[17]

Although some of these authors gradually dismantle certain elements of Aquinas's account of the nature of law, justice may be seen to control the idea of *ius* or law in the writings of virtually all legal philosophers between Aquinas and Thomas Hobbes, be they Thomists (such as Francisco de Vitoria[18] and Francisco Suárez[19]) or not (such as Hugo Grotius[20]).

Hobbes is known, among other things, as the first author to define *ius* as essentially a sphere of absolute liberty, and Finnis believes that this radical theoretical move is "so drastic so as to carry the right-holder, and his right, altogether outside the juridical relationship which is fixed by law (moral or posited) and which establishes *ius* in Aquinas's sense: that which is just."[21] Thus, Hobbes is the first author to posit the thesis that the nature of law (understood as *ius*) is conceivable as entirely detached from justice. This argument strikes me as even more drastic than Hobbes's claim that the concept of *ius* is essentially detached from any other conceivable content (thing, or *res*) besides liberty.

In Hobbes's view, the essence of law (*ius*) emerges in the context of the state of nature, which is radically devoid of justice. In the state of nature, "every man has a right to every thing; even to one another's body,"[22] and since there is no distinction in things between mine and yours that is characteristic of justice, "any man might say

17. *ST* II-II, q. 57, a. 1. See also his argument that "the just [*iustum*] and *ius* are the same" in *ST* II-II, q. 57, a. 2., arg. 2. For his interchangeable use of *ius* and *iustum* ("*ius sive iustum*"), see *ST* II-II, q. 57, a. 2.

18. Francisco de Vitoria, *Comentarios a la Secunda Secundae de Santo Tomás*, vol. 3, *De Iustitia (qq. 57–66)*, ed. R. P. V. Beltrán de Heredia (Salamanca, 1934), 4.

19. See Francisco Suárez, *A Treatise on Laws and God the Lawgiver*, in *Selections from Three Works*, trans. Gwladys L. Williams, Ammi Brown, and John Waldron (Clarendon Press, 1944), I, 2, 2.

20. Hugo Grotius, *The Rights of War and Peace: Book 1*, ed. Richard Tuck (Liberty Fund, 2005), I, 1, 3.

21. Finnis, *Natural Law and Natural Rights*, 207–8.

22. Thomas Hobbes, *Leviathan*, ed. John C. A. Gaskin (Oxford University Press, 1996), XIV, 4.

of every thing, *this is mine*."[23] Justice appears in Hobbes's theoretical account of the nature of law only at a stage subsequent to the state of nature, when positive law (*lex*) of the State is introduced after civil power has been established. It is only through positive laws that things or realities, to which these laws refer, are effectively attributed to persons as their *suum*, and consequently as owed as a matter of justice by others.[24] Hence, in Hobbes's framework, the realm of justice is the outcome of positive law, and a person performs acts of justice to the extent that she follows positive laws. Since, however, positive law (*lex*) in Hobbes system, by assigning things to determinate persons as owed by others, sets limits on the structure of *ius*, conceptualized as a sphere of absolute liberty (where virtually everything belongs to everybody),[25] justice and *ius* are seen as practically adversarial and antithetical ideas. Put simply, more justice means less *ius*. This is a radical breach with the paradigm of the preceding tradition regarding the decisive role of justice in the nature of law.

I will conclude this excursus by noting that legal positivism is rather Hobbesian in at least one important aspect. When positive law is seen to essentially capture the entirety of the phenomenon of law—all law (*ius*) is positive law (positivists differ from Hobbes on this point)—the intralegal standard of justice is, in important aspects, ultimately reduced to a purely formal category and subject to rather arbitrary determinations of humanly posited valid law. Legal positivists will often say that justice possesses a "peculiarly intimate connection with law"[26] or that "the idea that law is intertwined with justice lies so deep in our consciousness that it barely attracts critical attention."[27] However, a positivist intralegal concept of justice encompasses only its purely formal aspect at the stages of law's

23. Thomas Hobbes, *De Cive*, in *Three-Text Edition of Thomas Hobbes's Political Theory: The Elements of Law, De Cive, and Leviathan*, ed. Deborah Baumgold (Cambridge University Press, 2017), I, 11.

24. Hobbes, *Leviathan*, XXIV, 5. See also Hobbes, *Leviathan*, XV, 3.

25. Hobbes, *Leviathan*, XXVI, 43.

26. Hart, *The Concept of Law*, 158.

27. John Gardner, "The Virtue of Justice and the Character of Law," in *Law as a Leap of Faith*, 238.

application, expressed in maxims such as "treat like cases alike and different cases differently." The underlying standards of justice that determine what exactly should be treated with impartiality and equality, and according to the content of which we shall assess the similarities and differences of various cases, are established exclusively by posited valid law. In accordance with the positivists' separability thesis, nonposited (or, for them, extralegal) conceptions of justice, which rely on certain substantive moral or political values, may be important and even necessary for understanding whether legal rules are just or unjust. But these conceptions do not of themselves, based only on their merit, conceptually or necessarily structure the intralegal concept of justice.[28]

In sum, for pre-Hobbesian legal philosophy, justice models the nature of law (*ius*). In Hobbes's writings, justice is essentially detached from and antithetical to law (*ius*). For legal positivism, organized around the core thesis that all law (*ius*) is positive law, it is law that controls virtually all the important aspects of intralegal justice.

The Essential Properties of Justice

Let us now return to the explanation of the ways in which justice may be said to model the nature of law and to "juridicize" things, realities, relationships, actions, and other states of affairs that may come within its reach.

It is usually thought, probably under the influence of a positivistic mentality wherein all explanations of law's nature are ultimately grounded in norms or rules, that a natural-law theory of law identifies the quintessential carriers of juridicity with nonposited or metapositive rules, such as the norms of something akin to natural law. Things become relevant for the domain of law to the extent that they constitute objects of certain norms or rules, whether natural or positive. Only norms "juridicize." Juridicity rests entirely on the

28. For my analysis of the role of justice in a positivist account of law's nature, see Petar Popović, "Hart on the Role of Justice in the Concept of Law: Some Further Remarks," *Jurisprudence* 13, no. 4 (2022): 489–515.

existence of certain norms. According to Thomistic juridical realism, however, things become juridically relevant and involved in the domain of law not only because they figure as objects of certain norms, positive or metapositive, but above all on account of their being caught within the reach of the evaluative realm of justice. As discussed above, positive or metapositive rules are indeed relevant, insofar as they denote titles that attribute things to determinate titleholders. But the moment of attribution is not sufficient to constitute justice, and, consequently, neither is it sufficient to complete an account of the essence of law.

What is also needed is the second moment, the moment of obligatoriness, whereby persons aside from the titleholder are able to interfere, in some way, with the attribution of a thing to the titleholder. This second moment, obligatoriness, also does not arise only from the content of a positive or metapositive rule that attributes the thing to a titleholder, even if such a rule contains instructions to other persons to refrain from interfering in any way with said attribution or prescribes sanctions for such interference. Even in the absence of such norm-based instructions or sanctions, and regardless of their existence, whenever a person stands in a position to be able to interfere in any way with the attribution of a thing to a titleholder, the deontic "mechanism" or structure of justice is completed and becomes operative. And with it, the phenomenon of law appears: the objectively measurable just thing—that which is just—emerges and becomes intelligible as the object of justice.

However, if one wants to understand how justice models the domain of law in such a way that law is sufficiently distinguishable from the broader sphere of morality, other properties of justice must be explored and made explicit. In the absence of these further properties, any "thing'" attributed to some person as her own and consequently owed by others in any conceivable way would be deemed immediately relevant to law. Due to the lack of any determinate criteria for selection, the field of law would be so extensive as to include virtually all moral "things" or values. If this were, indeed, the claim of Thomistic juridical realism and of a natural-law theory of law, then Dworkin would be correct in criticizing these theories' denials of any essential difference between principles of law and principles of substantive morality; their proponents would erroneously conclude that substantive moral principles have a legal status simply in virtue of their objective moral truth or merit.[29]

As we already saw, according to Thomistic juridical realism, the truth or merit of moral values is insufficient to establish these values, and "things" related to them, as fully law. Neither is it sufficient, for that purpose, to establish the sheer evaluative status of these values or things in the realm of both constitutive moments of justice: attribution and obligatoriness. What is also needed are additional properties of justice that are apt to explain why and how exactly there really exist considerable differences, to use Dworkin's terms, between the domain of law and the sphere of substantive morality. In what follows, I will present these properties of justice by closely following Aquinas's insights in this field.[30]

A first property that further specifies the realm of justice and distinguishes it from the rest of morality is *other-directedness*, that is, the feature according to which justice is paradigmatically oriented toward another person. Acts or states of affairs that are exclusively oriented toward the acting person, such as duties to oneself, are thereby excluded from the realm of justice. As Aquinas says, "justice ... denotes essentially [*ex sua ratione*] relation to another [*ad alterum*]."[31]

29. For Dworkin's critique of what he deems "strong," "orthodox," or "extreme" versions of natural-law theory, see Dworkin, *Taking Rights Seriously*, 339, 342, 344, and Dworkin, *Law's Empire*, 35–36, 97–98, 102.

30. For more citations from Aquinas's texts that further confirm his stance on the arguments presented in this chapter and in the next chapter, as well as for an inquiry into Aquinas's sources for these arguments, see Petar Popović, "The Concept of *Ius* in Thomas Aquinas: Analysis of Central Texts and Sources," in *The Concept of Ius and the Nature of Law in Thomas Aquinas*, ed. Loïc-Marie Le Bot and Petar Popović (The Catholic University of America Press, 2025), 3–21.

31. *ST* II-II, q. 58, a. 2. See also his following claim: "It is proper to justice ... to direct man in his relations with others.... The right in a work of justice, besides its relation to the agent, is set up by its relation to others" (*ST* II-II, q. 57, a. 1).

Beyond serving as a distinctive feature of justice in relation to the broader sphere of morality, the property of other-directedness also provides us with important insights regarding the nature of law (*ius*) as the object of justice. The phenomenon of law essentially appears as a reality that is radically altruistic, other-directed, *ad alterum*. The only proper way to approach and understand the relational framework of justice and law is to envision it from the perspective of the acting person who ought to attain justice through operations by giving (*tribuendi*, from Aquinas's definition of justice, borrowed from Ulpian) the thing in question to its titleholder. As we saw before, the moment of obligatoriness arises when a person other than the titleholder stands in a position to at least potentially interfere with the attribution of a thing to a determinate subject, or with the precise mode according to which the thing is legitimately "in the hands" of the debtor (as agreed upon between the titleholder and the debtor). Thus, the person who is the subject of this potential interference is the agent under duty to perform acts of justice; the titleholder is on the receiving end of a relationship of justice. In sum, according to Aquinas, the exclusively altruistic orientation inherent to justice is built into the very nature of *ius*, so that *ius* is not primarily something that belongs to me and that requires others to respect my relational sovereignty over the thing that is my *ius*, but is rather conceptualized in terms of the correct—and always other-directed—end of my personal agency.

This, in turn, means that Thomistic juridical realism puts a pattern for personal agency at the very basis of the phenomenon of law, and this pattern may be referred to as *virtue jurisprudence*. Said differently, the distinctiveness of justice for human agency, arising from its being essentially a virtue, is built into the very nature of law. Knowing that the virtuousness of justice is instilled into law's ontology is crucial for locating Thomistic juridical realism on the conceptual map of legal-philosophical approaches to understanding law's essence. According to Lawrence B. Solum, the evaluative standards that serve to explain law's nature in various theories may be subdivided into three main categories: (1) *teleological* standards, which primarily focus on the final (good) end of law or the value-laden ultimate purposes that are essentially brought about by law; (2) *deontological* standards, which explain how legal "oughts" are ultimately founded upon certain architectonic moral rules or principles; and (3) *aretaic* standards, which elucidate law's nature from the perspective of virtue-centered human agency.[32] Of course, authors usually build their accounts of the nature of law by taking one set of standards as their starting point, but not to the exclusion of other standards, which they proceed to incorporate by way of a secondary reference in comparison to the architectonic standard.

Following this classification, Thomistic juridical realism is a predominantly aretaic approach to describing law's nature. It places the evaluative standard of the virtue of justice at the center of the efforts to understand what law is and how it emerges. As will become clear throughout the book, the evaluative standard of justice is not the sole criterion for establishing what law is, since Thomistic juridical realism acknowledges the importance of other causes of the emergence of the phenomenon of law, including the appropriate attention to law's descriptive social-factual features, namely, its positivity.

A second property of justice, and thereby also of the nature of law, is *outwardness*. This property delineates the field of agency in which justice—acts relative to giving to each titleholder his own *ius*—are performed.[33] In a paradigmatic textual locus where he defines the phenomenon of law (*ius*) as the object of the virtue of justice, and explains what law is in terms of its ontological fabric, Aquinas highlights that justice is established through operations "without taking into account the way" in which the rectitude of justice is "done by the agent" at the level of his purely internal dispositions.[34]

32. See Lawrence B. Solum, "Virtue as the End of Law: an Aretaic Theory of Legislation," *Jurisprudence* 9, no. 1 (2018): 7.

33. Outwardness is also a property of the thing or reality that is the object of justice, that is, of *ius* or law. I will have more to say about this property in the following chapter when it is considered in relation to the thing or reality that is the object of justice.

34. Aquinas mentions the example of "the payment of the wage due for a service rendered" (*ST* II-II, q. 57, a. 1).

He firmly holds that justice is "not about the entire matter of moral virtue, but only about external actions and things."[35] Thus, the property of outwardness further specifies the realm of justice and the nature of law within the broader context of morality. This property clarifies that the acts of fulfilment of an other-directed duty, which do not transcend the agent's purely internal subjective dispositions and do not become outwardly manifestable, cannot be considered to constitute acts of justice in the strict sense, and thus remain ultimately irrelevant for the juridical world.[36]

This provides Thomistic juridical realism with the necessary elements for a response to Dworkin's aforementioned critique. Substantive moral principles do not have an immediate legal status simply by virtue of their objective truth or merit but above all by virtue of their other-directedness and outwardness, and always under the condition that these principles and their objects (goods) are somehow caught in both constitutive moments of justice, namely, the attribution to titleholders through a determinate title and the corresponding obligatoriness. Additional criteria for outlining the realm of law, beyond the sole reference to the properties of justice presented here, will be treated in the following chapter when I consider the characteristics that a thing or a reality must have to be apt for becoming law.

Justice and the Goodness of Law

The specific quality justice has as a virtue adds another evaluative layer that is of considerable importance for understanding the nature of its object, namely, law (*ius*). As all virtues do, justice contributes to the moral flourishing of the person who performs acts of justice. However, the primary object of analysis of legal philosophy is not moral flourishing but understanding what law is. Still, an important aspect of the virtuousness of justice may be seen to significantly

35. See *ST* II-II, q. 58, a. 8.

36. For Aquinas's insights regarding this claim, see *ST* I-II, q. 60, a. 2; II-II, q. 58, a. 9; II-II, q. 60, a. 3, ad 3.

contribute to our apprehension of law's nature. This aspect lies behind the answer to the question of whether some objective form of good, brought about by justice, goes beyond its flourishing effect on the person who performs acts of justice. Since justice is essentially other-directed and outward, it is important to ask whether a corresponding form of other-directed and outward good is brought about when someone performs acts of justice.

We have already established that justice, as the perpetual and constant will to give to each person her own *ius*, pertains to the domain of human action. In Aquinas's view, the proximate principle of human actions relative to justice resides in what he calls the intellective appetite, which has the good as its object—the will.[37] The term "appetite" is used here to denote the dynamism according to which the will of the human person may be said to be captivated by *ius* upon apprehending that this object of justice, as Aquinas says, "regards a certain special aspect of the good [*respiciat quandam rationem boni specialem*]."[38] It is his understanding that a special aspect of human good is brought about when each person is effectively given the thing that is attributed to her on the basis of a certain title, and which is correspondingly owed to that person by those who ought to respect that order of attribution through their external operations. Thus, it may be said that from the viewpoint of justice, the human will desires a justice-based form of good, and it accordingly seeks to vacate, through operations, all the remaining potential that certain things or states of affairs have not yet been properly given to their titleholder (or otherwise respected). This form of other-directed[39] and outwardly manifestable good, which attracts the will of the acting person, is the constant and perpetual "motor" that operates in justice as a virtue: it is good to "give to each person her own *ius*," to use Ulpian's and Aquinas's description of this "motor." We may refer to this form of good as the good of justice or the juridical good.

37. *ST* II-II, q. 58, a. 4. See also *ST* II-II, q. 58, a. 5, ad 2.

38. *ST* II-II, q. 79, a. 1.

39. "Justice is somewhat [*quodammodo*] the good of another person [*bonum alterius*]" (*ST* II-II, q. 58, a. 12).

The same goods-based structure is then seen as impressed on the nature of law, since the object of the virtue of justice—the *ius* that ought to be given—is precisely the concrete manifestation of the good that is externally brought about and given to the titleholder by acts of justice. Law (*ius*) is, according to an aspect of its very nature, the carrier of the specific goodness pertaining to justice, and thus, whatever its full ontological identity, law participates in this goodness. Law is a juridical good. Therefore, according to Thomistic juridical realism, the most fundamental legal-philosophical question—"What is law?" or "What is law 'in'?"—can never be detached from considerations of the human good, and the link between the nature of law and the good is established already at the highest, conceptual level of analysis.

Differences in Approach from Finnis and from Other Nonpositivists

As will become obvious throughout this book, the contributions of Thomistic juridical realism are contextualized in the broader framework of natural-law theories of law. It could not be otherwise, given the ample reliance of these contributions on Aquinas's original insights. I do not hold that Thomistic juridical realism is the "only true" or "exclusive" interpretation of Aquinas's thought. Rather, I see it as a module—indeed, a module faithful to Aquinas's insights—that may serve as a fruitful complement to other Thomistic accounts of law's nature. It is not my intention to replace these other Thomistic accounts with my present analyses. Instead, I develop the ideas of this book in hope that they will trigger an exchange of ideas with other Thomistic natural lawyers and perhaps also contribute to a further development of the overlap between those ideas.

Having said that, it is only fair to acknowledge that there are, indeed, some differences between Thomistic juridical realism and certain other natural-law accounts of the ontology of law that rely on Aquinas's ideas. John Finnis's theoretical project is the first that comes to mind when I reflect on these differences, while keeping in mind considerable common ground that I share with him. I am insisting on highlighting these differences because I believe that there are important things to be learned from them, especially with a view to the fact that they are not irreconcilable but rather may be seen to gravitate toward a common understanding of law's nature.

The main differences between Finnis's approach and my interpretation of Aquinas's juridical realism are to be found, first, in Finnis endorsement of the thesis that all law is essentially posited, and second, in Finnis's estimation of the importance of justice for the constitution of the phenomenon of law. Finnis does not seem to think of justice in terms of an evaluative criterion that in any way juridicizes things and norms, since these become juridical, or enter into the domain of law, on account of their being posited as valid. It is the social fact of positivity that marks the threshold of juridicity for Finnis, and it is his firm conviction that even the most unjust and immoral laws are still valid and still fully laws from the social-factual viewpoint, though they do not evaluatively or morally correspond to the central case of law. Even the most borderline cases of law, evaluatively speaking, are still laws, descriptively speaking.[40] I will return to the problem of unjust laws, and to Finnis's assessment of this problem, in the sixth chapter of this book.

But even if we focus only on law's evaluative "life," justice does not seem to have the same foundational function in Finnis's account and in my line of argument. This is because justice is, according to Finnis, only a part of the evaluative aspect of law's nature, which covers a much larger field and includes the entire relevant range of principles of practical reasonableness that pick out the basic human goods as reasons for action on account of their constituting aspects of the whole human good. In Finnis's account, justice is only one of the requirements of practical reasonableness,[41] and the good that

40. For what is arguably Finnis's most successful synthesis of this view, see John Finnis, "What Is the Philosophy of Law?" *The American Journal of Jurisprudence* 59, no. 2 (2014): 140. See also Finnis, *Natural Law and Natural Rights*, 363–66.

41. Finnis, *Natural Law and Natural Rights*, 161.

pertains to justice is only a subset of the full range of the juridically relevant good of practical reasonableness. Granted, he does think that the evaluative realm of justice, with its emphasis on other-directedness and outwardness, is particularly apt to determine the precise scope of positive law, thereby distinguishing it from the rest of the moral sphere that is deemed nonpertinent for the content of positive law.[42]

In sum, when reading Finnis's texts, one remains under the impression that he ultimately places a predominant emphasis on practical reasonableness, or *prudentia*, when describing the evaluative aspect of law's dual nature, and that, for the purposes of elucidating the essence of law, he considers *iustitia* to be only a subset, however relevant, of *prudentia*. This emphasis then results in his position that considerations of justice, which form part of law's evaluative "life," are ultimately practically reasonable or moral considerations, without any decisive role in establishing the boundaries of law, since this role is reserved solely for the conditions pertaining to social facts of law's positivity and legal validity. Finnis does not seem to think of justice in terms of an evaluative criterion apt to constitute the domain of law beyond its posited features. This line of reasoning owes just as much to his quasi absorption of the virtue of justice in practical reasonableness as it does to his belief that all law must ultimately be posited to be fully law. He seems to think that his position is preferable to an understanding according to which justice denotes a central evaluative standard that distinguishes law in nature and scope from the rest of practical reasonableness and morality, thereby establishing the realm of juridicity.

Other nonpositivist legal philosophers also ground their theoretical accounts of law's nature in a line of argument wherein justice has a prominent or even central role. For Alexy, the idea of justice

42. Finnis, *Aquinas: Moral, Political, and Legal Theory*, 226–27, 232–33. For other examples in Finnis's texts where he attributes an important role to justice in conceptualizing law, as well as for an overall assessment of his account of juridically relevant justice, see Petar Popović, "Reading Finnis and Aquinas on Justice as the Evaluative Standard for Positive Law," *The American Journal of Jurisprudence* 68, no. 1 (2023): 65–69.

forms part of the evaluative point of law, and it may be adequately described as an overarching, organizing principle for the moral content included in the "ideal" dimension of law.[43] Moreover, he holds that when the evaluative standard of justice is radically betrayed in the content of a posited valid legal norm—paradigmatically so "in cases of extreme violations of human rights"[44]—the descriptive aspect of law's nature in that norm conceptually collapses: "Legal character is forfeited when norms or systems of norms cross a certain threshold of justice."[45] Regardless, the principles of justice share the nonjuridical status of the entire "ideal" dimension to which they pertain in the framework of law's dual nature. In other words, they are not of themselves law, and law may not be said to be "in" them unless they meet the demands of the "real" dimension of law, that is, unless they are positivized. Thus, and in a way that is strikingly similar to Finnis's position on this argument, even when viewed as only a part of law's "ideal" dimension, justice is understood to denote a moral criterion, a module of morality that subsists in the dual nature of law.[46] Granted, justice is still a powerful moral feature in Alexy's account of law's nature—since it is within the range of its conceptual force to render posited valid law non-law (as will be further explained in the sixth chapter)—but it is still of itself only a moral, nonjuridical feature.

In Dworkin's view, justice, or "what we all together owe others,"[47] in a political community is above all a set of rights that are ultimately compatible with the citizens' fundamental natural rights to equal concern and respect, which are founded upon human capacity to "give justice."[48] Dworkin, however, ultimately grounds this set of requirements of justice, which are already fully law even before

43. For instance, see Alexy, "The Dual Nature of Law," 37, 39–40, 43.

44. Robert Alexy, "Some Reflections on the Ideal Dimension of Law and on the Legal Philosophy of John Finnis," *The American Journal of Jurisprudence* 58, no. 2 (2013): 108.

45. Robert Alexy, *The Argument from Injustice: A Reply to Legal Positivism* (Oxford University Press, 2002), 28.

46. Alexy, "The Dual Nature of Law," 40.

47. Dworkin, *Justice for Hedgehogs*, 327–28.

48. Dworkin, *Taking Rights Seriously*, 182.

they are posited as valid norms, in the domain of political morality of concrete polities. For Aquinas, however, the interconnectedness between justice and law is substantive, rather than merely political-moral, and I will return to this argument and explore it in more detail in the sixth chapter. For the purposes of this chapter, suffice it to say that from the viewpoint of Thomistic juridical realism, justice juridicizes and introduces everything, each thing and norm that stands in or is caught within its realm, into the domain of law. Thus, from that same viewpoint, justice and law do not ultimately depend on what constitutes the best political-moral justification of posited legal norms, institutions, and practices in a particular political community, nor do they depend on his account of the right to equal concern and respect as the sole controlling nucleus of this Dworkinian justification.

Chapter 3

The Thingness of Law

A Premise: The Four Causes of Law (*Ius*)

To say that law is intertwined with the evaluative standard of justice is quite a common idea in legal philosophy. Of course, there are many ways and levels of intensity according to which the interconnectedness between law and justice can be envisioned. As seen in the previous chapter, Aquinas holds that the very nature of law is so intensely linked with the virtue of justice that the former is conceptually dependent upon the latter, so much so that he seems to suggest that describing what law is should start with the understanding of the properties of justice.

But this does not mean that for Aquinas all that law is according to its nature can be explained by understanding the evaluative features of justice. We saw that the other candidate for elucidating law is identifiable in law's social-factual features: the posited legal norms, the corresponding practices of legal officials, and the institutional or systemic consequences of law's source-based coercive nature. Does Aquinas's emphasis on law's evaluative features mean that he completely discards its descriptive features as irrelevant for grasping the nature of law?

Aquinas's answer to that question would be that the nature of law includes both the evaluative and the descriptive features. But even this bifurcation of features is insufficiently precise for grasping the totality of law's fabric, since law is something ontologically richer than the framework of its "dual" evaluative-descriptive life. This is why his account of the nature of law could seem idiosyncratic to those people for whom law is either something decisively descriptive, or essentially practical-reasonable, or ultimately explainable only through some broadly established combination of the two vectors of reasoning about its nature. In other words, Aquinas's proposal on what counts as law could seem rather peculiar to almost everybody in the present-day context of thinking about law. We can fully comprehend his proposal if we are prepared to be surprised by the ontological richness of his idea of law, without taking up the tendency to reduce it entirely to today's predominant categories of jurisprudential thinking. At the same time, Aquinas's conception of law is also not entirely different from these categories, and we will see that whatever law is in his view, it certainly includes some descriptive and evaluative features. But his account of law's nature is even more inclusive than this, and it is important to understand exactly how these features are interrelated and what else is included in law's ontological fabric aside from the obvious candidates on where we should start in elucidating this fabric.

Perhaps the most fruitful way to understand the position of Thomistic juridical realism on the complex ontological fabric of law is to present Aquinas's account of the essence of *ius* according to the Aristotelian framework of the four causes,[1] each of which provides us with an essential aspect of law's nature. We can fully understand what law is only by taking all four causes into consideration, that is, by understanding law as a unity of diverse phenomena, each revealing an aspect of the essence of law, rather than by reducing law to only one such phenomenon or aspect.

The *material cause* of law (*ius*) may be seen to answer the questions: "*Out of what* does law come to be?"; "What is the basic

1. For a comprehensive account of Aristotle's four causes, see Boris Hennig, *Aristotle's Four Causes* (Peter Lang, 2019). For Aristotle's presentation of the four causes, see Aristotle, *Physics: Books I and II*, ed. William Charlton (Oxford University Press, 1992), II.3, 194b16–35. For Aquinas's account of the four causes, see Thomas Aquinas, *Commentary on Aristotle's Physics*, trans. Richard J. Blackwell, Richard J. Spath, and W. Edmund Thirkel (Dumb Ox Books, 1999), II, lect. 10.

ontological fabric of law?"; or "Where do we find law?" A central tenet of Thomistic juridical realism, indeed, the ratio of its *realism*, corresponds to the claim that things themselves enter into the very definition of law. Things (*res*, that is, in the broadest possible sense, realities, states of affairs, etc.) are not devoid of juridicity, and they should not be considered to constitute nonjuridical content of valid legal norms or nonjuridical objects of legal rights. Rather, things (*res*) constitute the very essence of the phenomenon of law. They form part of the ontological fabric of what law is. Whenever things are in some way implicated in the domain of law, they thereby become juridical. As seen in the previous chapter, things or realities become implicated in the juridical domain whenever they are constituted as the objects of justice. Things, realities, acts, or states of affairs—such as a house, an amount of money, human life, a bottle of water, religious freedom, the act of performing a concert, driving either on the right- or on the left-hand side of the road—do not of themselves possess juridicity as part of their ontological identity. A bottle of water is not juridical merely on account of its being what it is, ontologically speaking, and juridicity is not an aspect of its "bottleness" or "waterness." A *res* becomes juridical only when it is apt to be viewed as caught in a relationship of justice (usually, each thing is implicated in a whole network of applicable relationships of justice). Whenever that happens, the *res* in question brings all the relevant aspects of its ontological identity to the juridical domain. In other words, it is justice that juridicizes a thing and introduces the ontological identity of the thing (such as the "bottleness" and the "waterness" of a bottle of water) in the juridical world.

According to almost all other approaches to law's essence, things, acts, or states of affairs constitute the content of valid legal norms or the objects of legal rights, and thus they are the primary purpose and the ratio of existence of these norms or rights. Norms are promulgated as valid, and rights are seen as brought into existence, for the purposes of establishing an order regarding certain things or acts to which these legal phenomena refer. However, in these approaches, things themselves are never considered to constitute law or to enter into the description of law's nature. In Thomistic juridical realism, however, *res* are given a more prominent role in explaining the juridical phenomenon: law cannot be thought of without assuming that *res* forms part of its very nature. Thus, law is not something that essentially concerns only the phenomena of legal norms and legal rights, which then in some way refer to certain nonjuridical things, acts, or states of affairs. Rather, things, acts, or states of affairs are juridical—are law—to the extent that they stand within the reach of the virtue of justice. Hence, both (1) the substance or the ontological identity of the *res* and (2) the relational perspective of the evaluative standard of justice play an essential role in understanding the complex nature of *ius*. For Aquinas, law is thing-centered, or *rei*-centric.

Hence, Aquinas's answer to the question "*out of what* does law come to be?" is that law is essentially "in" the things themselves, be they things that pertain to a natural (such as water) or to an artifactual kind (such as a bottle), provided that they somehow stand within the reach of justice. It is an essential part of law's intelligibility that it always, and essentially so, falls at the level of concrete things, acts, realities, or states of affairs. In his account of the essence of law—indeed of the primary meaning of the word *ius*—Aquinas is particularly interested in highlighting law's thingness:

> It is usual for words to be distorted from their original signification so as to mean something else: thus the word "medicine" was first employed to signify a remedy used for curing a sick person, and then it was drawn to signify the art by which this is done. In like manner the word *ius* was first of all used [*primo impositum est*] to denote *the just thing itself* [*ipsam rem iustam*], but afterwards it was transferred to designate the art whereby it is known what is just, and further to denote the place where justice is administered, thus a man is said to appear *in iure*, and yet further, we say even that a man, who has the office of exercising justice, administers the *ius* even if his sentence be unjust.[2]

But again, highlighting law's essential thingness is not sufficient for grasping the entirety of law's complex nature. If the answer to the

2. *ST* II-II, q. 57, a. 1, ad 1.

question of what law is "in" is that law is "in" the things themselves, additional questions must be further explored to fully understand what law is. Among the most pressing questions is the one concerning the conditions under which we may claim that a thing (*res*) is truly law, namely, the query of what it takes for a thing to be constituted as law.

The structure of this query roughly corresponds to exploring the so-called *formal cause* (the second of Aristotle's causes), namely, the form (the essential idea or the archetype) of what *ius* is. *Ius* is, yes, a thing (*res*), but not simply any kind of thing, and certainly not according to whichever evaluative standard of reference and identification. As Aquinas says in the passage cited above, and as we saw throughout the previous chapter, *ius* is always and necessarily a *just* thing, that is, a thing caught in a framework of the relationships of justice. He adds that the thingness of each manifestation of *ius* must be understood as "the term of an act of justice,"[3] namely, it must be brought within the evaluative reach of the actualization of a "particular just work [*opus iustitiae*]."[4]

Next, the question of the *efficient cause* roughly corresponds to the question of how exactly it is that things (*res*) are brought within the reach of the evaluative standard of justice, how they got there in the first place. We saw in the previous chapter that the title of *ius* establishes a thing as a *suum* of a titleholder, and that this attribution (together with other relevant evaluative considerations) then provides the basis for a corresponding debt by other determinate persons. The title of *ius*, which determines or at least provides sufficient elements for the determinability of all the relevant aspects of acts of justice with regard to a concrete thing (the measure of what exactly is attributed and owed, as well as the identification of the titleholder, and usually also of potential debtors), is the efficient cause of *ius*. As Aquinas says, the title, be it natural or positive,[5] is the *ratio* of *ius*, namely, that which causes a thing to be introduced in the juridical

3. *ST* II-II, q. 57, a. 1.
4. *ST* II-II, q. 57, a. 1, ad 2.
5. *ST* II-II, q. 57, a. 2.

realm, by positioning this *res* in the orderedness of acts of justice.[6] In the following chapters, more will be said regarding the variety of juridical titles and their specific roles in law's nature.

Finally, there is the question of the *final cause*, that is, of putting the previous three causes of *ius* in a telic perspective: "What is this all for?" There is no doubt that for Aquinas, the end of *ius* is a specific form of good brought about by giving each titleholder that thing which is his own *ius*, as seen in the previous chapter: the juridical good.

The framework of these four causes covers the most basic structure of Aquinas's legal reasoning. Reasoning and practice characteristic of law starts with the things themselves, then proceeds by inquiring into the relevant relationships of justice through the verification of the relevant titles and their details in order to secure the fulfilment of the acts of justice and the attainment of a specific form of good pertaining to that virtue. Said differently, whether one operates from within the context of a controversy regarding the correct juridical status of a thing (as a citizen or as a legal official), or in a pacific setting of everyday nonconflictual performance of the acts of justice, if we want to know whether in reference to a certain thing there exist some applicable relationships of justice, and thus also certain goods to be attained through operation, we must verify that existence by seeking out the details of a putative corresponding title.

Back to the Things Themselves: Which Things Are Apt to Become Law?

Aquinas specifies two further characteristics of a thing (*res*) required for its aptitude to be constituted as *ius*. Not every reality, entity, or thing is suitable for denoting an object of justice, and thus for its inclusion in the juridical domain.

First, a thing is apt to be constituted as *ius* only in its outwardly or externally manifestable aspects (*res exteriores*).[7] This necessary

6. *ST* II-II, q. 57, a. 1, ad 2.
7. *ST* I-II, q. 55, a. 4, ad 4; II-II, q. 58, a. 8.

characteristic of a thing—outward manifestability—corresponds to the requirement that the act of "giving" each person her own *ius*, from the very definition of justice, be performed in an outward way. For justice to be attained, the *suum* of the titleholder must be given or otherwise respected in all the relevant aspects of its outward manifestability. For example, a house is typically a thing that is outwardly manifestable, but for a concrete house to constitute an *ius*, and thus to form part of the juridical domain, it must be sufficiently outwardly manifestable, something that is at least potentially realistic and sufficiently determinable as such-and-such a house by the relevant juridical titles. The freedom of forming and performing an act of personal assent in matters of faith (i.e., religious freedom) typically pertains to a sphere of personal agency that is largely inward, deeply personal, and thereby to that extent escapes the perception of the senses of other persons. Regardless, in those outward aspects that concern the possibility of interfering with this freedom (e.g., by forms of outward social pressure or coercion by force), this freedom is sufficiently externally manifestable and intelligible and thus constitutes an *ius*, an outward setting of freedom that makes inward acts of faith and their outward social effects possible.

But even among the outwardly manifestable aspects of things, some *res* are still unsuitable for inclusion in the juridical domain. Aquinas refers to this further characteristic in terms of the "becomingness" of a thing (*convenientia rei in seipsa*) to be constituted as *ius*.[8] To be "becoming" or fitting as the object of justice, a thing must be apt (1) to be attributed as a *suum*, that is, as "mine" or "ours" in clear distinction to "yours" or anyone else's, according to the title of attribution, and (2) to be consequently owed or due as such by others, and demandable by the titleholder according to its determinate measure.[9] Aquinas highlights that there are certain duties regarding

8. See *ST* I-II, q. 60, a. 3.

9. Javier Hervada elaborated a rather useful account of the *measure* of the thing owed in justice (i.e., the measure of that which is just, of *ius*): "We understand the measure of [the *ius*] to be its intrinsic and extrinsic characterization and specification. It consists of: (1) the specification of the thing (be it corporeal or incorporeal): its quantity, quality, value,

outwardly manifestable things that do not pertain to justice but to other spheres of agency, such as charity or mercy,[10] the objects of which cannot be constituted as *ius*, since they lack some aspect of the thing's fittingness (e.g., a clear distinction between *suum* and non-*suum*, a sufficiently determinate attribution or debt with regard to the person of the titleholder, to the person of the debtor, or with regard to the concrete measure of the debt).

At this point, another issue must be settled regarding the requirement of the "becomingness" of a thing to be constituted as *ius*: if, according to Thomistic juridical realism, everything that stands within the reach of the evaluative standard of justice thereby becomes law, does that mean that every violation of justice, however small or even trifling, regarding an outward and other-directed thing or reality, really constitutes a breach of law, that is, something illegal? This issue must be settled by taking into account two interrelated but distinct questions: (1) whether, according to the relevant idea of what law is (i.e., the relevant features of juridicity), an act that is unjust is always also a violation of law, and (2) whether an unjust act is always apt to activate the coercive mechanism of law.

Regarding the first question, for Thomistic juridical realism, each unjust act is, indeed, also a violation of law, provided that it is truly an unjust act, that is, provided that it constitutes a denaturing of a sufficiently determinable just thing or reality (which is suitable to be owed in justice), that both the titleholder and the debtor are clearly identifiable, and that the thing in question is manifestable in the outward and intersubjective realm. From this viewpoint, the juridical domain is inherent in a great multitude of relationships between persons, and it is certainly much more pervasive in the fabric of human interactions when compared to other frameworks of what counts as law, for example, legal positivism.

---

nature, etc.; (2) the determination of the modalities according to which a thing belongs to the titleholder: as an owner, tenant, user, or administrator, as the first holder or as a delegate, etc.; (3) juridical faculties that pertain to the titleholder; and (4) the conditions of the exercise of [the thing owed in justice], etc." (Hervada, *Critical Introduction to Natural Right*, 27–28).

10. *ST* II-II, q. 23, a. 3, ad 1; II-II, q. 58, a. 6; II-II, q. 58, a. 11, ad 1.

As was already mentioned and will be presented in more detail in the following chapter, for Thomistic juridical realism, there are certain things that are constituted as law even before or beyond what is fixed by humanly posited valid legal norms. This means that certain things or realities become law because they somehow already enter into the reach of the virtue of justice, regardless of the fact that they are not fixed as law by positive law. Of course, as will be shown in chapter 5, the range of such metapositive juridical goods is rather thin and circumscribed only to those outward and other-directed things that are picked out as the objects of the precepts of natural law—the so-called basic human goods—to the extent that they are sufficiently determinable in all the relevant aspects to be owed in justice. So, for example, if a person says something offensive to her grandmother in the context of their private conversation, or if a person deliberately tells her friend something false about their mutual acquaintance, to the extent that such actions have the character of unjust acts directed against the objects of the relevant precepts of natural law (e.g., against certain basic human goods, such as the knowledge of truth and refraining from offending the members of one's society, in this case, of one's family), they thereby constitute an infringement of law, even if these behaviors do not enter into the positive-law determination of corresponding felonies, misdemeanors, or infractions under the relevant state law.

At the same time, with regard to the second interrelated question, not every unjust act is apt to activate the coercive mechanism supporting the legal practices in a community. It is up to the political community to establish, by way of positive-law determinations, the level at which a violation of justice constitutes an unjust act and activates the coercive mechanism of that community.[11] Below this level, a violation of law is left to legitimate and peaceful private

11. It could be said that in the case of some extreme offenses, which are gravely destructive for the whole of human society, the violation of law somehow immediately provokes the response from the community's coercive mechanism, even if the activation of that mechanism was not explicitly predicted by positive-law determinations, as was the case in the so-called Nuremberg trials after World War II for "crimes against humanity."

settlement and reparation (the parameters of which are also determinable by positive law). This line of reasoning is already established by the classical juristic maxim *de minimis non curat praetor* (or *de minimis non curat lex*)—"the [positive] law does not regard trifles"—the clear traces of which are already discernable in the texts of the Roman jurists.[12]

Aquinas's legal-philosophical texts also include a number of arguments that correspond to the elements of this maxim. It is his understanding that "human law [*lex humana*] does not forbid all vicious acts ... but it forbids certain acts of each vice, just as it prescribes some acts of each virtue,"[13] including "some acts" (but not all acts) of the virtue of justice. For prudential reasons and for reasons pertaining to the principle of toleration, he holds that human laws forbid "only the more grievous vices, from which it is possible for the majority to abstain; and chiefly those that are to the hurt of others, without the prohibition of which human society could not be maintained."[14] Paternalistic tendencies in understanding the aspect of the nature of law concerning the activation of the coercive mechanism of securing law's application could, indeed, provoke "breaking out into yet greater evils," according to Aquinas.[15]

In sum, Thomistic juridical realism takes the metapositive elements in the nature of law so seriously that it deems them instantiated in each outward and other-directed object of the virtue of justice,

12. See, for example, *Dig.* 4, 1, 4, and 4, 3, 9–11. For more information about the maxim, see Max L. Veech and Charles R. Moon, "De Minimis Non Curat Lex," *Michigan Law Review* 45, no. 5 (1947): 537–70.

13. *ST* I-II, q. 96, a. 3, ad 1.

14. *ST* I-II, q. 96, a. 2. See also his following claim: "Human law was unable to forbid all that is contrary to virtue; and it suffices for it to forbid whatever is destructive of human intercourse, while it treats other matters as though they were lawful, not by approving of them, but by not punishing them" (*ST* II-II, q. 77, a. 1, ad 1).

15. *ST* I-II, q. 96, a. 2, ad 2. As J. Budziszewski cleverly notes in the online *Companion* to his *Commentary on Thomas Aquinas's Treatise on Law*: "Law takes cognizance of truthfulness, but although it may command a public official to speak truthfully before a grand jury, it does not command a teenage girl to write truthfully in her diary." See J. Budziszewski, *Companion to the Commentary on Thomas Aquinas's Treatise on Law* (Cambridge University Press, 2014), 189, accessed October 23, 2024, https://www.cambridge.org/gb/files /1814/0898/2129/9781107029392online.pdf.

which is fixed not by positive law but by the relevant precepts of natural law. But it is certainly neither paternalistic nor exceedingly repressive when it comes to the activation of the coercive mechanism supporting the relevant legal practices in a political community.

A Brief Historical Excursus #2: The Thingness of Law and the Separation between *Ius* and *Res*

It is quite common nowadays to think of law (*ius*) as something describable without any necessary reference to the things themselves that law regulates and protects, as well as to think of *res* as nonjuridical entities. *Ius* is thought to be merely instrumental in securing certain forms of behavior regarding *res*, whereas *res* do not add anything essential to our understanding of *ius*. However, at the very beginning of the philosophical reflection on the juridical phenomenon, *ius* and *res* were envisioned as a conceptual unity, and *res* was considered a necessary aspect for our understanding of *ius*.

We have already seen that in book V of his *Nicomachean Ethics*, Aristotle refers to the nature of law (i.e., to what will later be called *ius*) by employing the neutral term *to dikaion*, a term that denotes an objective reality that is just—that which is just—a reality different from personal (moral or virtuous) qualities or faculties of a just man.[16] That which is just (*to dikaion*) is an objective term—that which is brought about in external reality—of acts of justice (*dikaiosunê*), and these acts are, in Aristotle's view, predominantly about external things and operations, rather than about internal passions.[17] The just thing, although established either by a natural title or by a title "laid down" in the form of humanly posited law, does not conceptually overlap with these titles.[18] Rather, Aristotle places the objective just reality, that which is proportionately equal (and thus not disproportionately excessive or deficient) with regard

16. See *Nic. Eth.* V.1, 1129a5–1129a10.
17. See *Nic. Eth.* V.2, 1130a25–1130b5.
18. See *Nic. Eth.* V.5, 1134a1–1134a15.

to the benefits or burdens fixed by the relevant natural and positive titles, at the center of relationships of justice.[19]

The Roman jurists further developed these Aristotelian insights regarding the thingness of law. In the Roman legal tradition, it is by starting from the things themselves and by subsequently following the relevant relationships of justice, gathered by verifying the relevant elements from the titles of these relationships, that we can attain the complete juridical perspective of what things (*res*) belong to which titleholders, by whom should they be given (or respected), in what ways, and according to which precise measure. This thing-based, classical Roman jurisprudential tradition was subsequently articulated, probably at the time of medieval glossators, in the dictum *res clamat domino* [a thing calls out for its rightful titleholder].[20]

According to that tradition, our current understanding of the relevant juridical titles is only one element in a broader foundational framework for knowing the concrete *ius*, which needs to be completed (and possibly even improved or developed) by gaining insight into the relevant aspects of justice in a particular case. The jurist Paul quite successfully conveys this thing-centered, or *rei*-centric, paradigm that underscores the Roman-law understanding of the nature of *ius*: "A rule is something which briefly describes how a thing is. The law may not be derived from a rule, but a rule must arise from the law as it is [*non ex regula ius sumatur, sed ex iure quod est regula fiat*]."[21] The same jurist highlights that *ius* does

19. In Aristotle's view, whenever a general law made for all applicable cases leads to an injustice when applied to some particular case, "the source of the error is not in the law or the legislator" but in "the nature of the object itself" that diverges from the scope of the posited legal norm, and it is then "correct to rectify the deficiency" of the norm by understanding and attaining that which is just, as this is gathered from the relevant aspects of justice concerning the thing itself in a particular case (see *Nic. Eth.* V.10, 1137b15–1137b25).

20. See Alain Sériaux, "Res clamat domino," in *Un droit en perpétuel mouvement: Mélanges offerts à Geneviève Pignarre*, ed. Christophe Albiges et al. (LGDJ, 2018), 761–70.

21. *Dig.* 50, 17, 1. As will become evident in subsequent chapters, this *rei*-centric approach to understanding what law is in a particular case does not mean that the relevant juridical titles, especially humanly posited valid legal rules, may be considered irrelevant or even disposable in a particular case. The *ius* that is established by the relevant natural

not conceptually overlap with subjective powers and faculties over a thing, or with purely subjective mental constructs regarding a thing, but rather with the thing itself as the center of the relevant relationships of justice: "If a buyer did not know that the seller was owner, facts [i.e., the objective status of the thing] are more important than belief [*plus in re est, quam in existimatione mentis*]. Hence, though he thought he bought from a nonowner, if the property is in fact transferred by the owner, he becomes the owner."[22] These dicta from the Roman juridical tradition, although devised on the occasion of concrete legal controversies or issues examined and resolved by the jurists, testify to the belief of the tradition that *ius* and *res* form a conceptual unity, that is, to a *rei*-centric account of *ius*.

This conceptual unity between *ius* and *res*—firmly held by Aquinas, as shown earlier in this chapter[23]—was ruptured at a very precise historical point of legal-philosophical development. The author primarily responsible for the possibility of understanding the essence of *ius* in its detachment from *res* is William of Ockham. Arguably the largest part of the legal-philosophical analyses dedicated to Ockham's writings aim to assess whether he was the first author to define the essence of *ius* in entirely subjectivist terms (i.e., as, so to speak, my faculties and powers regarding what is owed to me or what I am entitled to), thereby abandoning the prior framework wherein *ius* was understood to be primarily describable in terms of certain duties to others (i.e., what ought to be given to others according to some relevant objective criteria).[24]

However, I believe that reading the core claims of Ockham's

and positive titles remains a source of our understanding of that which is just in a particular case, although the legal officials have the task of verifying whether our current understanding and formulation of these titles perhaps ought to be somehow improved—not arbitrarily, but in congruence with the order of justice established by the relevant titles—in order to better secure the elements of justice pertinent to that case.

22. *Dig.* 22, 9, 4.

23. Already in his *Commentary on Aristotle's Nicomachean Ethics*, Aquinas argues that the specific property of justice is its thing-centeredness, since the basic evaluative criterion of justice is a certain equality to be established with regard to the things themselves: "*in iustitia accipitur medium rei*" (*Sent. Eth.* V, lect. 1, n. 886).

24. I will return to this question and provide more detail on the debate concerning the

account of *ius* solely through the lens of the debate on the origin of the language of subjective rights obscures one of his important parallel lines of reasoning. Ockham seems to be among the first authors (if not the first) who explicitly describes *ius* as something that may be completely envisioned as separated from the thing itself. This radical breach from the previous *rei*-centric framework of *ius* was contextualized in the early fourteenth-century dispute over Franciscan poverty between Pope John XXII and some distinguished members of the Franciscan order, Ockham being one of them. Briefly put, the controversy concerned the juridical status of the Franciscan monks' relationship with the things they were in contact with (such as food, religious clothes, monasteries, etc.) during their life and mission, both individually and communally, as a religious order. Since the vow to poverty and the corresponding renouncement of private property are central to the Franciscan way of religious life, Ockham advanced the claim that it is possible for someone (e.g., a Franciscan monk) to be only a simple user of a certain thing (i.e., to engage in what he calls "purely factual use [*simplex usus facti*]" of a thing) without being in any way implicated in the relationships of strict justice regarding that thing, and without the necessity to view the thing in question as an *ius* from any relevant viewpoint.[25] In other words, things (*res*) and our usage of them may be envisioned as carried altogether outside of the relevant relationships of justice and law (*ius*).

It is not entirely clear whether Ockham was, indeed, the first author to detach *ius* from *res*, and the question of the extent to which his arguments on this issue managed to widely influence subsequent authors is far from settled. Regardless, it is rather evident that the uniqueness of Ockham's historical and doctrinal context[26] provided

subjectivist/objectivist reading of *ius* in chapter 8 of this book, dedicated to the analysis of rights.

25. William Ockham, *The Work of Ninety Days*, in *A Letter to the Friars Minor and Other Writings*, trans. J. Kilcullen (Cambridge University Press, 1995), 26.

26. For more details on Ockham's historical context and on the ways this context influenced his legal theory, see Andrea Padovani, "Birth of a Legal Category: Subjective

him with an almost unprecedented possibility to advocate a radical conceptual breach between *ius* and *res*. This breach was never directly disputed by the post-Ockhamian theorists of law's nature, and it continues to exercise a decisive influence on our present-day legal mentality. Whatever *ius* is in the mindset of authors dedicated to elucidating its essence, it is usually thought to be something, so to speak, "hovering above" the things themselves. *Ius* is almost never, at least not in any elaborate way, envisioned as something that is essentially modelled by *res*. In the following chapters, I will present an alternative to this prevailing legal mentality, that is, I will argue that there are important ways in which *res* models *ius* according to the central tenets of Thomistic juridical realism.

Rights," *Divus Thomas* 116, no. 3 (2013): 37–53; Ferdinando Treggiari, "Il lessico giuridico della povertà: Ideale minoritico e diritto nel primo secolo dopo Francesco," *Ius Ecclesiae* 32, no. 2 (2020): 549–78.

Chapter 4

Ius and *Lex*—*Ius Naturale* and *Lex Naturalis*

Lex as the Efficient Cause of *Ius*

Having analyzed the material cause of law (its thingness), its formal cause (justice), and its final cause (juridical goodness), in this chapter and the following three chapters (chapters 4 to 7), I will present various elements that form part of the efficient cause of law understood as *ius*. Again, the efficient cause provides us with the understanding of how exactly things (*res*) are brought within the reach of the evaluative standard of justice—how they got there in the first place. We are already familiar with the claim that another word, specifically jurisprudential or lawyerly, for the efficient cause of *ius* is the legal "title."

But there is another, more general terminological issue that needs to be settled at this point of the book. From the beginning, I have explored the nature of law from the viewpoint of the line of argument organized around Aquinas's concept of *ius*. Now is the time to explain in more detail why this terminological and doctrinal choice is justified and preferable to other options.

What we today call "law" in the English language, and what lawyers, judges, and other legal officials normally refer to as "law," namely, humanly posited legal rules, the rulings of courts, the practice of legal officials, and so forth, does not exactly correspond to what Aquinas would have called "law." In fact, there is a longstanding and still ongoing debate regarding what the corresponding Latin word in Aquinas's texts for the reality or phenomenon that we today call "law" would be. We are already familiar with the two obvious candidates—*lex* and *ius*—and lawyers should certainly be familiar with these terms, since both expressions are abundantly used in the classical legal texts and are still operative in legal discourse. However, as the French Philosopher Yves-René Simon said during his lectures at the University of Chicago in the winter quarter of 1958: "A whole library could be filled with controversies as to whether it is felicitous or not that one and the same word 'law' should be used to express the two ideas which are expressed in Latin by *ius* and *lex*, . . . in French by *droit* and *loi*, in Italian by *diritto* and *legge*, in Spanish by *derecho* and *ley*."[1] Simon concludes this observation by saying that "what remains of primary importance are the meanings and relations of meanings behind the terms."[2]

The central argument of this book is that Aquinas referred to the reality that lawyers and legal officials today call "law" by using the term *ius*, which is broader than the term *lex*. The concept of *ius* includes a necessary reference to the semantic range of the term *lex*, but it also includes some other realities, some of which I have already identified in previous chapters, and others that will be explored in the remainder of the book. However, following Simon's conclusion, it is imperative to justify this preferential option for the term *ius* in exploring the nature of law by clarifying the meaning behind this term, and especially its connection to the notion of *lex*.

Contrary to the reputation of the term *ius* as denoting a moralized meaning of law,[3] when he uses the word *ius*, Aquinas is not only making moral observations on what the law (understood essentially as humanly posited *lex*) ideally should be. Rather, we could

1. Yves-René Simon, *The Tradition of Natural Law: A Philosopher's Reflection* (Fordham University Press, 1992), 119.

2. Simon, *The Tradition of Natural Law*, 119.

3. For example, see John Gardner, "Legal Positivism: 5½ Myths," in *Law as a Leap of Faith*, 50–51. See also H. L. A. Hart, "Are There Any Natural Rights?" *The Philosophical Review* 64, no. 2 (1955): 177–78.

envision him as trying to update and broaden our existing, largely positivistic, *lex*-centered idea of what law is. He is certainly not inviting us to unlearn all that we know about law, and neither is his idea of law entirely different from today's prevailing understanding of what counts as law. Indeed, Aquinas's conception of law certainly includes the *lex*-centered phenomena of humanly posited laws and corresponding legal practices, but he incorporates these phenomena into a much broader and more complex notion of law.

Perhaps because of today's predominant jurisprudential mindset, according to which the term "law" is almost automatically conceptualized in relation to a legal norm (be it positive or natural), it is usually considered that the crucial texts for Aquinas's account of what law is are to be found in the *Prima secundae* part of Aquinas's *Summa Theologiae*, in a section dedicated to exploring the phenomenon of *lex*.[4] However, even from a cursory reading of that section, it is quite obvious that the conceptual framework organized around the term *lex*, as elaborated there by Aquinas, is too broad to provide the criteria for understanding the juridical or jurisprudential meaning of "law," that is, for comprehending what jurists refer to in their discourse and reasoning about law and legal practices. Said differently, regardless of the multiple connections between the jurisprudential meaning of the term "law" and the notion of *lex*, the latter notion is not entirely suitable to describe the nature of "law."

For Aquinas, the term *lex* generally denotes an underlying rational order (*ratio*) that "moves all things to their due end."[5] This general characteristic of each instantiation of *lex* is then captured in Aquinas's more specific definition of *lex*: "An ordinance of reason for the common good, made by him who has care of the community, and promulgated."[6] He subsequently elaborates on the concept of *lex* by presenting its complex structure in terms of a hierarchical network of mutually inclusive and interdependent plural orders, which include eternal *lex*, natural *lex*, and positive *lex*. Thus, the term *lex*

4. *ST* I-II, qq. 90–108.
5. *ST* I-II, q. 93, a. 1.
6. *ST* I-II, q. 90, a. 4.

is used to describe the eternal law, through which God "governs *all the acts and movements* that are to be found in *each single creature*."[7] When he describes natural law, Aquinas uses the term *lex* to argue that the precepts of *lex naturalis* prescribe the attainment of "*whatever* the practical reason naturally apprehends as man's good."[8] The field of natural law is, therefore, roughly identifiable with the broad field of practical agency and morality, and it also includes the duties to oneself without any relational relevance, as well as duties that may be fulfilled exclusively at the level of the purely internal dispositions of the person. Thus, Aquinas does not seem to provide us with the sufficient criteria to delimit, within the sole realm of natural law, a specifically juridical domain, or, broadly speaking, a field corresponding to the conceptual reach of the term law in the thinking and practice of jurists.

What about human positive law? Of course, if readers are convinced that all law is positive law, then the fact of positivity should be enough for them to establish what jurists refer to when they speak about law and when they practice it. However, if readers remain unconvinced that positivity is the defining feature that marks the threshold of what it means to say that something is truly law in a jurisprudential sense of that term, they will find that the criteria for determining the juridical character of *lex* cannot be fully comprehended by focusing only on Aquinas's account of the phenomenon of human positive law. Aquinas firmly holds that if we remain at the level of analysis only of the concept of *lex*, it is impossible to grasp the central case or the focal meaning of human positive *lex* without reference to a higher legal order of natural law, and thus to the broad domain of morality.[9]

But this brings us back to the problem of the insufficient specification of the whole of natural law for immediate jurisprudential purposes. Let us suppose that the juridicity of positive law is established not only by its sheer positivity but also by its harmony

7. *ST* I-II, q. 93, a. 1 (emphasis added).
8. *ST* I-II, q. 94, a. 2 (emphasis added).
9. See *ST* I-II, q. 95, a. 2.

with the precepts of natural law. For example, the following norms, which may be said to be in harmony with the precepts of natural law, are accordingly apt to be considered law if they become positivized: "It is forbidden to nurture negative feelings towards people who wear glasses"; "Citizens must defy persisting in suicidal thoughts, by taking into account the available measures, including also those prescribed by the competent governmental office for health-related issues"; "Citizens must become members of at least one other society that is deemed necessary for their integral development, besides the political community and the family"; "All citizens must dedicate sufficient time every day to their personal search for the knowledge of the truth about God." It is almost counterintuitive to consider norms such as these to constitute law, in a jurisprudential sense of that term, even if similar norms were to be promulgated according to the conditions of intrasystemic validity in a legal system. The scope of natural law, which includes the norms that prescribe purely internal or essentially nonrelational duties, is simply too broad to provide the criteria for identification of what counts as law for the purposes of legal practice. Thus, even a combination of (1) positivity and (2) necessary reference to natural law is still insufficient to establish the properties of law in a juridical or jurisprudential sense of that term.

In sum, it seems that we need further criteria for identifying law that extend beyond law's positivity or social facticity, and which are also more specific than a broad reference to the entire domain of natural law. Aquinas provides us with these criteria in his description of the concept of *ius*.

Understandably, when one approaches the English translation of the *Summa*, one is easily led into thinking that since Aquinas speaks of "law" in the *Prima secundae* in reference to phenomena such as natural "law" and positive "law" (the original Latin term here is *lex*), the core of Aquinas's account of the nature of law in general is located in that section of the *Summa*. However, the bulk of Aquinas's understanding of the juridical phenomenon, of what law is, at the highest level of analysis, is outlined in another section of the *Summa*, in the *Secunda secundae.* It is here that Aquinas analyses the phenomenon of law (*ius*) by presenting his teaching on the virtue of justice, by outlining the basic features of the object of justice, *ius*, and by developing his account of the properties of juridicity, which, taken together, provide us with the criteria for the identification of law, for grasping its essential nature. And it is in this same section that Aquinas explores the efficient cause of *ius*, namely, the possible types of titles of attribution of certain things (*res*) as owed in justice.

As one of the four causes of *ius*—the efficient cause—the title of attribution of a thing to-be-given or to-be-respected in justice is essential for understanding law's nature. When Aquinas develops his argument on the legal-philosophical importance of a juridical title, he does not use the word "title" but the word *ratio*, which, for juridical purposes, roughly means an underlying or foundational idea (or orderedness) that is sufficiently intelligible for understanding that a thing is attributed to a titleholder. Regardless of all the significant ways in which the *ius* and *lex* are interrelated, he thought it important to highlight that these two terms are referred to distinguished conceptual domains. *Ius* denotes the thing-centered, justice-based phenomenon of law, while *lex* occupies a different structural place in the architecture of law (*ius*): a title of *ius*. In Aquinas's words, *lex* is not the same as *ius*, strictly speaking ("*lex non est ipsum ius, proprie loquendo*"); rather, *lex* is a certain *ratio* of *ius* ("*aliqualis ratio iuris*").[10]

In his view, each act of justice, of giving to each person her own *ius*, presupposes an underlying rational idea or order, which has the structure of a rule (*regula*),[11] and on account of which a thing is attributed, assigned, or, as Aquinas says, "adjusted" (*adequatum*)[12] to its titleholder. If we want to understand to whom a thing belongs, in a world (or in our immediate setting) full of things, we should trace each thing back to the title of its attribution to a determinate

10. *ST* II-II, q. 57, a. 1, ad 2.
11. *ST* II-II, q. 57, a. 1, ad 2.
12. *ST* II-II, q. 57, a. 2.

titleholder. In doing so, we will find that such a title, in the end, always has the structure of an underlying rational order: "this thing belongs to that person, and this specific type of belonging includes that precise measure of action regarding the thing." Said structure concerns the very concept of what I call a "title" and is thus in principle applicable to all types of titles.

Thomistic Juridical Realism as a Natural-Law Theory of Law: Preliminary Remarks

Now that we are familiar with Aquinas's teaching on *lex*—any suitable type of *lex*—as a title, *ratio*, or efficient cause of *ius*, we can proceed toward a better understanding of the various types of *lex*-centered titles of *ius*. In this chapter, I will elaborate on the natural law (*lex naturalis*) as a possible title of law (*ius*), and in the following three chapters the focus will shift toward positive law (*lex positiva*) as a possible title of *ius*.

But before presenting the ways in which the natural law (*lex naturalis*) can figure as a title of a specific form of *ius—ius naturale*—some preliminary remarks have to be made.

Exploring the ways in which Thomistic juridical realism may be seen to denote a version of a natural-law theory of law is only a secondary aim of this chapter. In fact, it seems to me that the phrase "natural-law theory of law" may be at least partially misleading, since it typically relies on the premise that the focus of a theory carrying that label amounts to explaining how morality may be said to be "in" law, provided that the term "law" be understood to reference exclusively humanly posited law.[13] As discussed above, a large part of contemporary natural law theory shares this premise with non-positivist approaches, as well as with legal positivism.

13. Indeed, John Finnis sometimes describes his natural-law theory of law in terms of a "natural-law theory of positive law." See John Finnis, "Natural Law Theory: Its Past and Its Present," *The American Journal of Jurisprudence* 57, no. 1 (2012): 101. See also John Finnis, "Legal Philosophy: Roots and Recent Themes," in *Collected Essays*, vol. 4, *Philosophy of Law*, 158.

The best way to understand Thomistic juridical realism and its account of natural law is to invert the elements in the phrase "natural-law theory of law," and to see that one of the aims of this legal-philosophical approach is to engage in a legal study of natural law, that is, to explore the juridical status of natural law, both within and outside of positive law.

In the remainder of this chapter, I will first explore the conditions under which it is possible to claim that, from the viewpoint of the basic tenets of Thomistic juridical realism, there are certain elements of juridicity beyond humanly posited valid law. I will then proceed to explore the Thomistic account of what those nonposited juridical elements really are. To do so, I will reread the classical arguments of Aquinas's natural law theory through the lens of Thomistic juridical realism.

It is important to distinguish these two lines of argument, for two reasons. First, this is a book about the *nature of law*, not a book about *natural law*. I am primarily interested in understanding the essence of the phenomenon that we call "law," and the ways in which the existence of the elements of juridicity beyond humanly posited valid law model our understanding of what law is. Second, I am aware that for many reasons a wide consensus on the existence of natural law, especially on Aquinas's version of a natural law theory, is rather unrealistic and unlikely to arise today or within the foreseeable future. By this I mean that I am personally convinced that Aquinas's natural-law reasoning on law and morality is at least in principle intelligible to all, and, as such, it is available for being assented to as true by everyone. However, I wish to take into serious consideration the evident social fact that for various reasons many people think that this theory (1) is not the best rational explanation of the complex phenomena of law and morality; (2) is not fully rational, that is, its rational character is somehow defunct; and (3) is unsuitable as the basis for common agreement in a political community, although it might even be the best fully rational explanation of law and morality. In chapter 6 of this book, I will have more to say about the possibility of simultaneously (1) subscribing to Thomistic juridical realism and (2) being aware of the fact that it is unlikely that our present-day political communities will readily adhere to all the postulates of this account of the nature of law and of the natural law.

Thus, again, I believe that it is justified and useful to proceed in two stages. First, I will analyze the conditions advanced by Thomistic juridical realism for the existence of nonposited elements of juridicity *in abstracto* (i.e., prior to a full elaboration of the natural-law content of these elements). Second, I will explore the thesis that the natural law, in its Thomistic version, possesses an immediate juridical status even beyond (or, indeed, abstracting from) its incorporation in the content of humanly posited valid law. The two lines of reasoning, although interrelated, should not be viewed as necessarily forming a single theoretical move. Since they denote two discrete stages of a broader argument, the reader may assess each stage based on its own merits.

Elements of Juridicity Beyond Humanly Posited Valid Law?

The subtitle is phrased as a question, because in today's legal-philosophical landscape, there seem to be very few approaches to elucidating law that might appear as eccentric as the one advocating the existence of true law that is not humanly posited according to the agreed upon conditions of legal validity. It is almost as if a legal philosopher who would argue that not all law is posited might be considered as operating with an account of law's nature that inhabits a parallel conceptual universe of legal philosophy, a universe that has little in common with the one that today's legal philosophers and practitioners populate.[14] Indeed, apart from Dworkin, who is seen

14. Such a legal philosopher may be subject to even stronger charges, along the lines of the following claim, the "inclusive" character of which leaves much to be desired: "The concept of law is the concept of an artifact, that is, something that necessarily owes its existence to human activities intended to create that artifact.... Those who might want to deny that law is an artifact concept are not my concern here; the extravagance of their

as one of the "giants" of contemporary legal philosophy,[15] it is rather difficult to find an author who would be prepared to systematically challenge the "all law is positive law" thesis.

On the other hand, the claim for the existence of metapositive legal content continues to be closely associated with the central tenets of a natural-law theory of law. In his already quoted exchange with Finnis, Waldron expresses his amazement that Finnis's natural law theory is really only a "natural law account of *positive* law," wherein "natural law" means nothing other than "a well worked out moral and ethical theory."[16] Waldron, however, wants to take the word "law" in the term "natural law" seriously, and he argues that a natural lawyer should be expected to support the claim that natural law is, indeed, fully law or at least law-like, namely, "something that is capable of fulfilling the governance functions of law in the absence of positive institutions,"[17] including the very institution of positive law. In a similar vein, in his overview of the natural-law theories in the twentieth century, Francesco Viola notes that the doctrines of natural law "are linked by the persistence of an identical problem," namely, "that of the existence of law not produced by man."[18]

---

metaphysical commitments would, I suspect, be a subject for psychological, not philosophical investigation" (Leiter, "The Demarcation Problem in Jurisprudence," 666).

15. Neil M. Gorsuch refers to the period when Ronald Dworkin, Joseph Raz, and John Finnis, among others, regularly gave lectures and participated in mutual debates at the University of Oxford as "a time when legal giants roamed Oxford's spires." See Neil M. Gorsuch, "Intention and the Allocation of Risk," in *Reason, Morality and Law*, 413.

16. Waldron, "What Is Natural Law Like?" 74 (emphasis added).

17. Waldron, "What Is Natural Law Like?" 74.

18. Viola really only confirms that the cited problem is indeed the main concern of the natural-law theories of law when he immediately adds that there is another, "more modest" aspect of the same problem, namely, "the presence in positive law of some strictly legal elements not posited by man." See Francesco Viola, "Introduction: Natural Law Theories in the 20th Century," in *A Treatise of Legal Philosophy and General Jurisprudence Legal Philosophy in the Twentieth Century*, vol. 12, *Legal Philosophy in the Twentieth Century—The Civil Law World (Tome 2: Main Orientations and Topics)*, ed. Enrico Pattaro and Corrado Roversi (Springer, 2016), 3. In the same text, he will again restate that "in the authentic tradition, ancient and modern alike, natural law is law in the strict sense" (Viola, "Introduction: Natural Law Theories in the 20th Century," 79). These claims are even more incisive when seen against the backdrop of Viola's essential agreement with Finnis that "all law is positive law" (Francesco Viola, *Il diritto come pratica sociale* (Jaca Book, 1990), 133) and that "if it exists as law and as a condition for its existence as law, natural law is indeed an

Therefore, it seems that the claim in favor of the fully juridical status of metapositive content is generally seen to be congenial with the natural-law theories of law. The question that remains is *how exactly* it is possible to hold that there are elements of true juridicity beyond humanly posited valid law. Before presenting an answer to that question, it is important to note that, if there is, indeed, a way to advocate the juridicity of nonposited normative content, this circumstance necessarily alters and models the very nature of law. Just as the "all law is positive law" thesis amounts to the conclusion that positivity is a necessary feature of law's ontology, so, too, the claim that there are nonposited elements of juridicity shapes our understanding of law's essence in the following way: not all law is humanly posited according to the relevant criteria for legal validity.

Given that it endorses the latter claim, Thomistic juridical realism supports the existence of an alternative account of law's nature when compared to the account of law's nature modelled according to the "all law is positive law" argument. What law is according to the "all law is positive law" thesis and what law is according to the "not all law is posited" thesis are two different accounts of law's nature. Throughout this book, I will highlight that regardless of the differences, there are surprisingly many overlaps and compatibilities between the two accounts of what law is. For example, both accounts advocate the claim that there exists, at the level of law's nature, the necessity (or the need) for having positive law. Nonetheless, it is important to note that we find ourselves before two significantly different positions regarding the nature of law, two dissimilar sets of properties of juridicity, and ultimately two divergent meanings of the term "law."

Under which conditions may one affirm that not all law is posited and that there are nonposited elements of true juridicity? The shortest answer advanced by Thomistic juridical realism is: the

element that is internal to positive law" (Francesco Viola, "Positivizzazione del diritto tra immanenza e trascendenza," in *Verità e prassi tra immanenza e trascendenza: Prospettive di etica, politica e diritto*, ed. Tommaso Allodi, Elvio Ancona, and Shaban Zanelli (Perugia Stranieri University Press, 2020), 151).

virtue of justice must be taken as the starting point in conceptualizing law. If it is possible to identify certain things or realities (*res*) that are attributed to determinate titleholders by nonposited titles, and if these things or realities stand in the sphere of at least potential interference of persons different from the titleholders, relationships of justice emerge, and the things in question are constituted as juridical phenomena, that is, as law (*ius*). In other words, whenever the evaluative standard of justice appears in reference to things that are attributed to their titleholders according to titles different than humanly posited valid law, these things constitute elements of true juridicity, regardless of the lack of positivization of these elements and of the fact that they stand beyond the reach of the conditions for intrasystemic legal validity. Again, according to Thomistic juridical realism, it is justice that juridicizes things, not their incorporation, by reference, into the content of valid positive norms.

Whatever the relevant posited or nonposited titles of attribution and duty in justice, it is important to keep in mind that for Thomistic juridical realism, law is essentially a thing, not a norm or a right in any subjective sense of that term. Thus, the elements of law or *ius* beyond (or in abstraction from) humanly posited legal norms are always certain concrete things (*res*), which are attributed as owed in the relational framework of justice between determinate persons. Accordingly, since the very nature of law is altered by the inclusion of metapositive elements of juridicity, the best way to understand this alteration is to envision, in the ontology of law, a structural openness to elements that are best described as nonposited things (*res*) owed in justice.

Ius Naturale: A Metapositive Law

In legal philosophy, Aquinas's natural law theory is famous for being, in Hart's words, the "clearest, perhaps, because it is the most extreme form of the expression" of the point of view according to which "between law and morality there is a necessary connection."[19]

19. Hart, *The Concept of Law*, 153.

Raz notes that the Thomistic version of the natural-law theory of law is a paradigmatic expression of the thesis according to which "law [is] good in its very nature."[20] These are very important claims, but they need some unpacking to correctly understand their complexity. What does it mean to say that Aquinas's account of natural law tells us something about the thesis that law is good in its very nature and that this natural-law account represents a strong version of the claim that law and morality are necessary connected?

There are certainly many ways to convey what these arguments might mean. One way to describe their meaning relies on the prior premise that all law is positive law, and that natural law imposes a series of moral constraints on the content of positive law. In that framework, roughly corresponding to Finnis's legal theory, the primary meaning of the term "law" is reserved only for positive law, and the natural law remains only analogically law to the extent that its precepts are not infused with the feature of positivity.[21] However, in a Finnisian framework, the presence of natural law "in" positive law—we could also say: the unity of law's evaluative and descriptive "lives"—does have certain effects on law's ontology. Natural law serves as an evaluative guide for the creation and interpretation of positive law, since the harmony of positive law and natural law amounts to what is called the "central case" of law. When that harmony is ruptured, that is, when positive laws run afoul of the requirements and constraints of natural law, the ontological unity of law's two "lives" enters the mode of, so to speak, schizophrenic disbalance, or a split between what law is and what law ought to be. Unjust and immoral laws thus denote peripheral cases of what law is, while still remaining law. In addition, when confronted with unjust and immoral laws, citizens' moral (not legal) obligations to obey these laws may collapse. Finally, according to Finnis, the infringement of moral constraints on law in the case of immoral or unjust

20. Raz, "About Morality and the Nature of Law," 167.

21. For Finnis's claim that natural law is "analogically law" only on account of its essentially moral status in the absence of the feature of positivity, and for an example of his claim that the fully juridical—or, as he says, "focal"—meaning of the term "law" is reserved only for positive law, see Finnis, *Natural Law and Natural Rights*, 276–81.

posited laws never amounts to a collapse of positive law's juridical character. Said differently, unjust posited laws retain their legal status regardless of their defects in justice and morality.[22] More will be said on the status of unjust laws in both Finnis's legal philosophy and Thomistic juridical realism in chapter 6 of this book.

Aquinas proposes various ways in which the goodness of law should be taken into account when conceptualizing necessary connections between law and morality. In the previous chapter, we saw that the final cause of all law is always a determinate justice-based form of human good, namely, giving to each person her own *ius*. Law's essential goodness may also be seen to be operative at another level, namely, in grasping how certain moral values or goods become constituted as law. Aquinas's proposal for this latter level of analysis is not primarily based on exploring the ways in which morality is somehow present in positive law, which is the strategy adopted by authors such as Finnis and Alexy. Rather, Aquinas suggests that there are important ways in which law can be said to be already present in certain segments of the moral realm, even prior to humanly posited declarations or determinations of such presence.

There are two basic kinds of *ius* titles, according to Aquinas's theory. As he says, "a thing can be adjusted [*adequatum*] to a man" (or "a thing can be made just [*aliquid facere iustum*]") in two ways. First, "by its very nature [*ex ipsa natura rei*]," and second, by acts of human will according to which the attribution of a thing to a titleholder is posited either by private agreement (e.g., a contract) or by a public agreement (e.g., a posited legal norm).[23] In this chapter, I will focus on the ways in which something may be adjusted to a person as owed by others in justice according to what Aquinas calls "nature" (*ex ipsa natura rei*), that is, according to a natural, nonposited title.

Aquinas makes it clear that what he calls a natural *ius* is brought into existence when a thing becomes an object of justice according to a natural, nonposited title. Keeping his thesis on the thingness of

22. For Finnis's line of reasoning on the legal status of unjust laws, see Finnis, *Natural Law and Natural Rights*, 351–68.

23. *ST* II-II, q. 57, a. 2.

law in mind, a natural *ius* is essentially a thing and thus not a legal norm, nor a subjective right of the titleholder. This is particularly important, since the English translation of *ius naturale* is "natural right," which should not be understood to denote subjective claims, powers, faculties, etc., and should not be comprehended according to a more objectivist reading of *ius* as essentially a set of duties to others. *Ius* is a concrete thing, and *ius naturale* is also a concrete thing, reality, or state of affairs that is attributed to a titleholder according to a nonposited title somehow corresponding to the nature of a thing, or to the human nature of the titleholder, to the extent that the thing in question forms part of the nature of the human person.[24] For example, life and psycho-corporal integrity, as well as other examples Aquinas provides of what natural lawyers refer to as instantiations of *ius naturale* are all concrete things or realities that are assigned to a human person as the titleholder, and which other identifiable persons may interfere with and denature, thereby "owing" them in justice. Thus, the term *ius* does not refer here to the faculties or powers that a person has *over* her life or to the cluster of norms the *content* of which may be said to attribute life to that person; rather, life itself *is* the *ius* in question, the concrete thing-centered manifestation of law.

Natural Law (*Lex Naturalis*) and the Identification of Natural Juridical Goods (*Ius Naturale*)

How exactly does Aquinas envision the attribution of a thing to titleholders in virtue of human nature, and thus not according to a

24. When this Aquinas argument from the *Summa* is read in light of his treatment of the same argument in the *Commentary to Aristotle's Nicomachean Ethics*, it becomes obvious that he envisions *ius naturale* to be grounded, as its title or *ratio*, not only in some abstract concept of the nature of a thing (*ex ipsa natura rei*) but also and more specifically in the primary precepts of natural law: "Natural justice does not consist in what seems or does not seem to be, i.e., it does not arise from human conjecture but from nature.... In practical matters there are some principles naturally known as it were, indemonstrable principles and truths related to them, as evil must be avoided, no one is to be unjustly injured, theft must not be committed and so on; others are devised by human diligence which are here referred to as that which is legally just" (*Sent. Eth.* V, lect. 12, n. 1018).

humanly posited title? How do we know that the reality of life is attributed to each human person as something owed by others in justice, for example, that life is so attributed to me writing this book, and to you reading it? According to Aquinas, understanding what is owed to me and what I owe to other persons in justice on the basis of human nature (e.g., the reality of life) begins with the understanding of which things or realities constitute aspects of human good. Of course, as we have seen before, the juridical phenomenon generally represents a form of human good, juridical good, or the good of justice, which is somehow harmonized with the whole human moral good. But when we speak about metapositive law constituted as such on the basis of human nature as the title of *ius*, to know that a reality pertaining to human nature is, indeed, a juridical good, I first have to know that it is truly a human good. Accordingly, it is a good thing that I respect the outward aspects of the reality of life of another person in my other-directed and external actions because I understand that life is something good for that person, indeed for all human persons.

After the initial understanding of what constitutes human good, attributed to the human person through metapositive titles such as the precepts of natural law, additional criteria are needed to limit the full range of moral inquiry of human goods to the specific field of law. These criteria are provided by the virtue of justice and its essential properties, such as other-directedness and outwardness. Thus, an object of the precepts of natural law (i.e., a basic human good) becomes *ius naturale* from the viewpoint of its constituting an object of justice. As is the case with any type of *ius*, things (*res*) that are constituted as *ius naturale* bring into the juridical domain that part of their ontological identity that is apt to constitute a term of an act of justice.

But how can we know which aspects of the human good, or which basic human goods, are constituted as *ius naturale*? And how is it possible to know their precise measure? A Thomist case for knowing the basic human goods, according to their practical-reasonable and moral status, typically includes a crucial reference to the tripartite order of the so-called natural inclinations of the will, that is, of the ways in which our will responds with its mechanism of rational desire or appetite to certain prospective ends of human agency, which our practical reason previously grasped as authentic particular aspects of the whole human good. This tripartite order of basic human goods that our will inclines to, as outlined by Aquinas in the *Summa*, concerns, first, the preservation of human life; second, marital union between one man and one woman, together with the generation and education of children; and third, the knowledge of the truth about God and life in society.[25] An updated, though still "open-ended," Thomistic list of basic human goods is provided by Finnis and includes the following "basic kinds of intelligible human good": "life and health, marital/procreative union, knowledge, friendly association, artistic accomplishment, friendship with the divine transcendent source of all these goods, and practical reasonableness in actualizing all these intrinsic, self-evident forms of human good, these aspects or elements of wellbeing."[26]

A lot of ink has been spilled, and some longstanding debates have been held in Thomist moral philosophy, on the cognitive conditions for knowing the basic precepts of natural law and the corresponding basic human goods, as well as on the possible lists of these precepts and goods. These issues are certainly of great importance and in need of adequate, highly nuanced elaboration. However, I do not think it is necessary to reiterate these arguments and revisit those debates here, especially because the study of the genesis of the basic precepts of natural law and of the corresponding basic human goods pertains to the scholarly research regarding the emergence of moral obligations.[27] Most of the debates between Thomist scholars

25. See *ST* I-II, q. 94, a. 2.

26. Finnis, "Aquinas and Natural Law Jurisprudence," 18–19.

27. For some of the main contributions to these debates, see Finnis, *Natural Law and Natural Rights*, 23–133; Russell Hittinger, *A Critique of the New Natural Law Theory* (University of Notre Dame Press, 1987); Steven J. Jensen, *Knowing the Natural Law: From Precepts and Inclinations to Deriving Oughts* (The Catholic University of America Press,

on these issues remain ultimately irrelevant for the realm of Thomistic legal philosophy, since the philosophers of law are primarily interested in understanding the emergence of the phenomena of goods in a juridical or jurisprudential context.

Consequently, from the viewpoint of Thomistic juridical realism as a strictly legal-philosophical approach, it is enough to know that certain goods are, indeed, somehow attributed, by virtue of the norms of natural law, to determinate titleholders as things (*res*) owed in justice, regardless of the specificities concerning the exact way in which the moral status of these goods emerges and becomes intelligible. This book is primarily dedicated to the study of the nature of law, and the inquiry of the present chapter is limited only to exploring what the existence of certain nonposited elements of juridicity that have the structure of *ius naturale* means for our understanding of law's nature. A short Thomist answer to the question "which human goods pertain to *ius naturale*?" begins by identifying the basic precepts of natural law (*lex naturalis*) and then proceeds to delimit the moral goods these precepts pick out—regardless of the diverse accounts of the exact way in which they are picked out—according to their pertinence to the outward and other-directed domain of justice.[28] This enables us to delimit and identify the goods picked out by the basic precepts of natural law precisely as natural *juridical* goods (*ius naturale*), which are sufficiently specified within the broader domain of morality so that their harmony with the whole human good is secured, while at the same time a confusion with the full range of the moral domain is adequately avoided.[29]

2015); and Stephen L. Brock, *The Light That Binds: A Study in Thomas Aquinas's Metaphysics of Natural Law* (Pickwick Publications, 2020).

28. I have dedicated my previous book to the analysis of this argument; see, especially, Popović, *Natural Law & Thomistic Juridical Realism*, 169–260, 280–82.

29. In other words, contrary to Dworkin's critique, there is an important difference in scope between principles of law and principles of substantive morality already at the level of *ius naturale*, and it is possible to note that substantive moral principles do not have a legal status simply in virtue of their objective moral truth or merit but also, and essentially so, on account of their pertinence to the domain of the evaluative standard of justice.

Justice and the Basic Human Good of Living in Society

There is, however, one argument that I wish to further analyze here that is relevant for a correct grasp of the natural juridical goods but that has not been sufficiently explored in Thomist accounts of the tripartite order of the basic human goods. Aquinas explicitly mentions that the third order of the natural inclinations of the will concerns "living in society," and he adds that "whatever pertains to this inclination belongs to the natural law," including the duty to "avoid offending those among whom one has to live."[30]

As is evident from Finnis's list of the basic human goods, practical reasonableness in actualizing all other basic human goods is to be counted among these fundamental human goods. We have already seen that in Finnis's view, justice is predominantly describable in terms of a subset requirement of practical reasonableness, which becomes operative in a social context. Accordingly, in his view, it is enough to stipulate that the duties arising from the third-order natural inclination of the will concerning living in society are sufficiently covered by social-context mode of the good of practical reasonableness.

In my opinion, however, there is considerable ground in Aquinas's texts for arguing that the evaluative standard of justice, together with its object *ius*, establishes a realm of goodness—juridical goodness, or the goodness of law in a jurisprudential sense—that is sufficiently discrete (though not separated) from the good of practical reasonableness. The juridical good and the corresponding duties of justice model, in rather important ways, Aquinas's third-order inclinational duty to avoid offending or harming those among whom one has to live. This especially includes the duty to avoid harming others by not giving them, or by otherwise disrespecting, their natural juridical goods pertaining to each of the three orders of basic human goods. In fact, it could be said that any instance of failing to

30. *ST* I-II, q. 94, a. 2.

give to others their *ius* registers as a harm to others among whom one has to live, and thus the third-order inclinational duty to avoid harming others in the context of societal life is broader than the sole reference to natural juridical goods and includes all possible kinds of juridical goods (including, especially, humanly posited juridical goods).[31] Aquinas seems to be referring to this *inclinatio* when, in one of his texts, he speaks of the inclination of justice (*inclinatio iustitiae*) that is perverted when an act is unjust (i.e., contrary to the rectitude of justice).[32] Thus, the domain of justice and law (*ius*) may be said to form part of the third-order natural inclination of the will regarding life in society and of the corresponding basic human good(s).

In sum, with the natural juridical goods, we have identified a first set of the phenomena of law (*ius*), namely, those things that are established as owed in justice (*res iustae*) by metapositive titles. These phenomena thereby denote the elements of juridicity that stand beyond—that is, their existence as law is independent from—the realm of humanly posited valid law. As Aquinas says, "written law," that is, humanly posited valid law, does not establish nor does it give force to *ius naturale*, "for the latter derives its force, not from the law [*lex*] but from nature [*ex natura*]."[33] This means that *ius naturale* does not derive its juridicity from the social fact of positivity, or from the sheer fact of positivity combined with its harmony with the whole of natural moral law. The juridical status of natural juridical goods originates in the state of affairs wherein things are assigned by the basic precepts of natural law (*lex naturalis*) to certain titleholders, as owed in justice by the relevant debtors, according to a measure determinable in reference to the outward and other-directed aspects of

31. "A thing is said to belong to natural *ius* [*esse de iure naturali*] … because nature inclines thereto: e.g., that one should not do harm [*iniuriam*] to another" (*ST* I-II, q. 94, a. 5, ad 3). In Roman law, the term *iniuria* denotes that which is not *ius*, that which is contrary to *ius*: "*Iniuria ex eo dicta est, quod iure non fit*" (*Dig.* 47, 10, 1). Aquinas uses the term *iniustum* (see *ST* II-II, q. 59, a. 1–4) and *iniuria* (see, for example, *ST* II-II, q. 65, a. 4) to denote that which is unjust or contrary to *ius*.

32. *ST* II-II, q. 60, a. 2.

33. *ST* II-II, q. 60, a. 5.

the basic human goods picked out by those precepts. The existence of these metapositive elements of juridicity constitutes a Thomistic answer to Waldron's "expectations" that natural law be "law-like," namely, that it be made manifest "as something capable of ordering our actions and interactions in something like the way that positive law orders our actions and interactions."[34]

Hence, this core of metapositive elements of juridicity models our understanding of what law is according to its nature. Said differently, what law is "in" according to its necessary manifestations influences the answer to the question of law's "whatness" and enters into the definition of law. A part of the fabric of law's ontology is necessarily instantiated in the circumstance that law is "in" certain metapositive, natural juridical goods. This is an important aspect of what law is "in," and thus also of what law is. However, the metapositive elements of juridicity are not the only elements that enter into the description of law's nature. Law is also "in" other things or realities that are not constituted by metapositive titles. Law's subsistence in those other things or realities also adds certain important, and indeed necessary, features to law's nature, thereby modelling what law is.

34. Waldron, "What Is Natural Law Like?" 73.

Chapter 5

The Need for Having Positive Law and the Nature of Law

Between Kelsen and Finnis: A Third Stance on the *Raison d'Être* of Positive Law

Jeremy Waldron is certainly not the only legal philosopher, among authors who are not natural lawyers, to understand that a natural-law theory of law should advocate a version of the thesis that not all law is positive law, but that at least some elements of juridicity can be established to exist beyond the realm of humanly posited valid law. Another legal philosopher to share that same understanding is Hans Kelsen, one of the most notable legal positivists.

Kelsen's line of argument is rather important, since he believes he has formulated a devastating critique of the entire family of natural law theories, including Thomistic juridical realism, especially of their account of the place of positive law in the wholeness of law's nature. The crux of Kelsen's challenge is the claim that according to a natural-law theory of law, all law must necessarily be natural law. This claim then denotes a sort of antipode to the "all law is positive law" central tenet of legal positivism, shared by some prominent nonpositivists and even by some leading natural lawyers. These latter theorists' endorsement of the core positivist thesis is in itself a refutation of Kelsen's critique. Thomist juridical realism's short response to Kelsen would be that, indeed, not all law is natural law, although, as we saw in the preceding chapter, the existence of certain metapositive elements of juridicity is so important that it constitutes an essential feature of law's ontology, and the realm of these elements does not cover the entirety of the ontological fabric of law's nature. Not all law is natural law because some law is necessarily posited. However, to correctly understand the claim regarding law's nature advanced by Thomistic juridical realism, it is necessary to grasp the full impact of Kelsen's critique.

According to an important interpretation of Kelsen's account of the natural-law theory of law advanced by his fellow positivist Joseph Raz, Kelsen would seem to have affirmed that the natural law consists of a set of norms that are "objectively valid" on account of their being "objectively just and good" in a moral sense.[1] "Kelsen correctly points out," continues Raz, "that according to natural-law theories there is no specific notion of legal validity [but] the only concept of validity is validity according to natural law, i.e., moral validity [and thus] natural lawyers can only judge a law as morally valid."[2] "Positive law," he concludes this interpretation of Kelsen's views, "derives its validity from natural law."[3] However, Kelsen seems to put forward a claim that is even stronger than its slightly watered-down version described in Raz's partially inaccurate interpretation. The unlikeliness of the existence of metapositive law in contemporary legal philosophy seems to have obscured Raz's line of analysis, and he thus understands Kelsen to affirm that the natural law establishes the standard of purely moral validity, which ultimately undermines any conceptual possibility that the criterion of legal validity be predicated of positive law. But Kelsen's texts suggest that he in fact had a more nuanced understanding of a central thesis of a natural-law theory of law, according to which the metapositive norms of natural

1. Joseph Raz, "Kelsen's Theory of the Basic Norm," in *The Authority of Law*, 129–30.
2. Raz, "Kelsen's Theory of the Basic Norm," 130.
3. Raz, "Kelsen's Theory of the Basic Norm," 130.

law not only establish the evaluative standard of moral validity for positive law but also inaugurate a set of properties of what is to count as law. Thus, both natural laws and positive laws ought to be considered law according to these natural-law properties of juridicity or of legal validity.

In other words, Kelsen understood that for natural lawyers, natural law is fully law. In his view, the "essence of the natural-law doctrine" amounts to the claim that "the law can be deduced from nature" and that this law is "an eternal and immutable law, in contradistinction to positive law which, created by man, is only a temporary and changeable order."[4] The natural law is, he says, "preexisting law"[5] in comparison to positive law. In his estimation, "the natural law teachers contend, in a version which has remained a stereotype from the church fathers down to Kant, that positive law derives its entire validity from natural law," that is, from "the true law which is already somehow in existence."[6] Kelsen is correct to assume that for a natural-law theory of law the juridicity (or legal validity) of natural law arises from its essential connection to the evaluative standard of justice,[7] although he is mistaken to conclude that the conceptual range of the term natural law is entirely overlapping with the realm of justice.[8]

Not only are Kelsen's texts unambiguous regarding the thesis that the natural law is fully law, but he also maintains that positive law may be considered fully law only according to the conditions of juridicity or legal validity installed by the natural law: "Positive law is 'law,' too; and as long as it is not proved to be at variance with natural

4. Hans Kelsen, "The Natural-Law Doctrine before the Tribunal of Science," in *What Is Justice? Justice, Law, and Politics in the Mirror of Science: Collected Essays by Hans Kelsen* (University of California Press, 1971), 138, 141.

5. Hans Kelsen, "Law, State, and Justice in the Pure Theory of Law," in *What Is Justice? Justice, Law, and Politics in the Mirror of Science*, 297.

6. Hans Kelsen, *General Theory of Law & State* (Transaction Publishers, 2006), 416.

7. For Kelsen's claim that the natural law is "absolute justice," see Kelsen, "The Natural-Law Doctrine before the Tribunal of Science," 141.

8. "The terminological identification of law and justice is one of the characteristic elements of the natural-law doctrine, which presents justice under the name of 'natural' law" (Kelsen, "Law, State, and Justice in the Pure Theory of Law," 297).

law it is to be considered as truly law."[9] This line of argument is premised on Kelsen's understanding that the legal status of norms, be they positive or natural, can be established according to a single framework of the criteria of juridicity or legal validity. Again, it is his firm conviction that according to a natural-law theory of law, that framework is laden with the criteria for juridicity installed by the conditions for the juridical status of natural law, which are basically identical to the evaluative criterion of justice.[10] This is part of why Kelsen, for the purpose of postulating his theses, supposes that positivity is a necessary feature of legal validity and that all law is ultimately positive law. He thus inhabits a post-Hobbesian legal-philosophical world, wherein law and justice are conceptually separated; indeed, as he says, "The Pure Theory of Law insists upon a clear separation of the concept of law from that of justice."[11]

It is now possible to closely examine the core of Kelsen's challenge concerning the main topic of the present chapter, namely, the status of positive law in Thomistic juridical realism. In Kelsen's view, "the existence of natural law makes the establishment of positive law superfluous."[12] In a natural-law theory of law, he maintains, all law is natural law, and this claim regards both the understanding of the very concept of law and the coverage of the range of issues suitable for the inclusion in the juridical domain. Positive law is "merely declaratory" of natural law, and it is nothing more than "a mere reproduction" of the natural law,[13] "a mere emanation" or a "copy" of "the model or archetype that is the natural law."[14] Kelsen even compares the role and the existence of positive law to "a foolish effort to supply artificial illumination in bright sunshine."[15] *Ius positivum* does not really add anything that would in any way be crucial,

9. Kelsen, "Law, State, and Justice in the Pure Theory of Law," 297.

10. "If one assumes the validity of a natural legal order, one cannot, at the same time, assume the existence of a simultaneously valid positive legal order with the same sphere of validity" (Kelsen, *General Theory of Law & State*, 411).

11. Kelsen, "Law, State, and Justice in the Pure Theory of Law," 301–2.

12. Kelsen, "The Natural-Law Doctrine before the Tribunal of Science," 142.

13. Kelsen, "Law, State, and Justice in the Pure Theory of Law," 297.

14. Kelsen, *General Theory of Law & State*, 416.

15. Kelsen, "The Natural-Law Doctrine before the Tribunal of Science," 142.

conceptually or content-wise, to the juridical relevance of natural law, or to the very nature of law:

> A positive law, then, beside natural law is not only impossible from the point of view of formal logic, it is also superfluous from a material-teleological point of view, if the assumptions hold which alone permit one to maintain the validity of a "natural" order. For, why should a human-arbitrary order be needed for the regulation of human conduct, if a just regulation can already be found in an order "natural," evident to all and in harmony with what all men of good will would propose?[16]

On the other end of the spectrum of the status of positive law in a natural-law theory of law, we find Finnis's natural-law theory, together with one of its central claims with which we are already very familiar—that all law is positive law. Finnis's reasons for criticizing Kelsenian positivism and for describing Kelsen's reading of the status of positive law in a natural-law theory of law as a "travesty" and a "misleading, and not uncommon, image of natural law juristic theory,"[17] do not prevent him from ultimately sharing Kelsen's view regarding positivity as the necessary feature of law's nature.

Thomistic juridical realism establishes a third stance between Kelsen's and Finnis's accounts of the status of positive law in the description of law's nature. In response to Kelsen's challenge, this legal-philosophical approach establishes that law's positivity is not merely a contingent feature of law's nature, nor is it only a copy of the content that is already juridically constituted and sufficiently secured at the level of natural law. In addition, Thomistic juridical realism appreciates some of Finnis's findings regarding the importance of positive law for understanding the nature of law (which will be presented in the subsequent section), but without arriving at the conclusion that this importance amounts to postulating that all law is ultimately positive law. The remainder of this chapter will thus be dedicated to exploring the argument that, both conceptually and content-wise, law is partly natural and partly positive.

16. Kelsen, *General Theory of Law & State*, 411–12.
17. Finnis, *Natural Law and Natural Rights*, 28.

What Is *Ius Positivum* and Why Do We Need to Have It?[18]

The simplest Thomist answer to this question is the following: We need to have posited law because the elements of juridicity entirely established at the level of *ius naturale* provide us with only a part of the totality of all the relevant juridical goods, that is, of the goods that need to be secured by law in a society. As important as these metapositive elements of juridicity may be, having in mind both the content of *ius naturale* and its architectonic implications for law's nature, they are only a part of a larger whole. Indeed, the goods that are fully constituted already at the level of *ius naturale*—that is, that are already fully law—solely on the basis of metapositive juridical titles comprise only a quantitatively small part of the entirety of the juridical goods in a society. This is because in a vast number of cases (perhaps the majority) concerning the matters somehow pertaining to the content of *ius naturale*, that is, to the basic human goods in the perspective of justice, the elements established by the so-called natural titles must necessarily be further specified and provided with additional details. This further specification is needed for said goods to be, so to speak, completed and fully determined in all the important aspects of the relevant relationships of justice (the details regarding the titleholders, the debtors, the concrete measure of that which is owed in justice, etc.) and thus rendered apt for their constitution as law. In fact, it could be argued that even the things to be constituted as *ius* that are most distant content-wise, from their pertinence to some of the basic human goods, may be seen to be somehow, even if only remotely, connected to the juridical domain of these goods and in need of further positive-law determination.

Therefore, already at the level that is somehow, even if distantly,

18. The line of reasoning presented in this section relies on the conclusions I arrived at in a previously published article in Italian. Here, I revisit those conclusions in a reworked way and by following a different sequence of arguments. See Petar Popović, "Le norme prese sul serio nel giusnaturalismo neoclassico: La necessità della legge positiva secondo John Finnis e il giusrealismo tomista," *Ius Ecclesiae* 35, no. 1 (2023): 83–108.

pertinent to the issues covered by the content of *ius naturale*, the vast number of goods to-be-constituted as *ius* have a composite structure—a hybrid, part natural, part positive ontology[19]—wherein the *ius naturale* aspects of these goods denote only pieces of this composite structure, which must be further determined by positive juridical titles, such as the norms of positive law. The classic textbook example of such a composite good is the positive-law determination of the lane in which it is obligatory to drive once a legislative choice has been made between the right and the left lane. This posited concretization between reasonable choices that are not fully specified and selected at the level of metapositive titles creates genuine obligations in justice only after it is determined by valid positive law. But it is certainly broadly demanded by and connected to the aspects of metapositive juridical goods (such as the basic good of life and bodily integrity) included in the highly complex good of traffic safety.[20]

19. I owe particular gratitude to Carlos José Errázuriz for this insight. See Carlos José Errázuriz, *Il diritto come bene giuridico: Un'introduzione alla filosofia del diritto* (EDUSC, 2021), 124–25, 160–64.

20. For the textbook use of this example, see Finnis, *Natural Law and Natural Rights*, 285. See also Finnis, *Aquinas: Moral, Political, and Legal Theory*, 268. Aquinas presents his paradigmatic example of a hybrid, part natural, part positive juridical good, in a textual locus dedicated to answering the question of whether *ius* is fittingly divided into *ius naturale* and *ius positivum*. He does so by presenting a possible objection to this division, based on an objector's insinuation that *ius naturale* cannot exist, since what is natural, in principle, ought to refer to things that are unchangeable and that are the same to all (this is an almost direct quote of Aristotle's definition of that which is just according to nature, from *Nic. Eth.* V.7, 1134b19), whereas according to the objection, "all the rules of humanly relevant law [*regulae iuris humani*] fail in certain cases," and they cannot be said to "obtain force everywhere" (*ST* II-II, q. 57, a. 2, obj. 1). Aquinas's answer to the objection presents the example of a reality that is, as he says, "natural to man" but which can in certain cases "sometimes fail," as is the case with "the restitution of a deposit to the depositor" that, although "in accordance with natural equality," may fail in the case of the return of the deposited weapon to a "madman or an enemy of the common weal," in which case "a deposit should not be restored" (*ST* II-II, q. 57, a. 2, ad 1). To the degree that a similar exception to *ius naturale* were somehow determined at the level of *ius positivum* by a norm of positive law or by other humanly posited authoritative determinations (see *ST* I-II, q. 97, a. 4, ad 3) in a political community, this would denote an example of a hybrid natural-positive juridical good. Another one of Aquinas's examples of such hybrid good revolves around the positive-law determination of the concrete punishment for the criminal, which is connected to a metapositive natural-law title, according to which it is demanded that corrective

The fact that our everyday life is full of such composite, part natural and part positive, juridical goods, and that there exists a corresponding need to declare and determine both the natural and the positive parts of these goods at the level of positive law, cannot be ignored in the analysis of the juridical phenomenon. And, in fact, Aquinas does not ignore it. To understand his account of *ius positivum*, it is necessary, as it was with *ius naturale*, to start with his treatment of the positive titles and their overall place in the virtue of justice and in the nature of *ius*, that is, to start with his legal-philosophical analyses in the *Secunda secundae* of his *Summa*. It is also necessary to keep in mind that, in Aquinas's view, law (*ius*) is primarily a thing (*res*), and thus *ius positivum* is always a thing or reality that is established and determined by positive legal titles, such as a positive legal norm (*lex positiva*), which he explores in the *Prima secundae* of his *Summa*.

We are already familiar with Aquinas's thesis that things can be attributed or adjusted to a titleholder on the basis of a positive legal title. The term "positive" here refers to the acts of the human will (i.e., the acts of positing)[21] that are directed at establishing and determining the relationships of justice. As Aquinas says, "the human will can … make a thing to be just … and it is in such matters that *ius positivum* has its place."[22]

justice be applied to the criminal in some way, without specifying the details of the punishment at the level of *ius naturale*. See *ST* I-II, q. 95, a. 2. Furthermore, Aquinas argues that a thing or reality pertains to *ius naturale* "because nature did not bring in the contrary," for example, in the case of "possession of all things in common" (together with the natural-law core of the presuppositions of private property), which is "said to be of the natural *ius* [*de iure naturali*], because, to wit, the distinction of possessions … [was] not brought in by nature, but devised by human reason for the benefit of human life" (*ST* I-II, q. 94, a. 5, ad 3). Hence, which things belong to determinate persons as their owners is further determined by positive law—and these determinations constitute posited "additions [*per additionem*]" to the natural law (*ST* I-II, q. 94, a. 5, ad 3)—while the natural core or underlying presupposition of such hybrid juridical goods consists of "what is brought in by nature," namely, the aforementioned common possession of all things and the capacity (and fittingness) of individual persons (or group-persons) to possess certain things in the form of individual or private ownership (see *ST* II-II, q. 57, a. 3; II-II, q. 66, a. 1–2).

21. *ST* II-II, q. 57, a. 2, arg. 2.

22. *ST* II-II, q. 57, a. 2, ad 2.

Of course, the constitution of positive law (*ius positivum*) is inherently related to natural law (*ius naturale*), since both types of *ius* have their proper place in the ontological fabric of *ius*. There are several important ways according to which the relatedness of positive law to natural law should be understood.

First, for Aquinas, *ius positivum* is always somehow, even if only very remotely, connected to the content of *ius naturale*, that is, to the natural juridical goods: "*iustum legale* or *positivum* always has its origin in that which is naturally just."[23] Things that are just according to a positive title thus typically—Aquinas uses the word "always"—contain a reference to a nucleus established by metapositive titles, which is relevant for the constitution of those manifestations of *ius positivum*. It may be said that to be constituted as *ius*, *ius positivum* needs to maintain harmony with the relevant aspects of *ius naturale*. Positive law, as the result of the human will's specification of that which is just, cannot be contrary to the content of those juridical goods that are already fully established as law (i.e., as that which is just) at the level of metapositive titles,[24] nor can it "diminish or annul the force" of that content.[25] The same can be said of the necessary positive-law determinations and specifications of the natural nuclei of hybrid "part natural, part positive" juridical goods, which must be fully harmonized with the content of those metapositive nuclei. Even the positive-law projections of exceptional cases in which "what is natural to man may sometimes fail," such as in the already mentioned case of the posited prohibition of restitution of a deposited weapon to a person who is likely to harm himself or others,[26] must be reasonably accounted for regarding their connection with the relevant metapositive relations of justice.

Second, *ius positivum* has its own range of issues and content that establishes and determines the relevant aspects of justice, and this field is significantly different from the domain of law that is

23. *Sent. Eth.* V, lect. 12, n. 1023.
24. See *ST* II-II, q. 57, a. 2, ad 2.
25. *ST* II-II, q. 60, a. 5, ad 1.
26. *ST* II-II, q. 57, a. 2, ad 1.

already fully constituted as such at the level of metapositive titles, that is, from the domain of natural juridical goods. Aquinas describes the field pertaining to *ius positivum* by following Aristotle's subject matter of legal justice: "[Aristotle] says that that justice is called legal which in the beginning, i.e., before it becomes law, is indifferent whether something is done in this way or that, but when it is laid down [*quando iam ponitur*], i.e., enacted into law [*statuitur lege*], then a difference arises because observing it is just, disregarding it is unjust."[27] Later in his *Summa*, Aquinas expands on the same line of reasoning and affirms that "*ius positivum* has no place except where it matters not, according to *ius naturale*, whether a thing be done in one way or another."[28] *Ius positivum* thus concerns a field of actions and things or realities regarding which *ius naturale* does not dictate all the relevant aspects of the relationships of justice, since there are a number of choices that can be made, all of which are in principle harmonized with the relevant elements of *ius naturale*. Before these choices are made, paradigmatically through positive legal norms (but also through other humanly posited titles), the metapositive aspects relevant for these choices are insufficiently determined for their autonomous constitution as law. But once these choices are made—as Aquinas says, when they are "laid down" and when they establish or determine the *ius positivum*—then "a difference arises"[29] because the selected posited options become *ius* and denote the corresponding duties in justice, while the other available options continue to be non-*ius*.

Third, there is something important to be learned regarding the relationship between positive *ius* and natural *ius* by observing the functions of the positive titles of *ius*. The positive titles, paradigmatically positive legal norms (*leges positivae*), exist, as Aquinas says, "for the purposes of manifesting both *iuris*," natural and positive, "but in different ways."[30] It is thus in the ratio of positive laws to add

27. *Sent. Eth.* V, lect. 12, n. 1020.

28. *ST* II-II, q. 60, a. 5, ad 1. See also *ST* II-II, q. 57, a. 2, ad 2.

29. *Sent. Eth.* V, lect. 12, 1020.

30. *ST* II-II, q. 60, a. 5.

something or to contribute with some peculiar feature to the existence of both natural *ius* and positive *ius*, according to the specific nature of each type of *ius*.

If one looks at the legal status of natural juridical goods, they are, as already mentioned, fully juridical also in the absence of wholly corresponding posited laws. What could a positive legal norm possibly add to an already fully juridically formed *ius naturale*? As Aquinas claims, such a norm adds a further manifestedness or declaration (*ad declarationem*), indeed a reaffirmation, of the content of *ius naturale* whenever it "contains *ius naturale*," without the aspiration to "establish it" anew.[31] Finnis maintains, quite correctly in my opinion, that even these positive legal norms are "not a mere emanation or copy of natural law," as Kelsen would suggest.[32] Beyond a useful declaration or restatement of what is already fully law at the level of *ius naturale* (of course, for Finnis this content is fully law only after its proper positivization), Finnis argues that a positive-law emphasis on the content of *ius naturale* also yields a better understanding of the crucial and systemic importance of this content, since it is thereby brought into even more palpable connection with a variety of positive-law issues in the whole of the juridical order of a community.[33]

A qualitatively different but important feature is added in the case of positive laws that represent the decisive titles of *ius positivum*, without which they would not have been constituted as *ius*. As said before, Aquinas maintains that there are no manifestations of *ius positivum* entirely detached from considerations regarding the applicable metapositive titles, and thus each positive *ius* has at least some distant connection to a *lex naturalis* nucleus of the relevant basic human goods. However, for its proper constitution as *ius*, each instantiation of a thing to-be-constituted as *ius positivum* necessitates the stipulation of a positive title, paradigmatically a promulgation of a positive legal norm (*lex positiva*) according to the

31. *ST* II-II, q. 60, a. 5.
32. Finnis, *Natural Law and Natural Rights*, 28.
33. See Finnis, *Natural Law and Natural Rights*, 282–83.

applicable standards of legal validity. In these cases, law's positivity constitutes a *conditio sine qua non*, indeed a threshold, of juridicity provided that the other relevant elements of justice are satisfied, such as the correspondence with *ius naturale* and with metapositive natural nuclei in a hybrid juridical good. Said differently, in Aquinas's own words, a positive legal norm "both contains *ius positivum* and establishes it by giving it force of authority."[34]

Again, the existence of an entire field of indispensable juridical goods that become law (*ius*) only when a corresponding positive title, such as a positive legal norm (*lex*), is stipulated, models the very nature of law. Not all law is necessarily posited, but some law, indeed, is necessarily posited, and it cannot become law unless it is appropriately posited. This means that we need positive laws, given that law's nature is necessarily partly instantiated through positivity. Without positive laws, we would not be able to establish or determine the essential elements of what is just (i.e., of what justice requires) in relation to many goods that are important or even necessary for the adequate functioning and coordination of a society. These laws are not merely instrumental. They are essential—essentially needed—for the purposes of a full understanding of the ontological fabric of the juridical phenomenon.

Aquinas develops the arguments on the need to have positive laws, a need originating from the very nature of law, in his exposition of *lex positiva*, in the *Prima secundae* of his *Summa*. As usual, he takes an objection as the starting point, which is in this case basically Kelsenian: "The natural law suffices for the ordering of all human affairs. Consequently, there is no need for a human law."[35] According to Aquinas's brief answer to that objection, human reason can participate of itself only imperfectly and incompletely in "particular determinations" regarding "individual cases" that flow downstream from the basic precepts of natural law.[36] In other words, while we as human persons can know the content and juridical value of the

34. *ST* II-II, q. 60, a. 5.
35. *ST* I-II, q. 91, a. 3, arg. 1.
36. *ST* I-II, q. 91, a. 3, ad 1.

natural juridical goods (*ius naturale*), human reason cannot have the same full and unified knowledge of the exact juridical range of goods that pertain to the field of *ius positivum* because these latter goods still need to be authoritatively determined at the level of human positive law.[37] There is thus, according to Aquinas, "the need for human reason to proceed further to sanction [these determinations] by law [*quasdam legum sanctiones*]."[38]

According to Aquinas's understanding, positive laws, as any other form of *lex*,[39] must exist simultaneously (1) in the mind of the lawgiver of positive laws (who respects metapositive titles of *ius*) and (2) in the mind of citizens, who thereby participate in the mind of the lawgiver (and who share the lawgiver's respect for metapositive titles of *ius*). The minds of both the legislators and the citizens who are the addressees of positive laws need to be synchronized in their clear and detailed knowledge of the *ius* contained in positive laws. But, as we have already seen, such synchronization is not possible until authoritative choices have been stipulated in valid positive legal norms by the competent lawgiver among viable options, all of which are in harmony with the *ius naturale*. This is the definitive reason underlying the need to have valid positive laws: to have a clear knowledge of all the relevant aspects of concrete objects of justice, the just things themselves. As Aquinas says, the citizens are in a position to "use that which is just [*utuntur iusto*]" and thus to give to each person her own *ius*, to the extent that the concrete demarcations of just thing itself or *ius* are completely "imparted to the human mind."[40] And it is precisely the purpose of posited human laws that the content of *ius positivum* be clearly manifested or declared in terms of things owed in justice.

Before concluding this section, a few words need to be said about

37. This is one of the arguments of a natural-law theory of law that Kelsen grossly misunderstands, since, as we have seen, he is convinced that the proponents of that theory maintain that all the issues resolved by positive law are, in fact, somehow already available at the level of natural law, thereby making positive law superfluous.

38. See *ST* I-II, q. 91, a. 3, ad 1.

39. See *ST* I-II, q. 90, a. 1, ad 1; I-II, q. 90, a. 3, ad 1.

40. *Sent. Eth.* V, lect. 12, n. 1017.

the role of the authority of the law-creating subjects in establishing *ius positivum*. The fundamental question that should be addressed is whether and to what extent the authority of the law-creating subject forms part of the deontic power inherent to the obligatoriness of *ius positivum*. Aquinas holds that the competence to authoritatively make laws pertains to the very definition of *lex*.[41] Furthermore, we are familiar with his argument that the posited *lex* both "contains" *ius positivum* and "establishes it by giving it force of *authority*."[42] Finally, as will be seen in more detail in the following chapter, one of the grounds for the injustice of positive laws is their deficiency relative to authority. A law is unjust when, among other reasons, the author of a law-aspiring posited rule altogether lacks the legislative competence or goes beyond the limits of legislative power.[43] Thus, authority is certainly essential for the constitution of *ius positivum*, since without, it a law-aspiring norm cannot be thought of as a *lex*, and in the absence of a positive *lex*, we lack the *ratio* of *ius positivum*. In other words, that which may become just only on account of the *ratio* established by positive law remains ultimately undetermined in the absence of law-making authority, and without such an authoritative determination, an *ius positivum* based on positive *lex* is not constituted.

However, it is also necessary to highlight that the phenomenon of authority to make positive laws pertains only to the efficient cause of *ius*, more precisely, to that part of the efficient cause of *ius* that concerns *ius positivum*. This means that the phenomenon of law-making authority forms part of the explanation of how exactly is it that things (*res*) are brought within the reach of the evaluative standard of justice and its specific form of obligatoriness and goodness, in the case of *ius positivum*. But the deontic power inherent to the obligatoriness of *ius positivum* depends not only on the efficient cause of *ius* (where the question of authority becomes relevant) but

41. *ST* I-II, q. 90, a. 1.

42. *ST* II-II, q. 60, a. 5 (emphasis added). See also his following argument: "A law cannot be made save by public authority" (*ST* II-II, q. 60, a. 6).

43. *ST* I-II, q. 96, a. 4.

also and essentially so on the pertinence of the *res* that is the object of positive laws to the formal cause of *ius* (justice) and to the final cause of *ius* (juridical goodness). Having been authoritatively determined as the object of positive laws, the things (*res*) must still be assessed by the evaluative standards of obligatoriness and goodness of justice to become *ius*. In this sense, authority is an essential part of *lex*, and to that extent, it is also an essential part of *ius*. What makes something law (*ius*), however, is the cumulative activation of all the four causes of *ius*.

Determinatio

From the viewpoint of Thomistic juridical realism, the process Aquinas refers to as *determinatio* concerns the selection of certain things or realities to-be-constituted as *ius* from multiple options that are available and in full harmony with the relevant aspects of *ius naturale* (e.g., driving in the left or right lane becoming obligatory once the authoritative positive-law choice is validly made). Aquinas distinguishes this process from that of deriving positive law from natural law by way of conclusions from prior premises or principles (*conclusiones ex principiis*). His example of a conclusion derived from prior premises is the inference that "one must not kill" from the prior premise or principle that "one should do harm to no man."[44]

Aquinas affirms that both modes of derivation are found in human law, but in a different way, since conclusions from prior principles "have some force from the natural law also," while determinations "have no other force than that of human law."[45] Aquinas's line of reasoning in this matter begins with the thesis according to which "the force of law [*lex*] depends on the extent of its justice."[46] It is thus possible to read his arguments on the legal "force" of conclusions and determinations in a way that is consistent with the analysis outlined throughout this section. According to this reading, positive

44. *ST* I-II, q. 95, a. 2.
45. *ST* I-II, q. 95, a. 2.
46. *ST* I-II, q. 95, a. 2.

laws that contain conclusions from the natural law's prior premises only refer to goods that are already fully juridical in virtue of metapositive legal titles. Indeed, as Aquinas says in the aforementioned quote, they "have some force from the natural law also."[47] Positive laws that contain determinations, on the other hand, refer to goods that become fully law only in virtue of the promulgation of valid positive laws, regardless of the fact that these laws contain certain connections to metapositive titles, or the fact that the positive juridical goods established as such by these posited laws possess a natural nucleus somehow related to *ius naturale.*

Usually, in a natural-law theory of law, the process of *determinatio*, which Finnis translates as "concretization"[48] or as a "making-more-specific,"[49] is understood to denote the activity of rendering the general moral norms of natural law juridical by making their content sufficiently elaborate by positing valid human norms to be applied in concrete, legally relevant situations. This process corresponds to the human need for determining all the relevant details concerning the coordination of societal life for the purposes of the attainment of the common good, since those details are insufficiently determined (or "underdetermined"[50]) at the level of natural moral law.[51] In Finnis's view, the system of positive law is a complex "artifact and artifice,"[52] and its norms are individual artifacts that are fundamentally "incomplete" until they are "fully" or at least sufficiently

47. This reading is further corroborated by Aquinas's own line of reasoning presented in his *Commentary on Aristotle's Nicomachean Ethics*, which contains another explanation of the two modes of derivation, *conclusio ex principiis* and *determinatio*. In that text, he operates with the concepts of *ius positivum* and *ius naturale* and describes how the former is derived from the latter. At one point of his presentation, he argues that "it is necessary that whatever follows from natural justice as a conclusion *will be natural justice* [*iustum naturale*]" (*Sent. Eth.* V, lect. 12, n. 1023 [emphasis added]).

48. John Finnis, "'Natural Law,'" in *Collected Essays*, vol. 1, *Reason in Action* (Oxford University Press, 2011), 208.

49. Finnis, "Aquinas and Natural Law Jurisprudence," 38.

50. Finnis, "A Grand Tour of Legal Theory," 114. See also Finnis, *Natural Law and Natural Rights*, 28.

51. For Finnis's analysis of *determinatio*, see Finnis, *Natural Law and Natural Rights*, 281–90.

52. See Finnis, "The Truth in Legal Positivism," 186.

"determined."[53] A similar norm-based understanding of *determinatio* may be found in the reasoning of other natural lawyers.[54]

I would argue, however, that the process of *determinatio* concerns above all the needed concretization and specification of the things or realities themselves that are to-be-constituted as *ius*. This concretization is, indeed, necessarily achieved by positive titles, paradigmatically by positing valid laws, but these titles are only the efficient cause of *ius positivum*, which must always be seen in concomitance with the other three causes of *ius*, wherein the material cause is the thing or reality itself (*res*), seen in the perspective of the relevant relationships of justice (formal cause), with a view to the attainment of the corresponding juridical form of good (final cause). What needs *determinatio* is not primarily a norm (or a cluster of norms) of natural moral law for the purposes of the positive-law juridical realm. Rather, all four causes of *ius* need *determinatio* through positive law, starting from the thing or reality itself and its status in the relationships of justice, the metapositive aspects of which are to a certain degree underdetermined for its constitution as law (*ius*). Keeping all four causes of *ius* in mind when exploring the concept of *determinatio* is important, since, from the viewpoint of Thomistic juridical realism, the juridical goods that are constituted as *ius positivum* are not purely positive: rather, they are predominantly or even necessarily hybrid—part natural, part positive. Thus, what is juridicized by positing valid law is not only the so-called positive part of those hybrid goods but also their natural metapositive nuclei, which are thereby rendered juridically effective for the relevant particular issues.

Perhaps it is possible to speak of the valid positive laws that represent the title of *ius positivum* in terms of "purely positive laws." By using this expression, Finnis[55] intends to highlight that these determinations, as Aquinas says, have no other force than that of human

53. Finnis, *Natural Law and Natural Rights*, 284.

54. See Adrian Vermeule, *Common Good Constitutionalism: Recovering the Classical Legal Tradition* (Polity, 2022), 9–11, 44–46, 151–54.

55. Finnis, *Aquinas: Moral, Political, and Legal Theory*, 268.

law, which means that certain things or realities become fully law only in virtue of the promulgation of valid positive laws. However, one should keep in mind that the "pure" positivity or artifactuality of these laws does not adequately reflect the hybrid (part natural, part positive) ontological fabric of the juridical goods that are determined through those laws. Accordingly, even if it is perhaps possible to speak of "purely" positive laws, it is not entirely accurate to refer to *ius positivum* as "purely" positive. Although positive juridical goods are indeed constituted as such on account of validly promulgated legal norms as the efficient cause of *ius positivum*, the juridical status of these goods, as well as of those norms, is also controlled by aspects pertaining to the other three causes, such as the material-cause aptitude of the thing or reality to be constituted as *ius*, the formal-cause capacity of said positive laws for establishing true relationships of justice, and the corresponding final-cause goodness of these *res* at the level of *ius positivum* (and in harmony with *ius naturale*).

Chapter 6

The Juridical Status of Unjust Positive Laws (*Lex Injusta*)

Justice as the Evaluative Standard for Positive Laws

Regardless of the significant differences among natural lawyers in defining the nature of law, the default natural-law position (and perhaps even more broadly, nonpositivism) usually includes an argument in support of the need to assess the content of positive laws against some set of substantive evaluative features. To give an example, for Finnis, understanding whether an instance of a positive legal norm pertains to the focal point or to the central case of law relies upon a previous evaluative assessment of whether that norm instantiates the requirements of practical reasonableness (justice being one of those requirements), thereby appropriately respecting the basic human goods.[1] Or, to provide another example, for Alexy, to identify a norm of positive law as instantiating the nature of law, said norm must be evaluated according to the criterion of what he refers to as justice, and especially according to the question of whether the

1. See his following claim: "The law's institutions—to the extent that they are reasonable—remain dependent upon foundational moral principles which pick out the requirements of a reasonableness attentive to the basic human goods" (Finnis, "A Grand Tour of Legal Theory," 118). See also Finnis, *Aquinas: Moral, Political, and Legal Theory*, 11–18, 276–81.

norm crosses the threshold of extreme injustice. In Alexy's estimation, the evaluative viewpoints of justice and "extreme injustice" are understood essentially in terms of respect (or violation) of human rights, especially with reference to the core or basis of these rights, which stipulates the necessity to treat persons according to their inherent dignity, expressed first and foremost in the ideas of maximum possible equality and freedom.[2] In both examples, justice is highlighted as an evaluative criterion for assessing the juridical status of positive law. However, in Finnis's framework, justice is only a subset of the broader relevant set of evaluative criteria organized around the virtue of practical reasonableness, whereas according to Alexy, although justice denotes the crucial evaluative criterion for positive law, it is understood in a minimalist sense of the core values of (or rights to) personal equality and freedom.

Aquinas assigns a more prominent role to justice as the evaluative criterion for assessing positive laws, in comparison to Finnis's corresponding estimation of the function of justice. In addition, as has already been discussed, Aquinas's substantive, value-laden setting of the virtue of justice is broader than Alexy's minimalist reference to the values of equality and freedom, since it also includes a necessary reference to other basic human goods or, more precisely, to the jurisprudential counterparts of those other goods (i.e., natural juridical goods).

In Aquinas's texts, we find a number of programmatic arguments in which he strongly supports the evaluative role of justice in assessing positive laws. Aquinas holds that it is indeed "necessary for laws [*leges*] to be framed" or posited in order that persons may achieve the corresponding virtues,[3] the most prominent of which—when we are talking about the juridical phenomenon—is justice, which has *ius* as its object. In fact, as he says, "it belongs to the law

2. For Alexy's rather complex argument on justice (and human rights, especially the architectonic rights to freedom and equality) as the evaluative standard for positive law, see Alexy, "The Dual Nature of Law," 39–40, 47; Alexy, "Some Reflections on the Ideal Dimension of Law," 108; and Robert Alexy, "Law, Morality, and the Existence of Human Rights," in *Law's Ideal Dimension*, 60.

3. See *ST* I-II, q. 95, a. 1; I-II, q. 96, a. 2, ad 2.

[*ad legem pertinet*] to direct human acts according to the order of *iustitia*."[4] We are already familiar with his firm conviction that the phenomenon of law (*lex*), including positive law (a "rule expressed in writing"), is the efficient cause—the underlying foundational idea or *ratio*—of *ius*.[5] He seems to advance an even stronger argument, with which he implies that positive laws have the specific *telos* of declaring or establishing *ius*, when he claims that "laws are written for the purpose of manifesting [*ad declarationem*] both these *ius* [natural and positive]."[6] Thus, it is their pertinence to the virtue of justice that provides positive laws with their particular juridical force: "the force of a law depends on the extent of its justice [*unde inqantum habet de iustitia, intantum habet de virtute legis*]."[7] In a sense, it could be said that laws are what they are on account of being just: "it is of the essence of law [*de ratione legis est*] to be just [*quod sit iusta*]."[8] Positive legal norms are created as legal artifacts, then are promulgated, and finally enter into force with the primary scope of addressing, with their content, the field that pertains to the virtue of justice, and hence, not first and foremost with the aim of structuring the other virtues: "human law [*lex humana*] makes precepts only about acts of justice; and if it commands acts of other virtues, this is only insofar as they assume the nature of justice."[9]

Being circumscribed by the cluster of its essential properties—namely, its unique form of obligatoriness, its outwardness, and other-directedness—the sphere of justice specifies and delimits the range of issues to-be-covered by positive law from the remaining content that falls within the broader domain of morality, beyond the strict sphere of justice. As Aquinas puts it, "moral matters are determinable by law [*sunt lege determinabilia*] insofar as they belong to justice [*inquantum pertinent ad iustitiam*]."[10] Thus, a posited

4. *ST* I-II, q. 91, a. 5.
5. *ST* II-II, q. 57, a. 1, ad 2.
6. *ST* II-II, q. 60, a. 5.
7. *ST* I-II, q. 95, a. 2.
8. *ST* I-II, q. 97, a. 1, arg. 3.
9. *ST* I-II, q. 100, a. 2.
10. *ST* I-II, q. 99, a. 5, ad 1.

legal norm that aims to establish an order for human action, which stretches beyond the field of strict justice and thereby regulates realities pertaining to the broader sphere of morality—for example, realities that lack the properties of outwardness,[11] other-directedness, or obligatoriness characteristic of justice[12]—may be considered to constitute only a moral exhortation or another type of evaluative directive but not an orderedness pertaining to justice, strictly speaking.

The evaluative standard of justice aims to secure that in every humanly posited valid legal norm, each thing (*res*) is properly attributed to its legitimate titleholder, and that the corresponding debt is sufficiently determinable. This is attained when the content of that legal norm further determines the implications arising from natural juridical goods, or from the natural-law core of a not-yet-constituted positive juridical good, by sufficiently identifying (1) the concrete measure of the thing that constitutes the debt in justice, (2) the titleholder(s), and (3) the debtor(s). A positive legal norm that lacks one of the aforementioned elements fails to sufficiently determine the relevant elements of the standard of justice regarding positive juridical goods to-be-constituted. Consequently, such a norm is deficient from the standpoint of justice, not only because it is perhaps in some way unjust or directly contrary to justice but also because it lacks one (or more) of the constitutive elements necessary for establishing the relationship of justice in the first place. We could say that what is established by such a deficient norm is not a thing or an

11. For Aquinas's argument that human law aims to regulate primarily outward human acts, see *ST* I-II, q. 91, a. 4; I-II, q. 98, a. 1.

12. The reference to "obligatoriness characteristic of justice" is meant to delimit the sphere of justice from other normative standards, such as, for example, those pertaining to the virtues of charity or liberality. The manifestations of these virtues may also be seen to possess the properties of outwardness, other-directedness, and may even constitute a peculiar form of debt, the precise measure of which is, however, ultimately determinable according to criteria that exceed the limits of strict justice. Aquinas refers to such broadly envisioned duty as, for example, "gratuitous favor" in the case of charity (*ST* II-II, q. 23, a. 3, ad 1) or "generous beneficence" in the case of liberality (*ST* II-II, q. 58, a. 11, ad 1). For example, a norm that prescribes that "citizens ought to have a positive inward and outward attitude towards helping the poor and needy" points to a certain moral duty, the precise measure of which is largely left to the determination of citizens (beyond what is already settled in terms of duties in justice regarding this matter in other positive legal norms).

order that is *unjust*, but simply a thing, reality, or state of affairs that is *not-yet-just*.

An unjust norm, or a norm contrary to justice, is first and foremost that positive legal norm that attempts to simply reproduce or declare certain aspects of natural juridical goods, but which, although it contains a reference to the aforementioned elements (measure of the *ius*, titleholder, debtor) of justice, is in some way deficient in comparison to what is reproduced or declared. Aquinas describes this type of unjust law as "containing something contrary to *ius naturale*,"[13] and this "cannot be made just by human will."[14] Next, unjust laws are those that further determine the natural-law core of a not-yet-constituted hybrid natural-positive juridical good in a way that runs contrary to that core (e.g., a norm that empowers each driver to arbitrarily choose the preferred lane within which to drive in each given moment). In my opinion, Aquinas has this type of injustice in mind when he presents the argument that a humanly posited law (*lex humanitus posita*) is unjust if it contains determinations from natural law that are not correctly harmonized with (or "derived from") the precepts of natural law.[15]

In addition, Aquinas affirms that a law is unjust when it is "contrary to human good" in three more cases: (1) on account of being opposed to "the end" of the law, which is the "common good," namely, when a posited legal rule illegitimately aims at the attainment of a particular or private good to the detriment of the common good, (2) when the legislator is enacting laws beyond the competence to

13. *ST* II-II, q. 60, a. 5, ad 1.

14. *ST* II-II, q. 57, a. 2, ad 2.

15. See *ST* I-II, q. 95, a. 2. As seen before, in this article, Aquinas introduces another mode of derivation from the precepts of natural law, besides determinations, which he calls *conclusiones ex principiis*. However, since he argues, in the same article, that the content of those human laws that pertains to the *conclusiones* mode of derivation from natural law "has some force from the natural law also" (*ST* I-II, q. 95, a. 2), there is good reason to hold that he in fact understands that the primary aim of these human laws is to reproduce and declare certain aspects of natural juridical goods. In other words, a deficiency of humanly posited laws derived from natural law by way of *conclusiones ex principiis* may be considered identical to the defects of positive laws containing something contrary to *ius naturale*.

legislate (*ultra vires*), and (3) when the principle of formal justice (or fairness) is violated, that is, when like cases are not treated alike according to the same underlying criteria of substantive justice (and different cases are not treated differently according to the same criteria), even if legislators act (or believe they act) with a view to the common good.[16]

A Brief Historical Excursus #3: *Lex Injusta Non Est Lex*

What are the consequences of the existence of an unjust positive law for that law, or for the legal system to which such a law belongs? Above all, do these consequences contribute something to our understanding of the nature of law? At some point in the history of legal philosophy, these questions were reformulated in a maxim—*lex injusta non est lex*—and individual authors started to give their answer to those questions by interpreting this maxim and addressing its possible meanings. For the purposes of my present analysis, I am predominantly interested in the second of the above questions, namely, the ways in which the diverse interpretations of the maxim contribute to our understanding of the very nature of law.

It is usually thought that the maxim is endorsed by natural lawyers and rejected by legal positivists. However, on closer inspection, both the maxim and the aforementioned questions to which it seeks to respond, are far more complex. H. L. A. Hart claims that the maxim represents a core contention of "the most extreme form" of the argument in favor of the necessary connection between law and morality, the form associated with, in his words, "the Thomist tradition of natural law."[17] In his interpretation, the meaning of the maxim is that "man-made laws which conflict with these principles [of true morality and justice] are not *valid* law."[18] Hart is thus convinced that the maxim erroneously aims to deny the legal validity of an unjust positive legal norm, that is, its intrasystemic status a law

16. *ST* I-II, q. 96, a. 4.
17. Hart, *The Concept of Law*, 156.
18. Hart, *The Concept of Law*, 156.

(*lex*).[19] He is aware, though, that even "some modern exponents of natural law," such as John Finnis, who he explicitly mentions in this regard, reject this "extreme" reading of the maxim as a "travesty of their doctrine and a misinterpretation of Aquinas."[20]

Hart is correct in his reading of Finnis on this point. Finnis, a proponent of a maximalist natural-law theory of law, indeed holds that the tradition of that theory, "even in its most blunt formulations," is not indulging in "a refusal to recognize evil laws as valid," that is, as authentic positive laws (*leges*) in force and readily applicable by legal officials.[21] Finnis thereby interprets said tradition similarly to Hart by framing the scope of the maxim in terms of the discussion in favor or against the legal validity of unjust laws. Faithful to his own account of the dual nature of law, Finnis holds that the injustice (even the most radical injustice) of posited legal rules may indeed expose these rules to a corresponding evaluative critique (even a radical critique) from the viewpoint of law's evaluative "life," thereby judging them as defective from the viewpoint of the focal sense of law. However, in his view, the injustice cannot extinguish the descriptive life of these rules, that is, their continuous existence as source-based social facts even in these peripheral or borderline cases of law. Thus, from the standpoint of the instantiation of law's nature in unjust laws, these laws continue to be both unjust and valid: they continue to participate in the nature of law, and they are law. Finnis presents these arguments not only as his own understanding of the issue but indeed as the traditional core claim of the natural-law tradition, including especially Aquinas's own account of the maxim.[22] Any other interpretation of the maxim would result in an unnecessary "dramatization,"[23] since in Finnis's view, denying

19. See also H. L. A. Hart, *Essays on Bentham: Studies in Jurisprudence and Political Theory* (Oxford University Press, 1982), 146.

20. Hart, *Essays on Bentham*, 146.

21. Finnis, *Natural Law and Natural Rights*, 364–65.

22. Finnis, *Natural Law and Natural Rights*, 364. For similar claims that "neither Aquinas nor any other natural law theorist holds that [unjust] laws are not laws at all, that is, in any event, for any purpose," and that an "unjust law is law only in a qualified sense," see Sean Coyle, *Natural Law and Modern Society* (Oxford University Press, 2023), 356–57.

23. Finnis, *Natural Law and Natural Rights*, 364.

"legal obligatoriness in the legal or intra-systemic sense" to an unjust norm, thereby "smudging the positivity of law," is "not conducive to clear thought, or to any good practical purpose."[24] Far from "denying legal validity to iniquitous rules," the tradition "explicitly (by speaking of unjust *laws*) accords to iniquitous rules legal validity."[25]

This line of reasoning leads Finnis to conclude that the maxim denotes no more than a "subordinate theorem" in any natural-law account of the nature of law.[26] He thus comes close to sharing Dworkin's estimation that the "ancient jurisprudential puzzle" concerning the legal status of "evil law" is "of almost no practical importance," although it has had (and arguably continues to have) a "prominent place in seminars on legal theory."[27]

The evident complexity relative to the correct understanding and impact of the maxim seems to warrant a reexamination of the history of its interpretations. In addition, I believe that some aspects of this complexity have not as yet been properly addressed, which prompts me to shed further light on this issue from the standpoint of the approach to law's nature expounded in this book.

Although Aquinas is not the first author to suggest that an unjust law (*lex*) seems to manifest certain important defects with regard to its ontology as *lex*, he seems to be enumerated among the authors with whom the *lex injusta non est lex* maxim is usually associated. Indeed, Aquinas explicitly refers to the version of the maxim more than once. Since this book approaches Aquinas's account of the nature of law by starting from his description of *ius* in the *Secunda secundae* of the *Summa*, let me start by presenting the version of the maxim that appears in that part of the *Summa*. In the textual locus, with which we are already familiar, where he analyzes the possibility that humanly posited law (he uses the term "a writing of the law," *scriptura legis*) "contains" something "contrary to *ius naturale*," in which case that law is unjust, Aquinas argues that such a "writing"

24. Finnis, *Natural Law and Natural Rights*, 357.
25. Finnis, *Natural Law and Natural Rights*, 365.
26. Finnis, *Natural Law and Natural Rights*, 351.
27. Dworkin, *Justice for Hedgehogs*, 410.

(*scriptura*) cannot be called "law" (*lex*) but rather a "corruption of the law" (*legis corruptio*).[28] His conclusion is reinforced when read in light of his earlier argument, according to which when a *ratio* of a particular work of justice is "expressed in writing," it is "called a law [*lex*]";[29] in the case when what is expressed in writing fails to denote a *ratio* of a particular work of justice, paradigmatically so when it contains something contrary to *ius naturale*, that specific writing (*scriptura*) cannot be understood to denote a *lex* at all.

Earlier in the *Summa*, in the treatise on *lex* in the *Prima secundae*, Aquinas introduces the version of the maxim that he explicitly attributes to Augustine: that [law] which is not just does not seem to be law at all ("*non videtur esse lex, quae iusta non fuerit*").[30] Since Aquinas holds that such a law-aspiring or law-appearing reality "has the character of a law" only "to the extent that it is just,"[31] it could be argued that, in his view, an unjust law amounts to something akin to violence, more than to a *lex*.[32] He also refers to laws that are just (*iustae*) as "legal laws" (*leges legales*).[33] From these arguments, it follows that for him, justice seems to enter into the very idea or

28. *ST* II-II, q. 60, a. 5, ad 1. It seems that already the purely exegetical analysis of this text resists Finnis's reading of Aquinas's understanding of the maxim, since Aquinas here does not say that an unjust *law* is not a *law*. That is, Aquinas does not say that an unjust and thus peripheral case of true and valid *law* is not a law in the focal sense. Instead, he argues that an unjust *writing* (*scriptura*) purporting to constitute a law (*lex*) cannot be called a *law* (*lex*) at all, but at best a *corruption* of *lex*. In other words, an unjust "law" is really just a *writing* that aspires to be referred to as *lex*, but which on account of its defects does not merit being denoted a *lex* in any focal or peripheral sense of that term. Such a law-aspiring norm can be categorized, from the standpoint of *lex*, only in terms of what it lacks when compared to a *lex*. Following the line of reasoning from Aquinas's text, the maxim could be formulated in the following way: a writing that is only an unjust less-than-law is not a law in any sense of that term.

29. *ST* II-II, q. 57, a. 2, ad 2. A similar chain of arguments would follow from Aquinas's reflections from the *Prima secundae* of the *Summa*, where he argues that "the volition of what is commanded" by the legislator may have "the nature of law [*legis rationem habeat*]" to the extent that it is "in accord with some rule of reason [*ratione regulata*]"—that is, with the relevant criteria of justice in case of human law—otherwise, "what is commanded" is more a "lawlessness [*iniquitas*]" rather than law (*ST* I-II, q. 90, a. 1, ad 3).

30. *ST* I-II, q. 95, a. 2; I-II, q. 96, a. 4.

31. *ST* I-II, q. 95, a. 2.

32. *ST* I-II, q. 96, a. 4.

33. *ST* I-II, q. 96, a. 4.

definition of *legality*, of what counts as *lex*, at the level of human law. Instead, unjust laws are more like law-aspiring realities that always remain something less-than-*lex*, realities that are deemed nonlegal *lex*[34] (or a law-appearing non-*lex*), already from the standpoint of the conceptual reach of the term *lex*, even before taking the conceptual reach of *ius* and the idea of juridicity into full account.[35]

As seen, Aquinas's direct source for his versions of the maxim is Augustine, more precisely, an argument from *De Libero Arbitrio*: "A law that is not just does not seem to me to be a law."[36] In another version of the maxim, from his *De Civitate Dei*, Augustine switches from the term *lex* to the term *ius* when describing the status of unjust human enactments: "For where there is not true justice, there can be no *ius*.... We are not to reckon as *ius* such human laws [*humana constituta*] as are iniquitous."[37] Of course, the juridical status

34. Finnis frequently justifies his reading of the maxim—an unjust *law* (still fully *law* in a peripheral sense) is not a *law* (in the focal sense)—by highlighting that it is rather normal to use similar idioms, for example, when someone says that "an insincere friend is not a friend" (see Finnis, "What Is the Philosophy of Law?" 140). But since Aquinas maintains that just laws are thereby legal laws (*leges legales*), it is equally possible to interpret his words in the following way: unjust laws are *leges* that are not *legales*, that is, they are nonlegal "laws" (where, by "laws," he actually intends merely the law-aspiring or law-appearing realities), and hence not laws at all. Or, if we take sincerity to enter into the very definition of what counts as a friend, one could say that an insincere friend is a nonfriendly "friend," and thus a nonfriend or not a friend at all.

35. Aquinas describes the unjust law-aspiring or law-appearing realities—retaining only "some appearance of law [*aliquid de similitudine legis*]" (*ST* I-II, q. 93, a. 3, ad 2)—as having some elements that pertain to law's nature ["*aliquid de ratione legis*"], namely, as having the character of an "ordinance [*dictamen*] made by a superior to his subjects," which "aims at being obeyed by them" (*ST* I-II, q. 92, a. 1, ad 4). Elsewhere, he will refer to such unjust ordinances as iniquitous "enactments [*statuta*]" (*ST* I-II, 94, a. 4, ad 3). Although at times Aquinas loosely calls these unjust norms "laws" (*leges*), a case can certainly be made for his understanding that the unjust *scripturae*, *dictamina*, *statuta*, or *constitutiones scriptae* (*ST* II-II, q. 57, a. 1, ad 2) cannot be referred to as laws (*leges*) in any proper sense of that term, since the elements that a law-appearing reality possesses with regard to the nature of law are of themselves insufficient to establish that reality as a *lex*. Accordingly, he may be said to sometimes use the term *lex* for unjust *scriptura*, *dictamina*, *statuta*, or *constitutio scripta* only to identify these latter phenomena as law-aspiring or law-appearing realities that are ultimately deemed less-than-*lex*.

36. Augustine, *On the Free Choice of the Will*, in *On the Free Choice of the Will, On Grace, and Other Writings*, trans. Peter King (Cambridge University Press, 2010), I, 5, 11, 33.

37. Augustine, *The City of God: Books XVII–XXII*, trans. Gerard G. Walsh (The Catholic University of America Press, 1954), XIX, 21.

of unjust laws was an object of legal-philosophical reflection before Augustine.[38]

The question of the status of *lex iniusta* becomes increasingly important in the Thomist tradition after Aquinas, especially as the authors from that tradition gradually shift the emphasis from Aquinas's *rei*-centric concept of *ius* understood as the *ipsa res iusta* toward the phenomenon of *lex* in their assessments of law's essential nature. Thus, Francisco Suárez, for whom the "proper connotation" of the term *ius* is "practically synonymous with *lex*,"[39] is even more motivated to explore whether an unjust law participates in the nature of the juridical phenomenon predominantly understood in terms of *lex*. This explains why Suárez is at the same time both (1) rather progressive in attributing to Aquinas a subjectivist interpretation of the term *ius* (as essentially a "moral faculty" one enjoys regarding *res*) when that term is not used to denote *lex*[40] and (2) rigorously conservative—and perhaps even more clear on this issue than Aquinas—in his insistence that an unjust law is not a *lex*, in any sense of that term. Since, in Suárez's view, "it is inherent in the nature [*ratione*] and essence [*essentia*] of *lex* that it shall prescribe just things [*iusta*],"[41] it follows that a law "not characterized" by sub-

38. "We deny that laws are true laws unless they are enacted in the interest of the whole State. But where the laws are enacted in the interest of a section ... the justice they ascribe to such laws is, we say, an empty name" (Plato, *Laws: Books 1–6*, trans. Robert G. Bury (Harvard University Press, 1961), IV, 715b). "Those constitutions which consider the common interest are right constitutions, judged by the standard of absolute justice. Those constitutions which consider only the personal interest of the rulers are all wrong constitutions, or perversions of the right forms" (Aristotle, *Politics*, trans. Ernest Barker (Oxford University Press, 1995), III.6, 1279a17–22). "Those who wrote decrees [*iussa*] that were destructive and unjust [*iniusta*] to their peoples, since they did the opposite of what they had promised and claimed, produced something utterly different from laws; so that it should be clear that in the interpretation of the word 'law' itself [*in ipso nomine legis*] there is the significance and intention of choosing something just and right [*iusti et veri*]" (Cicero, *On the Laws*, in *On the Commonwealth and On the Laws*, trans. James E. G. Zetzel (Cambridge University Press, 1999), II, 11). Norman Kretzman deems this last argument from Cicero the "fullest pre-Christian statement" roughly corresponding to the *lex injusta non est lex* maxim. See Norman Kretzmann, "Lex Iniusta Non Est Lex: Laws on Trial in Aquinas's Court of Conscience," *The American Journal of Jurisprudence* 33, no. 1 (1988): 100.

39. Suárez, *A Treatise on Laws and God the Lawgiver*, I, 2, 11.

40. Suárez, *A Treatise on Laws and God the Lawgiver*, I, 2, 5; II, 17, 2.

41. Suárez, *A Treatise on Laws and God the Lawgiver*, I, 9, 2.

stantive justice, on account of its being contrary to the precepts of natural law, "is not a law, nor does it possess any binding force."[42] Such an unjust law is "not a *lex*, but partakes of the name of *lex* by analogy (so to speak) in so far as it prescribes a certain mode of action in relation to a given end."[43] If Aquinas's texts perhaps left open the possibility for an interpretation that he considered unjust laws to still be valid laws in peripheral or borderline cases, Suárez eliminates this possibility by affirming that a law that is unjust, as it is contrary to metapositive standards of natural law, "cannot be valid [*non potest esse valida*]," because it "cannot validly [*valide*] prescribe anything save that which is just."[44]

Thomas Hobbes offers a radically different account of the conditions for the existence and juridical status of laws that are deemed contrary to the standard of justice. We have already seen that Hobbes quite consistently detaches the concept of *ius* from the idea of justice. He does so precisely by connecting the emergence of the idea of justice with the promulgation of positive laws, which limit *ius* understood as a sphere of total freedom, by assigning determinate things to persons as something that is due in justice by others. In this framework, interestingly enough, positive laws can never really be unjust (or at least substantively unjust[45]) because it is through them that justice—issues related to the question of which persons owe what to whom and how—is established. "They that have the sovereign power," claims Hobbes, "may commit iniquity; but not injustice or injury in the proper signification."[46] It is the positive

42. Suárez, *A Treatise on Laws and God the Lawgiver*, I, 9, 11. Faithful to his norm-based understanding of the nature of law, Suárez refers to *lex naturalis* instead of *ius naturale* when he speaks about metapositive standards relevant to humanly posited law in a jurisprudential sense.

43. Suárez, *A Treatise on Laws and God the Lawgiver*, I, 1, 6.

44. Suárez immediately adds that Augustine had in mind precisely this effect of injustice on the legality of a *lex injusta* in his reflection on the connection between justice and positive laws. See Suárez, *A Treatise on Laws and God the Lawgiver*, I, 9, 4.

45. Laws may still be assessed according to their harmony with criteria of formal justice: "The safety of the people, requireth further, from him, or them that have the sovereign power, that justice be equally administered to all degrees of people" (Hobbes, *Leviathan*, XXX, 15).

46. Hobbes, *Leviathan*, XVIII, 6.

laws, he adds, that constitute "rules of just and unjust; nothing being reputed unjust, that is not contrary to some law."[47] Accordingly, the question of the status of unjust laws becomes irrelevant in Hobbes's account of the nature of law: "To the care of the sovereign, belongeth the making of good laws. But what is a good law? By a good law, I mean not a just law: for no law can be unjust."[48]

Having thus laid the foundations for a positivistic understanding of the question of substantively unjust laws, Hobbes may be said to have influenced subsequent thinkers steeped in the tradition of legal positivism with regard to their assessments of the *lex injusta non est lex* maxim. In his reaction to William Blackstone's claim (practically identical to Suárez's corresponding thesis) that "no human laws are of any validity, if contrary to this [law of nature],"[49] John Austin notes that to claim that unjust laws are not laws—that is, to imply that they do not exist and produce law-like effects—is "stark non-sense," since even the "most pernicious laws ... have been and are continually enforced by judicial tribunals." Accordingly, we should distinguish "the existence of law" and "its merit or demerit," claims Austin, "whether it be or not be is one enquiry, whether it be or be not conformable to an assumed standard, is a different enquiry."[50] He concludes by saying: "A law, which actually exists is a law, though we happen to dislike it."[51]

With Austin's remarks, we seem to have come full circle, since at the level of understanding the nature of law, Austin's thesis seems to be shared by both the legal positivist Hart and by the natural lawyer Finnis. The only difference between a legal-positivist and a Finnisian natural-law account of the *lex injusta non est lex* maxim is that

47. Hobbes, *Leviathan*, XXVI, 4.

48. As Hobbes then continues: "The law is made by the sovereign power, and all that is done by such power, is warranted, and owned by every one of the people; and that which every man will have so, no man can say is unjust" (Hobbes, *Leviathan*, XXX, 20).

49. William Blackstone, *Commentaries on the Laws of England—Book 1: Of the Rights of Persons* (Oxford University Press, 2016), I, 41.

50. John Austin, *The Province of Jurisprudence Determined* (Cambridge University Press, 1995), 157.

51. Austin, *The Province of Jurisprudence Determined*, 157.

for legal positivists, the substantively evaluative content is normally external to the law's nature (with the possibility, conceded by soft positivists, that such content be explicitly invoked by legal sources, in which case it is thereby considered legally relevant), while for natural lawyers, such as Finnis, that content is internal to law's dual nature but ultimately unable to alter or eliminate the legal validity of an unjust law and its conceptual status as *lex*. The outcome of the maxim with regard to the nature of law is the same in both camps: an unjust law is a law, regardless of its injustice.[52]

There are some important dissenters from the foregoing, broadly shared thesis. We are already familiar with Robert Alexy's argument that the dual nature of law still allows for the exceptional possibility that even the real or descriptive aspects of law collapse in cases of extreme injustice, that is, under the conditions of radical breaches of the ideal aspects of law (or law as it ought to be). In Alexy's estimation, law is not "in" such radically unjust posited norms, which are deemed non-law (in German: *Unrecht*),[53] regardless of the fact that such norms exist as law-aspiring or law-appearing entities that pass the test of legal validity in their real or descriptive "life."[54] It could be said that while in Finnis's framework even the most radical

52. This is one of reasons why the maxim is considered to "fail on its own to mark any interesting conceptual or practical distinction between natural law and legal positivism." For this remark, see J. S. Russell, "Trial by Slogan: Natural Law and Lex Iniusta Non Est Lex," *Law and Philosophy* 19, no. 4 (2000): 434.

53. Alexy, *The Argument from Injustice*, 28.

54. Here, Alexy follows the German legal philosopher Gustav Radbruch quite closely: "There can be laws that are so unjust and so socially harmful that *validity*, indeed *legal character itself*, must be *denied* to them. There are principles of law, therefore, that are weightier than any legal enactment, so that a law in conflict with them is *devoid of validity*." See Gustav Radbruch, "Five Minutes of Legal Philosophy (1945)," *Oxford Journal of Legal Studies* 26, no. 1 (2006): 14. See also Gustav Radbruch, "Statutory Lawlessness and Supra-Statutory Law (1946)," *Oxford Journal of Legal Studies* 26, no. 1 (2006): 7: "Where there is not even an attempt at justice, where equality, the core of justice, is deliberately betrayed in the issuance of positive law, then the statute is not merely 'flawed law,' it *lacks completely the very nature of law*" (emphasis added). Sean Coyle advocates an exception to his own position that unjust laws are still laws (albeit in a qualified, nonfocal sense), which is quite similar to Radbruch's line of reasoning, at least with regards to the effect of radically unjust laws: "a law that is deeply contrary to the common good is indeed *ultra vires* ... and thus, in itself, non-law" (Coyle, *Natural Law and Modern Society*, 358).

tension between law's descriptive and evaluative lives never yields the conclusion that a law-aspiring norm ultimately fails to instantiate law (in any sense of that term, focal or peripheral), in Alexy's line of reasoning, an extreme failure in law's ideal "life" may carry even the descriptive social-factual aspects of law entirely outside of the conceptual reach of what counts as law. Alexy considers his view to represent "a classic non-positivistic argument," and one might also add, an argument almost equally distant from the Finnisian version of the natural-law theory of law: "An authoritatively issued norm, socially efficacious from the time of issuance, is denied validity or … legal character because it violates supra-statutory law."[55]

Regardless, Alexy and Finnis continue to share at least one important thesis on the nature of law—the thesis on the nonexistence of the elements of juridicity beyond humanly posited valid law. Indeed, what Alexy sometimes refers to as "supra-statutory law," or what I here call metapositive law, is never really "law" for Alexy in any sense but only denotes a set of moral standards. For Alexy, the question regarding the juridicity of unjust norms appears exclusively in connection to positive laws that have already passed the validity conditions in their real or descriptive "life," and the question only appears because moral standards are operative within the ideal "life" of those laws that are already posited. All law is still positive law in Alexy's juridical world, regardless of the possibility that certain legal norms be deemed non-law on account of grave moral concerns.

How is the *lex injusta non est lex* maxim interpreted by an author favorable to the existence of nonposited elements of real juridicity, such as Ronald Dworkin? We already saw that Dworkin is not very enthusiastic about the importance of that maxim, and it is revealing to understand why this is so. In Dworkin's view, the dilemma inherent to the interpretations of the maxim revolves around the presupposition that law and morality are two discrete systems of norms or values, morality being an external, nonlegal corrective of law. But *law as it ought to be*, or *law that is just* according to the

55. Alexy, *The Argument from Injustice*, 7.

Dworkinian principles of political morality, already forms part of the realm of *law as it is*. In Dworkin's framework, it is not decisive to settle whether an unjust legal norm is valid or not for the purposes of law's identification.[56] To say that unjust legal norms are valid at the stage Dworkin refers to as "preinterpretive" does not automatically mean that these norms are the entirety of what counts as law on the relevant issue.[57] This is because, in Dworkin's view, "explaining the evil law puzzle" relies on the prior understanding that identifying law on the relevant issue includes the process of interpretation that embraces both the valid positive legal norms (even unjust ones) and the metapositive rights to which the principles of political morality point, and which may ultimately trump legally valid but unjust norms. Thus, in the Dworkinian process of identifying law, a *lex injusta* may well be fully valid according to the applicable conditions of legal validity, and still not be the legal norm that ultimately settles the issue of what counts as law in a particular matter.

Several important authors, including Suárez, Blackstone, Radbruch, Hart, Alexy, Dworkin, and Finnis (as well as many other authors, whose arguments are not mentioned in this section) argue that the maxim has potentially significant or even decisive consequences not only for the understanding of the juridical nature of unjust laws but also for the distinct question of the legal validity of those laws. It seems that for some of these authors, the question of the legal validity of unjust laws overlaps entirely with the question of their juridicity. Thus, for Hart and Finnis, the legal validity of unjust norms means that they ought to be considered to constitute law. On the contrary, for Suárez and Blackstone, the injustice of positive laws (or, for Radbruch and Alexy, the extreme injustice of positive laws) results in their defunct legal character (i.e., their being non-law) and in their invalidity, which arguably amounts to the same thing within the respective theories of these authors. Given the peculiar constitutive features of Dworkin's legal theory, the status of intrasystemic legal validity of unjust laws does not necessarily

56. Dworkin, *Justice for Hedgehogs*, 411–12.
57. See Dworkin, *Law's Empire*, 65–66, 102–4.

coincide with the conclusion that the relevant law, all things considered, is (or is not) ultimately reducible to the content of those laws.

After the foregoing survey of the historical interpretations of the *lex injusta non est lex* maxim, at least one thing seems to be certain: each author reads the meaning and the scope of the maxim through the lens of his own account of juridicity (i.e., of what counts as law). This is also true of Aquinas's line of reasoning regarding the maxim.

Ius, *Lex*, and the Status of *Lex Injusta*: What Are the Options, Besides Aquinas?

Aquinas's arguments on the *lex injusta* maxim presented in the preceding section were circumscribed mainly to his analysis of the maxim from within his account of the concept of *lex*. Given that the main idea of this book is organized around Aquinas's thesis that the essence of law is best captured by the term *ius*, rather than by the notion of *lex*, it is evident that Aquinas's crucial ideas regarding the juridical status of unjust laws have yet to be disclosed.

The scope of this section is to explore some alternative options that have been advanced in contemporary legal philosophy regarding the possibility of taking into serious consideration a concept of *ius* that is both (1) broader than the notion of *lex* and (2) somehow seen to be relevant (or ultimately shown to be irrelevant) to the very nature of law.

Hart, Gardner, and Finnis on *Ius* and *Lex*

The occasional alliance between legal positivists and the Finnisian version of a natural-law theory of law may be seen to also include the quasi-overlap of ideas on the conceptual connection between the terms *ius* and *lex*. Thus, for Hart, the term *ius* denotes a morally laden perspective on law, that is, law as it ought to be.[58] The content

58. "[There are certain] moral implications latent in the vocabulary of the law and especially in words like *ius*, *Recht*, *diritto*, *droit* which are laden with the theory of natural law" (Hart, *The Concept of Law*, 208).

implied by this term "hovers uncertainly between law and morals," although it does in fact "mark off an area of morality (the morality of law) which has special characteristics," and is "occupied by the concepts of justice, fairness, rights, and obligation."[59] Hart envisions *ius* and *lex* as "two rival concepts of law"; the "narrow" concept of law as *ius* excludes "morally offensive rules" from the domain of law, while the "wider" concept of law (*lex*), that Hart prefers, "considers as law all rules which are valid" according to the formal tests of validity, "even though some of [these rules] offend against a society's own morality or against what we may hold to be an enlightened or true morality."[60] In short, the term *ius* is confined to extralegal (or extra-*lex*), nonposited standards for moral evaluation, which are not of themselves necessary for identifying what counts as law or what the relevant law is for a particular issue, except for the possible (but not necessary) case when certain standards of *ius* are explicitly invoked by posited law or by the relevant formal tests of validity (i.e., in Hartian parlance, by the rule of recognition).

Another positivist who reflects on the relevance of the concept of *ius* for understanding law's nature, John Gardner, seems to roughly agree with Hart's conclusions, while adding some further insights. For Gardner, there are two senses of the term "legal," corresponding to the two words for "law": *ius* and *lex*. The term *ius* stands for a "moralized sense of law" or a set of standards on law's moral merits, while legal positivism aims to "explain what it takes for a law to be valid in the thin *lex* sense."[61] As a positivist, Gardner sees no problem in allowing for posited laws to be assessed according to the standards of *ius* (whatever these stand for), provided we agree that what is evaluated according to the criteria established by *ius* is brought into reach of that evaluation by legal validity in the *lex* sense. In other words, to be tested regarding its conformity to the relevant standards of *ius* and judged as a success or failure in these terms, a candidate law-aspiring norm must first qualify as fully *lex*,

59. Hart, "Are There Any Natural Rights?" 178.
60. Hart, *The Concept of Law*, 209.
61. Gardner, "Legal Positivism: 5½ Myths," 50–51.

valid positive law. Accordingly, the question that legal positivism seeks to address is: "What is this *lex*, such that it ought to be *ius*?"[62] Thus, Gardner's openness toward the concept of law as *ius* is deeply positivistic. In his view, there is no doubt that "all law is positive law,"[63] that there is "no other type of law but positive law,"[64] and that "there is no such thing as non-positive law."[65] At the same time, his commitment to the concept of law as *lex* is inclusive: although he holds that there is only one concept of true law (*lex*), he concedes that approaches beyond legal positivism, such as the natural-law theory of law, may legitimately and fruitfully explore the conditions for considering a valid legal norm to pertain to the central case of law (which Gardner calls *ius*) or to its limit case (which he refers to as "*lex* that is not *ius*").[66]

Finnis seems to generally hold that legal positivists, such as Hart and Gardner, cannot escape being, in some way, natural lawyers, since both camps increasingly agree that in describing law's nature, one must resort to evaluative arguments.[67] But perhaps an opposite, and quite surprising, case could be made that Finnis, in fact, endorses a version of legal positivism. Gardner's account of the dual *ius-lex* nature of law, wherein the assessment of law's central

62. Gardner, "Legal Positivism: 5½ Myths," 53.

63. John Gardner, "Some Types of Law," in *Law as a Leap of Faith*, 88.

64. Gardner, "Some Types of Law," 54.

65. Gardner, "Some Types of Law," 86.

66. John Gardner, "Hart on Legality, Justice, and Morality," 228.

67. See his claim that "contemporary positivist theories are, it seems, natural law theories" in John Finnis, "Natural Law Theories," in *The Stanford Encyclopedia of Philosophy* (Summer 2020 ed.), ed. Edward N. Zalta, accessed April 9, 2024, https://plato.stanford.edu/archives/sum2020/entries/natural-law-theories/. See also Finnis, "Describing Law Normatively," 23–45. In addition, see also his following claim: "Though human law is artifact and artifice, and not a conclusion from moral premises, both its positing and the recognition of its positivity ... cannot be understood without reference to the moral principles that ground and confirm its authority or challenge its pretention" (Finnis, "The Truth in Legal Positivism," 186). Finnis holds that legal positivism is, so to speak, blinded by the thesis that "a purely descriptive, normatively 100 per cent inert theory of law [is] possible" (Finnis, "Describing Law Normatively," 32). Consequently, in his view, a positivist account of law "lacks the stable responsiveness to questions" concerning the aforementioned reference to moral principles, and to that extent fails "to count as a proper candidate or option in legal theory and philosophy" (Finnis, "Law as Fact and as Reason for Action," 98).

(*ius*) and peripheral cases (*lex* that is not *ius*) depends upon a prior identification of law as valid *lex* according to the relevant validity tests, does not seem to diverge much from the core of Finnis's theory. Gardner even compliments Finnis's thesis on law's central case as the "most important study" on the subject.[68] Together with that praise, Gardner notes that Finnis seems to take for granted the "one and only proposition as the distinctive proposition of legal positivism": "In any legal system, whether a given norm is legally valid, and hence whether it forms part of the law of that system, depends on its sources, not its merits (where its merits, in the relevant sense, include the merits of its sources)."[69] Indeed, Finnis admits that he sees "little to object" to Gardner's formulation of the "one and only" proposition of legal positivism.[70] Both Gardner and Finnis ultimately agree that, to be identified as law, moral content must necessarily be somehow invoked by the posited legal norms and/or be included among the conditions for validity by something like a Hartian rule of recognition.[71] In other words, for both authors, the juridicity of moral standards ultimately rests on its source-based positivity. This is the default positivist position, although Finnis considers it to be the default natural-law stance.[72]

68. Gardner, "Legal Positivism: 5½ Myths," 53. Gardner claims to be under Finnis's influence regarding the account of the central-case thesis of law and the very possibility that law has a dual nature (Gardner, "Hart on Legality, Justice, and Morality," 228).

69. Gardner, "Legal Positivism: 5½ Myths," 19, 21.

70. Finnis, "Describing Law Normatively," 44.

71. For Finnis's accommodation or at least his noncritical usage of the concept of the rule of recognition as the set of social-factual criteria for identifying law, see, for example, the following argument: "The legal system ... is ... open ... to the unrestricted flow of practical reasoning, in which a stipulation, valid according to the system's formal criteria of validity ('rules of recognition'), may be judged to be, or to have become, unjust and, therefore, after all, wholly or partially inapplicable" (Finnis, *Natural Law and Natural Rights*, 356).

72. Gardner explicitly describes his views as pertaining to hard positivism (Gardner, "Legal Positivism: 5½ Myths," 22, 50). Perhaps Finnis's potential (and inadvertent) alliance with legal positivism is closer to the "soft" or "inclusive" version of positivism, since, beyond endorsing the "all law is positive law" positivist thesis, he also seems to hold that, first, it is conceptually possible (or even desirable) that the legal validity of a norm can sometimes depend also on its consistency with some moral norms (provided, of course, that such consistency is picked out by positive law), and that, second, such dependence

The sense that Gardner gives to the words "law" and "legally valid" in the aforementioned distinctive proposition of legal positivism is, in Finnis's view, "*precisely* the sense needed to give sense to the well-known slogan … 'an unjust *law* [something legally valid in its making but seriously unjust] is *not a law* [lacks something essential to law's central purposes].'"[73] Finnis's frequent collaborator Robert P. George quite correctly notes that the only relevant effect of the *lex injusta* maxim, on a Finnisian reading, concerns the moral (not legal) obligatoriness to obey a *lex injusta*:

> The truth of the proposition *lex iniusta non est lex* is a moral truth, namely, that the moral obligation created by authoritative legal enactment—that is to say, by positive law—is conditional, rather than absolute. The *prima facie* moral obligation to obey the law is *defeasible*. Finnis does not claim that unjust laws are in no legitimate sense laws, nor does he argue that judges enjoy as a matter of natural law some sort of plenary authority to invalidate or even to subvert or ignore laws that they regard (even reasonably regard) as unjust.[74]

In other words, the criteria for evaluating that a valid posited norm is *ius* (in Gardner's parlance) are neither operative in the concept of *lex* to the effect that they can invalidate valid laws, nor in any way fully juridical prior to their being posited. To be law, for Finnis (and for Gardner), it suffices that the norm be *lex*, that is, a valid posited law. When analyzing the concept of *ius*, Finnis is quite consistent

---

is only possible and by no means necessary. For the first claim, see his following remark: "That part of our positive law that is, as it were, adopted from, or carries over from, or quasi-read off, the natural moral law *is natural law*. Not to forget: it is at the same time positive law, and this latter truth about it—its positivity—is the truth that directly concerns the judge, in a generally just legal order" (John Finnis, "Coexisting Normative Orders? Yes, but No," *The American Journal of Jurisprudence* 57, no. 1 (2012): 116). For the second claim, consider the following thesis: "Some laws are utterly unjust, utterly immoral; the fact that something is declared or enacted as law by the social sources authorized or recognized as sources of valid law in no way entails that it is … morally acceptable or is even relevant to a consideration of someone's moral responsibilities" (Finnis, "A Grand Tour of Legal Theory," 105).

73. Finnis, "Describing Law Normatively," 44 (emphasis in original).

74. Robert P. George, "Introduction: The Achievement of John Finnis," in *Reason, Morality and Law*, 5 (emphasis in original). For Finnis's own detailed explanation of this purely moral effect of the maxim, see Finnis, *Natural Law and Natural Rights*, 354–62.

in his claim that besides denoting subjective rights, the term is practically synonymous and interchangeable with *lex*, for both him and Aquinas: "Aquinas … treats human positive law as the central case of law and focal meaning of *lex* and (in one of its two main senses) *ius*."[75]

Thus, the only difference between Gardner and Finnis seems to be that the positivist Gardner holds that law "may," "in some contexts," refer to *ius*, whatever that term might mean ("whatever it is"), and thus the nature of law "must capture" the possibility of assessing valid legal norms according to the applicable standards of *ius*, thereby judging that law as a success (central case of valid law) or failure (limit case of valid law).[76] On the other hand, the natural lawyer Finnis holds that law (*lex*, practically synonymous with *ius*, when this latter term is employed for specific lawyerly purposes) must necessarily appeal to substantive moral principles in its evaluative "life" in order to constitute law's central case (Gardner's notion of *ius*), and he provides a detailed account of what these principles are. But this thesis does not seem to be sufficient to defend Finnis against the claim that he shares virtually the same view on what constitutes juridicity with at least some legal positivists (i.e., the so-called soft positivists). Perhaps he does not even want to be so defended: "*why deny* that the facts which are referred to as 'human positing' … can all be identified by lawyerly historical"—that is, social-factual—"methods, without moral argument?"[77] The reluctance to attribute real juridicity to at least some nonposited standards (such as those I call natural juridical goods), leaves a natural lawyer vulnerable to the accusation of being in fact a legal positivist (most likely a soft positivist), at least from the viewpoint of grasping the nature of law.

75. John Finnis, "Grounding Human Rights in Natural Law," *The American Journal of Jurisprudence* 60, no. 2 (2015): 223. See also Finnis, *Aquinas: Moral, Political, and Legal Theory*, 134.

76. Gardner, "Legal Positivism: 5½ Myths," 52.

77. Finnis, "The Truth in Legal Positivism," 185.

Ius as a Set of Principles of Political Morality: Dworkin and Vermeule

In a recent revival of interest in classical jurisprudence, Adrian Vermeule, together with other frequent collaborators, perhaps most notably Conor Casey, advocate an integral understanding of what counts as law (*ius*), which they envision as extending beyond merely positive law (*lex*), including certain nonposited content. Vermeule's approach to understanding law's nature seems to position him in the camp of those authors who maintain that there are certain elements of juridicity beyond valid positive law and beyond the reach of the purely social-factual conditions for recognizing what counts as law. Thus, the Vermeulean approach to grasping law's ontology—which could be called "common good constitutionalism," following the title of Vermeule's important book on the contemporary restatement of classical jurisprudence—seems to stand alongside Aquinas and Dworkin in holding that not all law is posited. Vermeule not only enjoys the company of those authors but also actively borrows certain elements from their respective theories.

From Aquinas (and, more broadly, from the tradition of classical authors, which also includes the Roman jurists, as well as the medieval civil and canon lawyers), Vermeule claims to borrow the paradigmatic reference to *ius* for understanding what law is, in its essence. It is thus imperative that I analyze Vermeule's theoretical and practical proposal in more detail, since it will gradually become evident that it represents a highly influential, present-day alternative to my reading of Aquinas.

In his interpretation of Aquinas, positive law (including all posited instantiations of law's nature), to which Vermeule refers as *lex*, "while worthy of great respect in its sphere," is ultimately "contained within a larger objective order of legal principles," which he labels *ius*; consequently, positive legal norms (or *lex*) "can only be interpreted in accordance with these principles" (or with *ius*).[78] In other

78. Vermeule, *Common Good Constitutionalism*, 2–3.

words, while "*lex* is the enacted positive law," "*ius* is the overall body of law generally, including and subsuming *lex*, but transcending it."[79] On first sight, this line of analysis seems very promising, at least from the viewpoint of the basic ideas of this book.

Vermeule suggests that the integral conception of law (*ius*), together with all its posited and nonposited manifestations, is or at least should be ultimately ordered to the common good, which is the end of law according to the classical tradition, programmatically captured in Aquinas's definition of *lex*.[80] This decisive argument of the Vermeulean revival of classical jurisprudence enters to form part of the label of his legal theory: *common good* constitutionalism. The substantively moral part of the common good that defines the boundaries of law is, on Vermeule's reading, the natural law, which denotes a set of "principles of objective natural morality," or "*ius naturale*."[81]

At this stage of analysis, it is already possible to signal certain shortcomings of Vermeule's theory. These shortcomings are not merely exegetical misconstructions of Aquinas's original arguments on certain nuances; rather, they concern important conceptual issues.

Starting from the top of the classical framework, it seems that for Vermeule, *ius* is broadly based on the injunction of justice.[82] But Vermeulean justice is not exactly the decisive criterion that juridicizes things, thereby rendering them law or *ius*. In fact, Aquinas's paradigmatic definition of *ius* as the *ipsa res iusta* is mysteriously absent from the Vermeulean account of law's nature. For Vermeule, justice is "built into law from the ground up and from the start," but only as an aspirational criterion that points law toward a certain part of political morality: "This does not mean, it should go without saying, that justice and law are identical. Although law is a department of political morality, it is a distinctive part of political morality."[83] If

79. Vermeule, *Common Good Constitutionalism*, 4.

80. Vermeule, *Common Good Constitutionalism*, 2–3.

81. See Vermeule, *Common Good Constitutionalism*, 8, 24.

82. Vermeule, *Common Good Constitutionalism*, 6. See also his claim that justice is the ultimate aim of law (114).

83. Vermeule, *Common Good Constitutionalism*, 179.

Vermeule consistently understands the term "law" in the *ius* sense, as I believe he does or should, the foregoing passage reveals his conviction that the domain of *ius* corresponds to a specific part of political morality marked off by legally relevant justice. Now, in his view, justice becomes legally relevant in connection to that part of political morality concerned with rendering to each person and group their own due, which "takes into account distinct considerations arising from the *institutional embodiment of the legal system*."[84]

It is quite symptomatic that in this first part of his legal theory —which borrows from Aquinas and classical jurisprudence—Vermeule neither provides a detailed account of whether and how justice models the nature of law[85] nor explains how exactly to delimit the specific part of political morality that refers to law (*ius*) in Thomistic or classical terms. He chooses to settle that part of his account of law's nature—an account of the properties of juridicity and the conditions for identifying law (*ius*)—in the second part of his theory, where he borrows from Dworkin. In the quote at the end of the previous paragraph, Vermeule already signals certain Dworkinian aspects of his legal theory when he says that the sphere of legally relevant justice is somehow ultimately delimited by considerations of the institutional embodiment of the legal system.

Downstream from Aquinas's foundational interconnectedness between justice and law (*ius*), other Thomistic or classical concepts are also somewhat flattened in Vermeule's analysis. To name only one example, he says: "On the classical conception, rights are *iura* (the plural of *ius*) because *ius* is justice—affording to each what is due to each. Crucially, what is due to each, on the classical view is itself determined by the common good, right from the ground up."[86]

84. See Adrian Vermeule, "Common Good as a Legal Concept," *Ius & Iustitium* (blog), November 16, 2022, accessed October 29, 2024, https://iusetiustitium.com/the-common-good-as-a-legal-concept (emphasis added).

85. Based on his texts, including those cited above, a case could be made that Vermeule thinks that law, with its distinct properties, specifies the domain of justice that is legally relevant. This would be contrary to Aquinas's position that justice models law and defines its distinct domain.

86. Vermeule, *Common Good Constitutionalism*, 166.

In other words, rights are *ius*, *ius* is justice, and justice is determined by the common good, which is in turn shaped (at least regarding to its substantive moral content) by the natural law, and natural law is identified with *ius naturale*. But these concepts are far more sophisticated and nuanced in Aquinas's legal theory than in Vermeule's line of reasoning. The only concept that Vermeule analyses in more detail is the common good,[87] almost as if the other concepts (*ius*, *lex*, justice, natural law, etc.) are instrumental notions in the service of promoting the central value of *bonum commune* in his legal theory.[88] He admits that some of his arguments could have been developed with more attention paid to the richness of its basic concepts,[89] but he does not seem to be as equally aware that the underdevelopment of crucial Thomist concepts—for example, presupposing their interconnectedness or interchangeability as something obvious, almost self-evident—may compromise his project in significant ways.

As already mentioned, one of the examples of how undercooked Thomist arguments contribute to muddled results may be found in the second stage of Vermeule's line of argument, namely, where he explains why something counts as law or *ius* (i.e., where he elaborates on his thesis on the properties of juridicity). The fact that he builds this part of his account of law's nature by borrowing from Dworkin, instead of from Aquinas or the classical jurisprudential tradition, is certainly a legitimate scholarly option. However, it makes one wonder whether Vermeule was aware that Aquinas offers some convincing arguments on the issue, and if he was, why he ultimately opted for Dworkin's approach to understanding juridicity and law.

As Vermeule himself puts it, the main goal of his theory is to understand "how this classical view of law relates to the constitutional

87. Vermeule, *Common Good Constitutionalism*, 26–38. See also Conor Casey and Adrian Vermeule, "Myths of Common Good Constitutionalism," *Harvard Journal of Law & Public Policy* 45, no. 1 (2022): 109–14.

88. The structure of his arguments seems to suggest as much: for example, see Vermeule, *Common Good Constitutionalism*, 7–8, 190.

89. Vermeule, *Common Good Constitutionalism*, 25.

theory today."[90] In other words, he wants to understand how the account of the essence of law offered by Aquinas and other authors steeped in the classical tradition (according to Vermeule's reading of that account) becomes workable within the law of a particular political community, namely, the United States of America. With regard to the passage from theoretical issues to practical arrangements and considerations, he highlights: "I offer an account that aims to put our constitutional order … in its best possible light, given our whole history—not merely our most recent history.… I suggest that the best overall interpretation of our public law requires us to revive the principles of classical law, looking backward so that we may go forward."[91] This overall direction of the more practical part of his legal theory highly resembles Dworkin's general jurisprudential argument. Indeed, Vermeule admits that Dworkin's ideas on identifying law "fit like a glove with the classical conception of law."[92] Although Vermeule claims to not offer an "argument about jurisprudence"—that is, about the nature of law—"in the technical academic sense,"[93] his endorsement of the Dworkinian account of the nature of law reveals Vermeule's conviction that Aquinas's legal theory is insufficient (or that it is too "theoretical") to provide that explanation *per se*.

By espousing Dworkin's "practical" considerations on identifying law, Vermeule cannot escape adopting the overall Dworkinian account of the nature of law and juridicity. For Dworkin, law (roughly, Vermeule's *ius*) is the result of the interpretation of posited legal norms (roughly, Vermeule's *lex*) against the backdrop of relevant justifying legal principles and rights—including nonposited or

90. Vermeule, *Common Good Constitutionalism*, 4.

91. Vermeule, *Common Good Constitutionalism*, 5.

92. Vermeule, *Common Good Constitutionalism*, 6–7.

93. Vermeule, *Common Good Constitutionalism*, 4. Vermeule clearly refutes Dworkin's predominantly liberal "set of substantive moral commitments and priorities" and his "account of rights" in favor of "a classical theory of rights" (Vermeule, *Common Good Constitutionalism*, 6). It is Vermeule's understanding—and a correct one, in my opinion—that Dworkin's ideas on the substantive content of rights and of metapositive legal principles may be separated from his overall account on the nature of law, which includes due appreciation for the fully juridical status of nonposited rights, values, and principles.

metapositive principles and rights—that provide the best political-moral justification of legal practices in a particular political community. This interpretation defines what law is according to its nature by determining the properties that render norms, values, principles, and realities *juridical*. When Vermeule claims that his account is basically "a work of interpretation," a work with an essentially Dworkinian character, this description of the interpretive meaning of legal practices inevitably leads to theoretical repercussions, including some he may not have predicted.[94]

Vermeule's commitments to Dworkinian arguments on law's nature leave him vulnerable to some of the same critiques that may be advanced against Dworkin's theses from a Thomist perspective. For example, it seems to be Vermeule's understanding that the main thread of Dworkin's line of reasoning on the predominantly political-moral nature of law is highly compatible with the classical tradition.[95] But Aquinas does not hold that *res* and *lex* are rendered juridical, or rendered law (*ius*), on account of the interpretations of the best political-moral justifications of that *res* or *lex* in the overall legal practices of a concrete political community. On the

94. Occasionally and without further analysis, Vermeule does venture into more abstract jurisprudential arguments: "I believe that Dworkin's major critiques of Hart ... are essentially correct" (Vermeule, *Common Good Constitutionalism*, 188–89). Whatever his reasons for adopting Dworkin's path to understanding law's nature, a case could be made that Vermeule sees in Dworkin's theory further concepts and ideas that might be instrumental to his central project of securing the common good through law: "Since, on Dworkin's view, law is a distinctive department of political morality, it is perfectly possible to speak of promoting goods of political morality within law. The relevant goods are goods inside the law" (Vermeule, *Common Good Constitutionalism*, 73).

95. For example, see his following claim: "The classical tradition thus claims that principles of political morality are themselves already part of law and internal to it" (Vermeule, *Common Good Constitutionalism*, 19). See also his similar thesis: "Dworkin reinvented a version of the classical legal tradition without knowing it, especially when toward the end of his career he categorized law as a department of political morality—albeit a distinctive department, itself including distinctive moral considerations such as qualified continuity with past decisions and respect for institutional roles. That framing would have both Aquinas and the classical lawyers nodding in approval" (Vermeule, *Common Good Constitutionalism*, 69). Perhaps this conviction of the quasioverlap between Dworkin's ideas of what law is and the corresponding arguments of classical jurisprudence (in Vermeule's reading of those arguments) partly explains why Vermeule resorts to Dworkin's jurisprudential theory.

contrary, Aquinas maintains that *res* and *lex* become law (from the perspective of *ius*) when they are brought within the reach of the domain of justice, with its specific properties, in a framework where *ius naturale* forms part of the obligatory evaluative standards for determinations of *ius positivum*. Aquinas's account of the juridical phenomenon is not political-moral but conceptual: it concerns the instantiations of law's nature at all levels of the sources of laws, in all political communities.[96] This means that his proposal is not a purely theoretical module awaiting practical application in the legal practices of a concrete political community for its proper juridical force. Rather, Aquinas envisions his account of law's nature as an already practical and applicable juridical framework for the circumstances and arrangements of each concrete legal system.

Now, it is Vermeule's understanding that his implementation of Dworkinian jurisprudential arguments, which allow for a rehabilitation of key concepts of classical legal theory in the United States of America, points to the path that other political communities may or should take.[97] Dworkin was heavily criticized for making his account of law dependent on the political-moral values and priorities of concrete political communities. This Dworkinian line of argument would mean that even deeply immoral and unjust

96. Of course, Aquinas does not offer all the details of how exactly his jurisprudential framework ought to be implemented in the institutional arrangements and dynamics of legal practices of concrete legal systems. But he is rather clear in his claim that his account of the nature of law should not be diminished in that implementation. Even Brian McCall, lauded by Vermeule for his "essential treatment of the natural law and its relationship to the classical law generally" (Vermeule, *Common Good Constitutionalism*, 188), frames the nature of law as *ius* on the basis of Aquinas's legal theory in something more than only political-moral terms. McCall's view on the four causes of law is significantly different from the one I propose in this book. For him, the material cause of law are "individual laws"; the formal cause is "justice" considered in its object, *ius* (we seem to agree on that point); the efficient cause are the "lawmakers"; and the final cause is again "justice," but now considered in its telic perspective as that which "makes people act justly." Thus, "justice is the beginning and end of law." See Brian M. McCall, *The Architecture of Law: Rebuilding Law in the Classical Tradition* (University of Notre Dame Press, 2018), 375–79. Despite his correct emphasis on the architectonic importance of justice and *ius*, McCall's account of law's nature fails, in my opinion, to take into sufficient account the implications of Aquinas's thesis that law (*ius*) is a thing (*res*), which corresponds to a specific form of justice-based good.

97. See Vermeule, *Common Good Constitutionalism*, 5.

political-moral justifications of legal practices of a particular political community form part of the process of interpretation, which ultimately identifies the relevant law on a specific issue.[98] Dworkin's answer to these critiques, although elaborate, is ultimately weak from the perspective of understanding the ontology of law. The first part of his answer is a restatement of his overall theory of law. He seems to hold that in cases of unjust laws in the legal systems of overall legitimate and mostly just regimes, the best political-moral justification of legal practices in that particular political community will ultimately point to rights that persons have, and these rights will juridically trump (and protect against) unjust legal norms, without the need to declare these norms invalid (since their invalidity does not alter the outcome: the triumph of just rights over unjust laws).

However, in the second part of his answer to said critique, he deals with the extreme case of profoundly unjust regimes, their deeply immoral political moralities, and their equally unjust norms. In these radical circumstances, Dworkin proposes that legal officials use their powers to declare such unjust norms invalid on the basis of substantive moral principles and rights, which are not embedded in the political moralities of those regimes but disconnected from them.[99] In other words, the legal officials are called to appeal to mor-

98. For one such critique, see Hart, *Essays on Bentham*, 150–53.

99. See Dworkin, *Taking Rights Seriously*, 326–27, 341–43; Ronald Dworkin, "A Reply by Ronald Dworkin," in *Ronald Dworkin and Contemporary Jurisprudence*, ed. Marshall Cohen (Duckworth, 1984), 256–60, 299, and Dworkin, *Justice for Hedgehogs*, 411. For an overall analysis of this question in Dworkin, see also David Dyzenhaus, "Dworkin and Unjust Law," in *The Legacy of Ronald Dworkin*, ed. Wil Waluchow and Stefan Sciaraffa (Oxford University Press, 2016), 149–54. In Dworkin's view, the aforementioned legal official's decision, grounded in moral principles and rights, relies upon an underlying presupposition that the regime is so unjust that the unjust norms promulgated in that regime do not create even prima facie legal rights and duties—at least not legal rights and duties in Dworkin's interpretive sense of "legality" and "law" (see Dworkin, *Justice for Hedgehogs*, 411). But it remains unclear how such a decision, its grounds, and presuppositions might be "law" in any Dworkinian sense. Such a position rather resembles Alexy's and Radbruch's theory, according to which a moral (nonjuridical) criterion invalidates an unjust legal norm that passes the threshold of extreme injustice. The only difference between Dworkin, on the one hand, and Alexy and Radbruch, on the other, is that for Dworkin, the decisive moral criterion for the invalidity of unjust norms stands entirely outside of his account of the nature of law, whereas for Alexy and Radbruch, that criterion is somehow

al principles and rights that cannot be considered to constitute law according to Dworkin's own theory of law's nature. In those cases, a legal official's decision rules against both unjust positive laws and unjust underlying legal principles of those laws by appealing to morality that is beyond (and disconnected from) both the positive laws and the political moralities of that community. Dworkin has one option available here, namely, to follow his theoretical premises on the existence of the architectonic "natural" right to equality (and of the connected, similarly "natural," rights) to the systematic conclusion that these rights are already fully law in each political community on account of their being truly natural rights inherent to all human persons. But that option would undercut his preference for the political-moral ground of nonposited rights, and he never avails himself of it.

In a similar vein, we could ask how exactly Vermeule envisions legal systems in which deeply embedded legal practices are based on political moralities hostile to or disconnected from the ideas of natural law and common good, or alien to the concepts of classical jurisprudence. If he argues that these ideas and concepts have juridical relevance in those systems under the described circumstances (hostility, disconnection, etc.), then he would have to provide a detailed account of how exactly they are juridical, because no Dworkinian explanation for their immediate juridicity seems to be available.

But Vermeule seems to hold that the ideas and concepts of classical jurisprudence are indeed deeply embedded in the best political-moral justification of the legal practices of the United States of America, and he is in fact convinced that the same could be said for the legal traditions of many other political communities. His defense of that claim sometimes comes close to holding that regardless of the occasional historical disconnections from common good constitutionalism in legal practices (which he explicitly acknowledges[100]), a

present and operative in the unjust norm's dual legal life (i.e., it is explainable in the framework of their theory).

100. Vermeule, *Common Good Constitutionalism*, 2.

case could be made that the crucial elements of classical jurisprudence were never "purged" from American legal practices[101] but instead "remained vital"[102] and even continued to exercise a "pervasive influence."[103] He argues that in the periods of explicit historical disconnection from common good constitutionalism, its core features have only "ceased to be defended" or "recognized,"[104] indeed, they "went underground" and "changed into a kind of disguise"[105] while continuing to be highly operative in the legal system.[106] Now if Vermeule's assessment is true, his overall account of the nature of law resembles more of a Hartian version of soft positivism than Dworkinian interpretivism. Hart's soft positivism allows for the possibility of the social-factual incorporation of moral standards into law not only by way of morally laden legal norms, or by way of legal norms that explicitly point to extralegal moral standards for their correct interpretation, but also through the inclusion of certain moral values into the conditions for the validity of legal norms by a rule of recognition. As Hart puts it,

> The question of whether a rule of recognition exists and what its content is, i.e., what the criteria of validity in any given legal system are, is regarded ... as an empirical, though complex, question of fact ... established [by] the actual practice of the courts and officials of the system when identifying the law which they are to apply.[107]

101. Vermeule, *Common Good Constitutionalism*, 4.

102. Vermeule, *Common Good Constitutionalism*, 3.

103. Vermeule, *Common Good Constitutionalism*, 30, 52.

104. Vermeule, *Common Good Constitutionalism*, 3.

105. Vermeule, *Common Good Constitutionalism*, 60.

106. See also Vermeule's following claims: "The lawyer who is skeptical or hostile to the idea of the common good fails to understand not only the history but also the present practical reality of the law" (Vermeule, *Common Good Constitutionalism*, 35); "How deeply the classical legal tradition has always infused our law, it is hardly some sort of alien intrusion" (Vermeule, *Common Good Constitutionalism*, 53); and "The principles of the classical legal tradition are our own principles, written into our own traditions" (Vermeule, *Common Good Constitutionalism*, 53).

107. Hart, *The Concept of Law*, 292–93. Julie Dickson offers an excellent further description of the Hartian rule of recognition as the social fact manifested in the practice of legal officials: "According to Hart, legal officials must accept as binding and follow this rule of recognition in identifying valid law in order for a legal system to exist.... Officials must exhibit an attitude of acceptance or an internal point of view with regard to what

With this in mind, it is quite possible to categorize Vermeule's insistence on legal officials' continuous support for the implementation of moral standards that form part of classical jurisprudence in their actual practices—a support that seems to amount to the existence of a rule of recognition—as a form of soft positivism. Vermeule uses quite strong words when describing the legal officials' perhaps tacit or ambivalent but nonetheless identifiable commitments to the crucial features of classical jurisprudence:

> Judges and others unavoidably and unmistakably work with some account or other of the common good and of law's ordering to that good.[108]
>
> The official commitment to legal positivism that is the main common characteristic of the reigning approaches is itself consistently belied by the actual behavior of judges and other interpreters, who are far more classical than they know.[109]

Vermeule is, of course, aware of the central theses of positivism in general[110] and soft positivism in particular,[111] but he seems to be unaware of the vulnerability of his arguments to soft positivism's conflation of *ius* with *lex*, wherein a rule of recognition must appeal (at the level of *lex*) to legally relevant moral standards for these latter to constitute law (at the level of *ius*).[112]

---

they are doing, that is, they must treat the rule requiring them to recognize certain things as constituting valid law as binding upon themselves and upon other officials." See Julie Dickson, "Is the Rule of Recognition Really a Conventional Rule?" *Oxford Journal of Legal Studies* 27, no. 3 (2007): 375.

108. Vermeule, *Common Good Constitutionalism*, 4.

109. Vermeule, *Common Good Constitutionalism*, 53.

110. "For the positivist, background principles are law only insofar as they are recognized and incorporated into law as a matter of social fact. The classical tradition, however, holds that these principles are law *ipso iure*, binding of their own force. . . . To understand those principles as binding only insofar as they are incorporated into law on positivist terms is to conflate *ius* with *lex*." See Adrian Vermeule, "The Bourbons of Jurisprudence," Harvard Public Law Working Paper No. 22-31, August 22, 2022, accessed October 29, 2024, https://papers.ssrn.com/sol3/papers.cfm?abstractid=4192796.

111. Vermeule, *Common Good Constitutionalism*, 189.

112. Vermeule's argument that "principles of political morality are themselves already part of the law and internal to it" may be read in a way that is compatible with both soft positivism and Dworkinian interpretivism. Two scholars, John Tasioulas and Conor

An objection to Vermeule's case for soft positivism could certainly be made on the following basis: the history of American legal practices, in its periods of explicit disconnection from classical jurisprudence (but implicit usage of its core concepts), found itself, at best, in a situation of disagreement among legal officials regarding the criteria for whether classical moral principles and natural rights count as law. In the case of disagreement, according to this objection, soft positivism is excluded because there is no harmonized practice between the legal officials, and hence the rule of recognition cannot be said to incorporate said moral standards and rights. However, it seems that Vermeule, perhaps inadvertently, had responded to this objection when he argued: "it is irrelevant that there was, is, and will be disagreement" between legal officials on the specific points of classical jurisprudence—that is., "over the content of the common good and the natural law, in hard cases" (such as the "split almost down to middle" between the justices of the U.S. Supreme Court)—because in those cases, the disagreement concerns the positive-law determinations and not the natural-law general principles, which remain undisputed.[113]

Now, if Vermeule's accidental response to this objection is tenable, then it is likely that he is in fact a soft positivist, since the second part of his legal theory, wherein he explains what counts as law (*ius*) and why, may be more Hartian than Dworkinian. On the other hand, he may be seen to argue that historical disconnections, together with past and current disagreements in legal practices regarding the moral standards of classical jurisprudence, amount to the implausibility of the rule of recognition's inclusion of these standards and instead point to the plausibility of an interpretivist argument, since there is

---

Casey, read this argument as the core thesis in favor of Vermeule's nonpositivism, but they do not consider the possibility of a soft-positivist reading of the same thesis, such as the one I explore in this section. See John Tasioulas, "'Law as the Art of Justice': On Vermeule's *Common Good Constitutionalism*," *The American Journal of Jurisprudence* 69, no. 1 (2024): 61–76; Conor Casey, "Continuity and Evolution in Vermeule on Legal Interpretation," *The American Journal of Jurisprudence* 69, no. 1 (2024): 29–43.

113. Vermeule, *Common Good Constitutionalism*, 20.

good ground in his texts for that claim, too.[114] If this latter claim is closer to his legal-theoretical preferences, then he certainly seems to follow Dworkin[115] more than Aquinas.

Ultimately, the question of whether he is a soft positivist or a Dworkinian interpretivist is less relevant compared to the conclusion that, in the end, he is not following arguments advanced by Aquinas or by classical jurisprudence regarding the nature of law and the properties of juridicity. Otherwise, again, why would he feel the need to borrow from Dworkin (or from Hart, for that matter) when it comes to explaining the conditions of why something counts as law?

Vermeule's preference for non-Thomist accounts of juridicity influences his interpretation of the *lex injusta non est lex* maxim, which floats somewhere between Dworkin's and Finnis's understanding of the maxim: "As Aquinas observed, a law that is out of step with natural justice (procedural or substantive) does not simply become no-law, as though it had never been created; rather, it results in a perverted caricature of law."[116] In other words, in Vermeule's view, an unjust law represents a certain (however bad) instantiation of law at the preinterpretive stage (*lex*), and it becomes not only

114. See Vermeule's following arguments: "The classical tradition should be explicitly recovered and adapted as the matrix within which American judges read our Constitution, our statutes, and our administrative law" (Vermeule, *Common Good Constitutionalism*, 1); "This classical tradition embodies the best of our own tradition … and if anything has a claim to capturing the 'original understanding of the Constitution', this does. The classical law *is* the original understanding. In that sense, the book is as much a matter of memory and recovery as of theory" (Vermeule, *Common Good Constitutionalism*, 2); and "The core theoretical insights and jurisprudential principles of the classical legal tradition can be recovered, adapted and translated into our world, so as to yield a better interpretation of the past and present of our operative constitutional order" (Vermeule, *Common Good Constitutionalism*, 3).

115. Dworkin holds that the content of law cannot be settled by "any uniform behavior or conviction" of legal officials, that is, by something akin to a Hartian social-factual rule of recognition, because these officials often "disagree fundamentally about the criteria for identifying valid law," and thus "they do not share a convention that stipulates criteria for identifying valid law" (Dworkin, *Justice in Robes*, 197). As seen before, he maintains that even in the context of controversy and disagreement, legal officials arrive at a correct legal solution by picking out the best political-moral interpretation of the legal practices in their polity (Dworkin, *Justice in Robes*, 188–89).

116. Vermeule, *Common Good Constitutionalism*, 120–21.

non-law (or non-*ius*) on the sole account of its injustice but may also be overridden in the process of identifying law (*ius*) by way of broader interpretivist considerations of the political-moral justifications of the relevant legal practices.

Aquinas's Position: *Lex Injusta Non Est Ratio Iuris*

It is finally time to present Aquinas's complete account of the juridical status of unjust positive legal norms. As the course of this book suggests, this status cannot be resolved by only considering Aquinas's arguments regarding the status of unjust laws as *lex*. Of course, it is also necessary to take into consideration the likelihood that for Aquinas, unjust law-aspiring or law-appearing norms fail to qualify for inclusion in the concept of *lex* since he presents strong arguments in favor of the claim that justice enters into the definition of the concept of *lex*. On this reading, *lex injusta* would fail to qualify as *lex*.

However, the central question in this matter is whether a *lex injusta* participates in the juridical phenomenon as the efficient cause or the title of *ius*, that is, as a *ratio iuris*. In other words, if a norm fails to properly establish a certain reality (*res*) as a *ius*—because (1) it stretches beyond the field of strict justice for lack of some of its essential properties (outwardness, other-directedness, obligatoriness) or constitutive elements (measure, titleholder, debtor); (2) it is in direct contrast with *ius naturale* or with the natural core of hybrid natural-positive goods to be constituted as *ius positivum*; (3) it is contrary to the common good by illegitimately favoring particular or private goods; (4) it is enacted *ultra vires*; or (5) when the principle of formal justice (or fairness) is illegitimately violated—what is the status of that norm? Aquinas's answer would be that these norms, on account of their injustice (at least for reasons 2 to 5) or their irrelevance to justice (i.e., their nonjustice, for reason 1), do not constitute a *ratio* of *ius*, and that therefore these norms are not juridical in that they do not participate in the juridical phenomenon.

The *res* to which the content of those norms refers remain non-*ius* or non-*law* despite the positivity of the norms.

Aquinas explicitly claims that there may indeed exist some corollary reasons why citizens should obey at least some unjust law-aspiring posited norms (I will have more to say on this topic in the next section). But these reasons do not alter his understanding that, at the level of the nature of law, said norms are ultimately *not law* from the viewpoint of *ius* (because they fail to correctly establish a *ius*) and most likely also from the viewpoint of *lex* (because these norms, at least for reasons 2 to 5 mentioned in the preceding paragraph, fail to denote an instance of *lex*, on account of their defects with regard to justice, provided that justice may be said to enter into the definition of *lex*).

Of course, Aquinas never makes the absurd claim that unjust, posited, law-aspiring norms do not exist; they certainly exist, and they aspire to establish an order of "justice" under the appearance that they are qualified to do so. He seems to leave to the individual legal systems the determination of concrete practices, which aim to both identify the unjust law-aspiring norms and settle their status after that identification. Understanding the status of these norms and the effects they produce before they are identified, or before their unjust effect is neutralized by the relevant mechanisms of the legal system, is a complex and important question. But it is a question that exceeds the primary focus of this book: the ontology of law.

Unjust Law-Aspiring Norms and Reasons for Action

Law-Like Effects of Unjust Non-Laws: Introductory Remarks

In this section, I will explore the question of whether a law-aspiring, validly posited norm, which is deemed non-law on account of its injustice (according to Aquinas and the tradition of juridical realism), may still produce law-like effects in a legal system for certain reasons.

The bulk of Aquinas's reasoning on the possible law-like effects of unjust laws, on account of their somehow constituting reasons for action, may be found in his analysis of the concept of *lex* in the *Prima secundae* of the *Summa*. In the *Secunda secundae*'s analyses of justice and *ius*, Aquinas may be seen to argue that unjust, posited, law-aspiring norms that are directly contrary to *ius naturale* never provide good reasons for action.[117] This argument is based in both the content of these norms and other applicable corollary considerations. In other cases, it is his understanding that there may be some corollary causes, beyond the content of unjust law-aspiring posited norms, that may constitute good reasons for actions that amount to the observance of those laws. As Aquinas puts it, "such laws do not bind in conscience, except perhaps [*nisi propter*][118] in order to avoid scandal [*scandalum*] or disturbance [*perturbationem*], for which cause a man should even yield [*debet cedere*] his *ius*."[119] In other

117. "If the written law [*scriptura legis*] contains anything contrary to *ius naturale*, it is unjust and *has no binding force*" (*ST* II-II, q. 60, a. 5, ad 1, emphasis added). In a similar argument form the *Prima secundae* of the *Summa*, Aquinas does not speak directly of *ius naturale*, but he does say that when the injustice of laws is directly "opposed to the Divine good," "contrary to Divine law," or "contrary to the commandments of God," laws that are unjust for those reasons "must nowise be observed" (or "should not be obeyed") (*ST* I-II, q. 96, a. 4). Now, the argument explaining how certain realities that constitute the content of what Aquinas calls "Divine law" also, at least partially, fall under the scope of *ius naturale*, is rather complex. Perhaps it suffices to note that the precepts of the Decalogue, which are of divine origin, concern, among other things, the goods secured by the precepts of the natural law, which may be seen to take into consideration the specific perspective of justice. For a more detailed analysis, see Popović, *Natural Law & Thomistic Juridical Realism*, 201–9. Thus, when Aquinas speaks of laws that run afoul of "Divine good" or "Divine laws," it is possible to conclude that he also has in mind an important and well-defined number of goods constituted as *ius naturale*, besides other goods that are accessible only through supernatural modes of cognition by faith. When he shifts the perspective from *lex* to *ius* in the *Secunda secundae* of the *Summa*, Aquinas notes that *ius divinum* concerns those things that are promulgated by God as that which is just. He adds that "such things are partly those that are naturally just" because they are "promulgated" through natural law, while other things form part of the *ius divinum* on account of being "made just" exclusively "by God's decree" because the latter category of things (*res*) "transcends human nature" (*ST* II-II, q. 57, a. 2, arg. 3 and ad 3).

118. In his comment on this passage from Aquinas, Finnis notes that the Latin words "*nisi propter*" are more correctly translatable as "except no doubt" or "except of course" (Finnis, *Aquinas: Moral, Political, and Legal Theory*, 274).

119. *ST* I-II, q. 96, a. 4. See also *ST* II-II, q. 69, a. 4; II-II, q. 104, a. 6, arg. 3 and ad 3.

words, although such law-aspiring norms do not themselves constitute reasons for action because they are non-law, there are other collateral considerations that point to some extrajuridical reasons for action, which may even outweigh the relevant considerations of *ius* relative to the question of whether said norms produce law-like effects. Such law-aspiring, validly posited norms do not become *ius* (or *lex*, for that matter, at least in Aquinas's sense of that term) on the basis of these corollary considerations. But there is something about them that may give rise to certain reasons for legally relevant action and may even lead to producing law-like effects in a legal system.

The Value of Legal Validity

In my opinion, the question of what it is about such norms that produces the aforementioned collateral, extrajuridical reasons and law-like effects may be answered by starting from the set of arguments that form part of the concept of *intrasystemic validity*.[120] To understand this answer, it will be beneficial to first analyze how John Gardner, Maris Köpcke, and John Finnis understand the concept and value of intrasystemic validity of posited norms.

For John Gardner, the question of legal validity overlaps entirely with law's ontological existence: if it is valid, it is law. Considerations regarding issues other than validity, such as those relative to law's moral merits, do not alter a posited law's ontological status, that is, they do not render it non-law on account of a defect in its moral merits, just as they do not render it law only on the basis of its moral merits if there are defects at the level of its validity. What is particularly interesting in Gardner's position is that he considers the concept of legal validity to denote a specific value, something that is valuable for understanding law's nature. In his view, the nature of law includes more values than legal validity. Indeed, a "thesis about legal validity" is "compatible with any number of further theses

120. Throughout this section, I will use the term "intrasystemic validity" interchangeably with the term "legal validity" since (as explained before) for Thomistic juridical realism, intrasystemic validity does not necessarily yield legality (in the *lex* sense) or juridicity (in the *ius* sense).

about law's nature," such as the theses on the moral merits of laws.[121] Gardner claims that it is a good and valuable thing to dedicate at least a portion of the research on law's nature to the question of legal validity and its conditions, and in his view, this field of research corresponds to the specific aims of legal positivism.[122] He further holds that studying the validity of legal norms "in the agnostic way," that is, without aprioristically including an assessment of the moral merit of the content of these norms in the validity-conditions, could be of significant interest to natural lawyers.[123] Now, as mentioned in the previous section, Thomistic juridical realism does not share Gardner's enthusiasm for the study of legal validity if that study aims to offer conclusive arguments about what counts as law. But I do think he has a point when he highlights the importance of considering the idea of legal validity as a specific value that is in some way relevant for understanding law's nature in more detail.

Maris Köpcke's important work explores the reasons for considering legal validity to denote a special, legally relevant value. For Gardner, the value of legal validity is reflected in its capacity to identify legal norms (and to identify nonvalid norms as non-law), which then enables us to assess the moral merits of those norms that count as law. While generally agreeing with Gardner's overall direction in this matter,[124] Köpcke addresses a question that explores the premises of his interest in the value of validity, namely, the question of how (1) having positive laws and (2) knowing which posited norms count as law—through the specific technique of legal validity—corresponds to certain human moral needs. Since law's positivity denotes a response to human moral needs, it belongs to the essence of legality that law-aspiring norms be posited.[125] As she says, "political communities morally need law's positivity" because there is value

121. Gardner, "Legal Positivism: 5½ Myths," 33.

122. See Gardner, "Legal Positivism: 5½ Myths," 49.

123. Gardner, "Legal Positivism: 5½ Myths," 51.

124. "Moral business starts where legal validity ends." See Maris Köpcke, *Legal Validity: The Fabric of Justice* (Hart Publishing, 2019), 163.

125. Maris Köpcke, "Finnis on Legal and Moral Obligation," in *Reason, Morality and Law*, 385–86, 389.

to be found in the state of affairs where "legal positions persons are in are determined by the legal meaning of valid acts rather than by moral considerations that are not part of the legal meaning of valid acts."[126]

In Köpcke's view, positivity achieved through the technique of validity is preferable to an alternative wherein law is identified on the basis of the moral merits of law-aspiring norms. This is because positivity ensures the sufficient determinacy and the relatively easy identification of legal content, especially in situations of moral controversy and disagreement. The technique of legal validity detaches the question of what counts as law from moral debates in pluralist societies.[127] In addition, validly posited law is, in her view, the morally valuable outcome of the self-determining choices of a political community (made through established procedures), and it further allows individuals and groups to make similar self-directing, targeted choices within the framework of that law.[128] Köpcke's analyses differ from Thomistic juridical realism in that she seems to deny the existence of nonposited elements of juridicity, and accordingly to deny that positive-law determinations ought to be harmonized with those elements for their constitution as law.[129] However, there is an important aspect of her line of reasoning on the value of legal validity that is relatively autonomous from these differences.

In my opinion, John Finnis comes closest to identifying that aspect of the value of legal validity, which perhaps remains implicit in

126. See Köpcke, *Legal Validity*, 124.

127. See Köpcke, *Legal Validity*, 124, 129.

128. See Köpcke, *Legal Validity*, 132–33.

129. While for Thomistic juridical realism justice is the decisive factor in establishing the existence of nonposited elements of juridicity (as well as of subsequent aspects of this approach to the nature of law), for Köpcke, the relevance of justice for identifying legal norms (and, in this sense, for the nature of law) is almost entirely exhausted in the argument according to which the value of legal validity is itself a requirement of justice, indeed, its "fabric" (Köpcke, *Legal Validity*, 163). Precisely because "validity serves to mark specific conduct as due, even in the face of moral controversy," thereby legally positing the requirements of justice (i.e., establishing who exactly owes what to whom, and how), it "can help a large community to foster justice precisely by helping it bypass concerns about justice and other concomitant matters" (Köpcke, *Legal Validity*, 3, 5).

Gardner's and Köpcke's arguments. Finnis argues that there is "good reason" to introduce the technique of legal validity into legal theory and practice, as well as to understand that technique precisely as the set of criteria for grasping "not moral" but intrasystemic "legal obligatoriness."[130] In his view, "everyone everywhere" may be said to assent to the claim that there exists a certain value in a

> technically confined and intra-systemic sense of legal validity such that validity in this sense can be predicated of a supposed rule by reference only to social-fact sources, without reference to what ought to be the law (or the sources of law) according to some standard not based on social-fact sources.[131]

What is so valuable about legal validity, in Finnis's view? Just like Köpcke, he is convinced that the "main reason for wanting to introduce positive law" and to operate with the idea of legal validity "is to resolve disputes within a political community about what morality (especially justice) requires, recommends, or permits."[132] Since it is his argument that all law is positive law, a valid positing of legal norms (through promulgation of laws, through customary practice, or through the practice and decisions of legal officials) constitutes the only truly juridical way to establish what morality and justice require in a political community.

I agree with some of Gardner's, Köpcke's, and Finnis's insights in this matter, since I also hold that that legal validity is indeed crucial for the juridical status of *ius positivum*, which is authoritatively determinable only through valid positive laws or other humanly posited, legally relevant law-creating or law-determining acts. Indeed, not all law is metapositive, and some or most law needs to be validly posited. But neither is all law positive law, in my opinion, and this is the difference between my account of the value of legal validity in conceptualizing law and the approaches of these three authors.

130. Finnis, "What Is the Philosophy of Law?" 140.

131. John Finnis, "On Hart's Ways: Law as Reason and as Fact," in *Collected Essays*, vol. 4, *Philosophy of Law*, 247. See also Finnis, "Describing Law Normatively," 44.

132. Finnis, "What Is the Philosophy of Law?" 140.

Legal Validity and Civic Responsibility

But there seems to be more to the value of legal validity than the secured certainty at the stage of the identification of law. In fact, Finnis argues that legal validity corresponds to an important communal line of practical reasoning for the citizens in a polity: "the fact that others treat these laws as legally valid or demand that they be treated as such is an important fact, to be taken into account when deciding what are one's responsibilities as a participant in the legal order of one's society."[133] So in Finnis's view, legal validity goes beyond conclusively resolving the issue of what counts as law in a political community. Besides this feature, Finnis holds that the concept of legal validity introduces another highly important consequence, namely, the fact that citizens treat intrasystemically valid norms as reasons for action and that they demand these norms be treated as such by all other citizens. He envisions this consequence of the value of intrasystemic validity to form part of the responsibilities that a citizen has as a participant in the legal order of a political community, referring to this aspect of legal validity as "taking the burdens of the practice of citizenship under the rule of law as well as its benefits—the burdens of complying with the law as well as the benefits that flow to me from others' willingness to comply with it."[134] In short, an important part of the value of legal validity pertains to its representing a *commitment* to the political community, which for Finnis involves both the idea of justice and the concept of the common good:

> The fully reasonable premise for acknowledging positive law as a reason for action now (as judge, administrator or other subject) is a moral premise: *justice* as a fundamental aspect of promoting *the common good* of my political community presumptively requires me, in reason, to respect the commitments articulated in the rules, and by the institutions, of our law.[135]

133. Finnis, "Law as Fact and as Reason for Action," 107.
134. Finnis, "Aquinas and Natural Law Jurisprudence," 40.
135. See Finnis, "Aquinas and Natural Law Jurisprudence," 51 (emphasis added).

Of course, Finnis is well aware that the technique of intrasystemic validity, being systematically detached from evaluation of the moral merits of laws, can be used and deployed for bad or immoral purposes.[136] One of the main theses of his legal theory is that the law, of itself, "does not claim to be morally obligatory" in all cases,[137] in the sense that immoral positive laws indeed exist and should be identifiable as valid laws "prior to any question about" their subsequently examined "relation to morality."[138] It is only in this sense that, in Finnis's view, it is true that "there is no necessary or conceptual connection between positive law and morality."[139]

In sum, then, unjust laws for Finnis are intrasystemically valid norms and thus must be considered law and produce standard legal obligations, while they generate only defeasible moral obligations. Finnis, of course, acknowledges that for Aquinas, unjust laws may indeed provide the occasion for the genesis of reasons for action, not on account of the content or moral merit of those laws but in virtue of collateral considerations, such as those of giving a "corrupting example"[140] that "leads others into wrongdoing"[141] (Aquinas's *scandalum*) or the "occasioning of civil disorder,"[142] which upsets the "inner balance"[143] of the political community (Aquinas's *turbatio*). In Finnis view, the identification of these extralegal reasons for action relative to unjust laws has its origin in the value of reciprocity of the citizens' commitments and responsibilities as members of the same political community.[144]

On my reading of Aquinas, unjust laws fail to constitute law (from the viewpoint of both *ius* and *lex*), do not of themselves give

136. Finnis, "Aquinas and Natural Law Jurisprudence," 46.
137. Finnis, "Reflections and Responses," 553.
138. Finnis, "The Truth in Legal Positivism," 185–86.
139. Finnis, "The Truth in Legal Positivism," 184.
140. Finnis, *Natural Law and Natural Rights*, 360.
141. Finnis, *Aquinas: Moral, Political, and Legal Theory*, 273.
142. Finnis, *Natural Law and Natural Rights*, 360.
143. Finnis, *Aquinas: Moral, Political, and Legal Theory*, 273.
144. Finnis, *Natural Law and Natural Rights*, 476; Finnis, "Aquinas and Natural Law Jurisprudence," 42.

rise to any legal obligations, and thus present normally no moral obligation to follow them—they do not of themselves constitute reasons for action in either a juridical or a broader moral sense. In some cases, however, for causes or motives relatively disconnected from considerations of their justice and juridicity, these unjust, validly posited law-aspiring norms may still constitute valid reasons for action: *scandalum* and *turbatio*. Aquinas maintains that if the injustice of these law-aspiring norms originates in their being directly contrary to *ius naturale*, collateral considerations of *scandalum* and *turbatio* cease to be relevant. In other cases of defects in justice, considerations of *scandalum* and *turbatio* may provide the citizens with extrajuridical reasons for action (i.e., they may require the citizens to yield their *ius*, as Aquinas says[145]) in their response to the question of whether the relevant norms produce law-like effects in a polity. In the latter case, considerations of *scandalum* and *turbatio* do not alter the status of unjust norms: their content remains non-*ius*, and the norms themselves may be said to remain non-*lex*.

The Value of Civic Friendship

One promising way to approach and explain the law-like effects of all kinds of unjust law-aspiring posited norms—that is, the fact that some citizens and perhaps even a predominant number of legal officials continue to recognize law-like reasons for action in such norms—takes as its starting point the understanding that an important aspect of the value of their intrasystemic validity may be seen to rely on *civic* or *political friendship*. Aquinas, it seems, did not operate with a developed concept of what we now call "legal validity": he was more focused on the individual aspects of that concept, such as the issues pertaining to positivity, authoritative promulgation, legislation that is not *ultra vires*, etc. However, it may be said that Aquinas was generally familiar with that aspect of the value of legal validity that roughly corresponds to the notion of civic or political friendship. As some recent studies in the natural-law tradition

145. *ST* I-II, q. 96, a. 4.

show, there are various points of contact between the nature of law and the value of friendship.[146]

My present contribution to the analysis of the points of contact between law and friendship concerns the viewpoint from which we can better understand the range of the extrajuridical reasons for action that arise in connection to the existence of unjust, validly posited law-aspiring norms.

Aquinas argues that "the principal intention of the human law is to create friendship between man and man."[147] We are already familiar with his claim that even an unjust law-aspiring norm has something of law's nature if it denotes "an ordinance [*dictamen*] made by a superior to his subjects" and "aims at being obeyed *in a good way* [*bene obedientes*] by them, which is to make them good, not simply, but with respect for that government."[148] Of course, in my reading of Aquinas, these fragments of the nature of *lex*, instantiated in an unjust law-aspiring norm, are not enough to establish that norm as a *lex*, or as a *ratio iuris*. But they certainly do not amount to nothing, especially if we are aware that these unjust norms provide "reasons for action" for some or even for most citizens and legal officials.

Furthermore, it is useful to take into consideration that obeying the same set of positive laws that establish certain fixed common goals generally contributes to the good of shared action in a political community—acting together "in a good way," to use Aquinas's words. He refers to this form of good as *the intrinsic aspect of the common good* of a polity—it corresponds to civic friendship.[149]

146. For example, see Michael P. Moreland, "Friendship as the Primary Purpose of Law," *The American Journal of Jurisprudence* 67, no. 2 (2022): 279–92; Seow Hon Tan, *Justice as Friendship: A Theory of Law* (Routledge, 2016). See also John Finnis, "Reason, Authority, and Friendship," in *Collected Essays*, vol. 1, *Reason in Action*, 123.

147. *ST* I-II, q. 99, a. 2.

148. See *ST* I-II, q. 92, a. 1, ad 4.

149. A fundamental text for Aquinas's account of the intrinsic aspects of the common good is the following: "For good, inasmuch as it is the end or goal of a thing, is twofold. For an end is extrinsic to the thing ordained to it, as when we say that a place is the end of something that is moved locally. Or it is intrinsic, as a form is the end of the process of generation or alteration; and a form already acquired is a kind of intrinsic good of the thing whose form it is. Now the form of any whole which is one through the arrangement of its parts is the order of that whole. Hence it follows that it is a good of that whole....

Common good, as such, including its intrinsic aspect of the good of shared action, is an essential element and the final cause of *lex* in Aquinas's legal theory.[150]

The question is how much of this aspect of *lex*—that is, of the good of shared action in respecting positive laws because of the commitments to civic friendship—remains in a law-aspiring reality that is deemed non-law on account of its being unjust?

Let us first return to the issues relative to considerations of corrupting examples (*scandalum*) and civil disorder (*turbatio*). It seems to me that both considerations may be seen to belong to a broader framework of civic friendship. Giving a corrupting example that leads others into transgression of posited laws is problematic, as is providing occasion for civil disorder by disobeying an unjust norm that does not violate *ius naturale*. This is precisely because both sets of behavior run contrary to the good of shared action in conformity to certain fixed common goals in a polity. Collateral considerations and corresponding reasons for action, such as those relative to *scandalum* and *turbatio*, correspond to that fragment of law's nature instantiated in an unjust norm, which invites citizens to respect and

We see this, for example, in the case of an army; for the good of the army is found both in the order itself of the army and in … the purpose of achieving the good of … attaining victory." See Thomas Aquinas, *Commentary on Aristotle's Metaphysics*, trans. John P. Rowan (Dumb Ox Books, 1995), XII, lect. 12, n. 2627, 2630. For subsequent Thomistic development of the concept of the intrinsic common good, see, for example, Gregory Froelich, "The Equivocal Status of *Bonum Commune*," *The New Scholasticism* 63, no. 1 (1989): 49–53; Matthew S. Kempshall, *The Common Good in Late Medieval Political Thought* (Clarendon Press, 1999), 99–101, 127–29; Russell Hittinger, "The Coherence of the Four Basic Principles of Catholic Social Doctrine: An Interpretation," in *On the Dignity of Society: Catholic Social Teaching and Natural Law* (The Catholic University of America Press, 2024), 6–20; Finnis, *Natural Law and Natural Rights*, 459; Michael Baur, "Law and Natural Law," in *The Oxford Handbook of Aquinas*, ed. Brian Davies and Eleonore Stump (Oxford University Press, 2012), 240; and V. Bradley Lewis, "Catholic Social Teaching on the Common Good," in *Catholic Social Teaching: A Volume of Scholarly Essays*, ed. Gerard V. Bradley and E. Christian Brugger (Cambridge University Press, 2019), 241–47.

150. *ST* I-II, q. 90, a. 2. Scott Roniger correctly notes that the various descriptions of the end of *lex*, such as friendship or the common good, "add nuance" to Aquinas's analysis of law, and he adds that they "are not unrelated to each other." However, in his view, it is precisely friendship "that has a kind of governing role over the other descriptions of the end of law." See Scott Roniger, "Natural Law and Friendship with God," *The Thomist* 83, no. 2 (2019): 238.

follow the norm in a good way with regard to their polity, provided, of course, that the norm in question is not contrary to *ius naturale*.

But what if an unjust, validly posited, law-aspiring norm is in fact contrary to *ius naturale*, and what if, in a political community in which that norm is promulgated, many citizens and even a predominant number of legal officials are convinced that the norm is in fact not unjust and continue to somehow recognize certain "reasons for action" in its content, or at least do not recognize reasons for disobeying or invalidating that norm? The question is pertinent to this study of law's nature because the response to it may enable us to better understand and assess the law-like effects arising in a polity from law-aspiring norms that Thomistic juridical realism deems non-law. The above-described situation creates the following framework of reasoning for persons and legal officials who adhere to Thomistic juridical realism (or to other accounts of law's nature that lead to similar conclusions): (1) they hold that an unjust, validly posited, law-aspiring norm is not law (from the viewpoint of both *ius* and *lex*), and, at the same time, (2) they are aware of the impossibility to ignore the intrasystemic validity of such a norm, which produces law-like effects and is somehow considered to provide sufficient "reasons for action" by other citizens and legal officials.[151] This is certainly a less than satisfactory factual situation in the eyes of the adherents to a Thomist natural-law theory of law, or to Thomistic juridical realism. Perhaps considerations based on civic friendship may shed some further light on this challenging, far-from-ideal state of affairs.

Friendship, in its essence, constitutes a specific standpoint from which relationships between persons are considered. In Aquinas's view, both friendship and justice have the structure of an other-directed principle of action oriented toward the attainment of specific forms of good for another person. It is his understanding that justice seeks the good of another person "under the aspect [*sub ratione*]" of juridical due (i.e., of *ius*), while friendship seeks to attain the

151. As Peter Geach says, "an unjust piece of legislation exists *de facto*, as an institution: but it is no debt of justice to observe it, though it may be imprudent to ignore it." See Peter Geach, *The Virtues* (Cambridge University Press, 1979), 128.

other-directed good "under the aspect of a friendly or moral duty, or rather that of a gratuitous favor [*beneficii gratuiti*]."[152] Accordingly, as Michael Moreland correctly notes, civic friendship resists the reduction of relationships in a polity to a pattern of shared action defined entirely in terms of "competing instrumentalist concerns" in which citizens "merely seek to manipulate [one] another by way of rhetorical persuasions."[153] Civic friendship aims at transcending social conflict, in full awareness of the differences between the citizens' competing worldviews, by establishing a viewpoint that makes a common pattern of shared action possible. Indeed, as Moreland puts it, "legal discourse ... cannot begin from a standpoint of cynicism, skepticism, or hostility among citizens but can only be in pursuit of the human good when conducted in the mode of friendship."[154]

Thus, friendship introduces a perspective from which to view and live out the commitments to common projects and to shared action in a political community, as well as ways to overcome frictions that threaten those commitments and bonds. This perspective is well captured by Finnis:

> Just as the unknown time of one's prospective death is, in thought, a vantage point from which to distinguish some reasonable alternative plans of life, so friendship establishes an analogous vantage point. In friendship one is not thinking and choosing from one's own point of view, nor from one's friend's point of view. Rather, one is acting from a third point of view, the unique perspective from which one's own good and one's friend's good are equally in view and in play.[155]

How does the perspective of civic friendship contribute to our present problem? First of all, friendship does not obliterate the demands of justice. Accordingly, unjust valid norms remain non-law, at least from the viewpoint of Thomistic juridical realism. Injustice can certainly diminish or even obliterate friendships, since nobody can claim to be someone's friend if they are being unjust to that person,

152. See *ST* II-II, q. 23, a. 3, ad 1.
153. Moreland, "Friendship as the Primary Purpose of Law," 281.
154. Moreland, "Friendship as the Primary Purpose of Law," 283–84.
155. Finnis, *Natural Law and Natural Rights*, 143.

and injustice can thereby also diminish or obliterate the value of shared action in a polity as a whole. However, Aristotle may have a point when he says that it is friendship that "hold cities together," and that there is a viewpoint from which it may be said that legislators are more concerned about friendship than about justice.[156]

Here is my estimation of that viewpoint for the purposes of this study. Civic friendship requires us to safeguard and hold together a common pattern for shared action, even in situations of moral controversy and disagreement, that is, in the context of divergent views on whether the posited pronouncements regarding what ought to be done in a polity really provide sufficient juridical or extrajuridical reasons for action. Certainly, an account of justice and law that is in conformity with Thomistic juridical realism constitutes a desirable outcome of that common pattern. It is certainly the outcome that I personally advocate. Ideally, the Thomistic set of natural juridical goods (or natural rights) should be awarded the status of full metapositive juridicity and immutability in a polity, and it should be treated as a set of juridical absolutes,[157] the alteration of which is out of the question.

But what is the optimal course of action in the case of a different, undesirable outcome, when the aforementioned conception of justice and law is not fully attained or is not predominantly attained? In this latter situation, it is crucial that the legal system offer opportunities for citizens to politically argue for their ideas of justice (e.g., those based on Thomistic juridical realism) and to implement these ideas in positive laws, as well as to criticize unjust valid norms in the public forum, and to consider and put into motion the institutional options to strike down the law-like unjust effects of such non-law

156. *Nic. Eth.* VIII.1, 1155a25. Aquinas moves in the same direction in his commentary to this Aristotle text. See *Sent. Eth.* VIII, lect. 1, n. 1542.

157. The term "juridical absolutes" is partially and analogously borrowed from Finnis's term "moral absolutes," and it is terminologically adapted to the specific field of morality that pertains to juridicity. See John Finnis, *Moral Absolutes: Tradition, Revision, and Truth* (The Catholic University of America Press, 1991). I am indebted to professor Carlos José Errázuriz for the invention of the term "juridical absolutes." See Carlos José Errázuriz, *Cos'è il diritto divino nella Chiesa? Essenza e rilevanza pratica* (EDUSC, 2025), 98–101.

valid norms. It is also equally crucial that the legal system simultaneously secure the possibility of peaceful civil disobedience and conscientious objection (and similar proactive exempting options) regarding the norms that impose obligations or burdens to citizens who deem them unjust.

In the meantime, however, when total or partial abrogation of law-like effects of valid unjust norms is not possible for reasons that are out of the hands of the citizens who deem them unjust, I do not see any viable alternative to maintaining the bonds of civic friendship that prevent moral controversy and disagreement from collapsing into civil disorder, while continuing to hold together other friendly commitments to all members of the polity. The foregoing line of reasoning on civic friendship is, however, entirely suitable only for predominantly just legal systems that also contain some unjust laws. In the contexts of extremely unjust and corrupt legal systems, the expressions of both legitimate civic disobedience and civic friendship will have to assume suitably "radical" forms.

Chapter 7

Declaring and Determining Law in the Interpretive Practice of Legal Officials

Law's Indeterminacy and the Nature of Law

It is a feature of law's nature that it is indeterminate at least in some cases and, to that extent, needs to be interpreted for the juridical solution of a particular case. There seems to be considerable consensus on this argument in legal philosophy,[1] regardless of the differences in various approaches on what the nature of law is, on what constitutes indeterminacy (as well as on how much of law may be said to be really indeterminate), and on what it means to interpret law.

This chapter has two objectives. The first is to show that conceptualizing "indeterminacy" and "interpretation" of law ultimately depends upon a legal philosopher's account of the nature of law (i.e., of what counts as law). The second is to present the way in which

1. On this practical consensus, see, for example, Lawrence B. Solum, "On the Indeterminacy Crisis: Critiquing Critical Dogma," *The University of Chicago Law Review* 54, no. 2 (1987): 503. For a suggestion that legal theory should generally accept the claim that law is indeterminate, and that this claim is in fact implicit in the arguments of those authors who seem to explicitly advocate a contrary approach, see Timothy A. O. Endicott, *Vagueness in Law* (Oxford University Press, 2000), 57–75.

Aquinas's juridical realism envisions both the interpretation of law and the determination of law's occasional indeterminacy in the activity of authorized legal officials from the viewpoint of his account of the nature of law. In this section, I will focus on the first objective.

It is one of the core arguments of this book that the map of approaches to understanding law's nature may be beneficially divided in two basic groups: one consisting of those authors who hold that all law is positive law, and the other consisting of those who hold that certain nonposited elements of juridicity may indeed be established beyond and in abstraction from the conditions for identifying humanly posited valid law. Membership in one of these groups can be seen to model an author's position on what it means (1) that law may be indeterminate and (2) that, to that extent, it needs to be interpreted and/or determined. As seen in the first chapter, the last five decades of legal-philosophical analysis yielded H. L. A. Hart as the emblematic proponent of the first group, while Ronald Dworkin is typically deemed as representative of the second group.

For Hart, all law is positive law, and validly posited norms of a legal system, "however smoothly they work over the great mass of ordinary cases, will, at some point where their application is in question, prove indeterminate; they will have what has been termed an open texture."[2] Stumbling upon a case of law's open texture is a consequence of the uncertainty inherent to the use of "general classifying terms" in the language of posited legal norms: these terms always remain both (1) relatively indeterminate with regard to their aim and (2) relatively ignorant of facts and events, so that the reality continues to always be more variegated than our ability to adequately and conceptually predict all its cases in legal language.[3] Despite certain imminent areas of law's open texture, Hart is convinced that "a very large extent" of "life of the law" consists of cases where both legal officials and ordinary citizens will be sufficiently guided by certain and determinate rules.[4] He thereby rejects the so-called "rule

2. Hart, *The Concept of Law*, 128.
3. See Hart, *The Concept of Law*, 128–36.
4. Hart, *The Concept of Law*, 135.

skepticism," namely, "the claim that talk of rules is a myth, cloaking the truth that law consists simply of the decisions of courts and the prediction of them,"[5] where this latter category (predictions of courts' decisions) points only to nonlegal sources of law. In short, Hart rejects the claim that all law is ultimately dependent upon judicially made law.

In the open-texture cases, however, when law seems to reach its limits or the limits of its determinacy, which Hart refers to as the "penumbra of uncertainty,"[6] the legal officials vested with law-applying authoritative competence, typically in judicial (and occasionally also in administrative) organs, create new law to be applied in a particular case. But even when they exercise their law-creating (or law-interpreting) power, courts do not act as if in a complete legal vacuum. In Hart's view, the legal officials still exercise their discretion in a limited way, by taking into necessary consideration (i.e., by "interpreting"[7] the facts of the case in light of) the relevant rules of the legal system, "which are determinate enough at the center to supply standards of correct judicial decisions."[8]

Hart is, of course, aware of the existence of alternative approaches to the (at least partial) indeterminacy and open texture of law. He says that if one avoids the "great exaggerations" of "formalism and rule-skepticism," which are "the Scylla and Charybdis of juristic theory," then one can see that "the truth lies between them."[9]

However, having survived the Scylla and Charybdis of juristic theory, Hart must still face his "arch-rival": Dworkin's approach to the indeterminacy of law may likewise be seen to lie between formalism and rule-skepticism. As always, Hart is aware of this potential adversary to his theory of judicial discretion. In his own words,

> the sharpest direct conflict between the legal theory of this book [*The Concept of Law*] and Dworkin's theory arises from my contention that

5. Hart, *The Concept of Law*, 136.
6. Hart, *The Concept of Law*, 134.
7. Hart, *The Concept of Law*, 274–75.
8. Hart, *The Concept of Law*, 145.
9. Hart, *The Concept of Law*, 147.

> in any legal system there will always be certain legally unregulated cases in which on some point no decision either way is dictated by the law and the law is accordingly partly indeterminate or incomplete. If in such a case the judge is to reach a decision … he must exercise his discretion and make law for the case instead of merely applying already pre-existing settled law.[10]

For Dworkin, law is virtually always identifiable as determinate. As he says, there are "no gaps" in the law, or, at the most, "gaps in the law are very rare": "there is almost always a right answer to a legal question."[11] In his view, the law may be found to be indeterminate, or, said differently, we might stumble upon gaps in law, only in the following situation: "when there are two interpretations, two ways to read a statute (for example), one way would give you the decision for the plaintiff in the case, the second reading would give you the other decision, and there is no way to choose the better interpretation between the two."[12] Dworkin is alert to the fact that our position on the existence or nonexistence of law's indeterminacy necessarily relies on the account of law's nature that one supports: "our decision about the gaps-in-the-law question is going to depend upon the answer we give to the following question of ontology: what kind of facts are legal facts?"[13] Hence, according to Dworkin's analysis, if we think of law as an "institutional fact," namely, if we are convinced that "the manner in which law comes to exist" is "fixed" exclusively by the history of social facts of "customary practice and decisions made by institutions," then we will "of course think there are gaps in law."[14]

We are already familiar with Dworkin's account of law's nature, to which he refers as an "interpretive view": "any proposition of law which is true, is true because it figures in, or is the consequence

10. Hart, *The Concept of Law*, 272.

11. Ronald Dworkin, "On Gaps in the Law," in *Controversies about Law's Ontology*, 84, 89.

12. Dworkin, "On Gaps in the Law," 88.

13. Dworkin, "On Gaps in the Law," 84–85.

14. Dworkin, "On Gaps in the Law," 85–86.

of, the best interpretation of a community's political history."[15] If a posited legal norm is insufficiently determinate to fully control the facts of a given case, the correct legal answer to those facts may be arrived at by considering the principles of political morality that provide the best interpretation of that legal norm and the relevant facts of a particular case. These principles, in Dworkin's view, form part of the law, given that his answer to the ontological question of "what kind of facts are legal facts?" is interpretive, not institutional (i.e., positivistic).[16]

Even in the easiest of particular cases—"even when it goes without saying what the law is" in a given case[17]—Dworkin is convinced that interpretivism offers a better account of the way in which law is applied to that case than legal positivism. In his view, instead of positivism's simple conclusion that a posited valid rule fully "controls" the facts of the case (and if it does not, then "the judge must decide by exercising discretion"),[18] "we do better" to explain even the phenomenon of easy cases "by speaking of a convergence on a single interpretation, or at least, on interpretations that have the same results in most cases."[19]

The textbook example of a simple, validly posited rule that may prove indeterminate in some cases is "no vehicles in the park." In Hart's view, if the relevant positive law, consisting of sources such

15. Dworkin, "On Gaps in the Law," 85.

16. Hart was mindful of the fact that Dworkin operates with an alternative concept of law: "On [Dworkin's] interpretive view, the law is never incomplete or indeterminate, so the judge never has the occasion to step outside the law and exercise a law-creating power in order to reach a decision.... [In Dworkin's account] the lawyers address the judge as if he was always concerned to discover and enforce the existing law and the judge speaks as if the law were a gapless system of entitlements in which a solution for every case awaits his discovery, not his invention" (Hart, *The Concept of Law*, 272, 274). Probably because of Dworkin's alternative concept of law as something broader than the humanly posited conditions of what counts as valid law, Hart considers Dworkin to be a much bigger rival than Finnis, for whom Hart claims: "Finnis's flexible interpretation of natural law is in many respects complementary to rather than a rival of positivist legal theory" (Hart, introduction, in *Essays in Jurisprudence and Philosophy*, 10).

17. Dworkin, "On Gaps in the Law," 88.

18. Dworkin, *Taking Rights Seriously*, 33.

19. Dworkin, "On Gaps in the Law," 88.

as statues, precedents, and customary practices, does not entirely provide a judge with all the necessary criteria for deciding whether a bicycle may be included in the general classifying term "vehicle" in this particular case, that judge will have to exercise discretion and create law with regard to said inclusion in this case.[20] According to Dworkin, applying even this simple rule to any particular case, however easy or hard, necessarily entails interpretation, more precisely, an assessment of how this rule and the facts of the case figure in the best interpretation of the relevant community's political-moral practices.[21]

In sum, both Hart and Dworkin hold that law's nature entails a possibility that it be indeterminate at least in some cases. The radical differences between these two authors regarding what constitutes the indeterminacy of law and on how to establish or determine law in those cases may be seen to ultimately arise from their fundamentally diverse accounts of the nature of law, that is, of what law is "in." As seen before, the divide in question is not circumscribed to the positions of only these two authors but indeed concerns the entire catalogue of legal-philosophical stances on the nature of law in light of the question of the existence (or nonexistence) of the nonposited elements of juridicity. Thus, at least from the viewpoint of the question "what is law in?" it is possible to affirm that an account of law's indeterminacy may be seen to be dependent on the author's stance on law's ontology.

Aquinas and the Interpretation of Law in the Practice of Legal Officials

What does Aquinas say of the indeterminacy of law? What are his suggestions on how to approach and resolve this phenomenon? As with Hart and Dworkin, the answers to both questions are dependent on Aquinas's understanding of law's nature. In the previous

20. For Hart's reflection on this case, see Hart, *The Concept of Law*, 126–27.

21. For Dworkin's analysis of the "no vehicles in the park" rule, see Dworkin, "On Gaps in the Law," 90.

chapter, we saw that in Aquinas's view, both *ius naturale* and *ius positivum* provide the relevant juridical goods that shape the juridical order and, as such, conceptually enter into the understanding of the nature of law. In addition, *ius positivum* was analyzed as arising from the efficient cause of law—the juridical title of posited legal norms.

Following Aquinas's account of law's nature, law (*ius*) can be indeterminate in those cases where neither *ius naturale* nor *ius positivum*, to the extent that this latter form of *ius* arises on the basis of posited general legal norms, are sufficient to determine all the relevant cases of *ius* in a community.[22] Accordingly, determining *ius* in these cases pertains to the competence of legal officials who are authorized to perform such a determination through suitable legal practices upon establishing the relevant facts, which are either controversial or simply not fully available without these practices. From this chain of arguments, it follows that the ontology of law necessarily includes both (1) the possibility of the underdetermination of law at the level of *ius naturale* and of positive-law-based *ius positivum* and (2) the need for further authoritative determination of *ius* in those cases.

Aquinas has a name for the authoritative act of determining those just things that remain underdetermined at the level of *ius naturale* and positive-law-based *ius positivum*: determination by judgment (*iudicium*). The purpose of a judgment in general is to assert the *ius* (*ius dicere*).[23] Now in Aquinas's view, *iudicium* asserts the *ius* in question either (1) by declaration, when the facts of a particular case are interpreted as falling under the scope of *ius* fully constituted at the level of *ius naturale* or positive-law-based *ius positivum*, or (2) by determination (*determinatio*) of an *ius* in a particular case, when the aforementioned levels of *ius* are insufficient for understanding what is just, given the facts of the case.[24] In the latter case,

22. I will not here analyze the determination of *ius* by voluntary juridical acts *inter vivos*, such as contracts, or by voluntary juridical acts *mortis causae*, such as those pertaining to testamentary succession. Nor will I study the phenomenon of the indeterminacy of law occasioned by or connected to these juridical acts.

23. *ST* II-II, q. 60, a. 1.

24. See *ST* II-II, q. 60, a. 1. When he says that the original meaning of the word

namely, when a *iudicium* determines *ius*, what is thereby determined may be said to pertain to a specific form of *ius positivum*, established not by positive laws but by judgment.[25] In that case, the *iudicium* is the decisive ratio of the constitution of *ius*, rather than positive laws (or natural laws): "A judge's sentence is like a particular *lex* regarding some particular fact."[26]

Aquinas's position is that the activity that yields an *iudicium* implies the work of *interpretation*, and this work concerns both (1) establishing the relevant facts of the case and (2) arriving at a clear conclusion on the relevant *ius* by declaring or determining it.[27] With this argument, Aquinas joins what Timothy Endicott refers to as a "consensus" among authors who hold that "every application of the law requires an interpretation of the law."[28] In other words, the search of legal officials for that which is just in every particular case includes clarifying the facts of that case in light of the relevant

iudicium is a "*definition*" or "*determination*" of *ius*, Aquinas does not provide us with the details relative to the meaning of his use of the terms *definitio* and *determinatio*, or regarding the potential difference between them. It is not incompatible with his texts to claim that he calls *definitio* what I refer to as declaration of *ius*, which does not have to be further determined by the *iudicium*. This possible reading is based (1) in Aquinas's general meaning of *determinatio*, which must imply the specification of something left indeterminate, and (2) in the need to establish a form of *iudicium* that does not have the structure or the purpose of *determinatio*. In this light, we may read Aquinas's claim (in *ST* II-II, q. 60, a. 1) that one "defines" the things that pertain to the virtuous actions in a good way when one already possesses a virtuous habit and, presumably, already knows what the object of that virtuous action exactly consists in, while an *iudicium* that "determines" that object may also be said to pertain to justice. A reference to both *definitio* and *determinatio* may be found also in *ST* II-II, q. 60, a. 4, ad 3, and in *ST* II-II, q. 60, a. 5. However, even if he ultimately understands the terms *definitio* and *determinatio* to be synonyms, it is still necessary to distinguish a *iudicium* that is merely declaratory of *ius*, which is fully formed at the level of *ius naturale* and positive-law based *ius positivum*, from a *iudicium* in which *ius* is further determined by its author.

25. See *Sent. Eth.* V, lect. 12, n. 1022: "Sentences passes by judges are called a kind of legal justice [*iusta legalia*]."

26. *ST* II-II, q. 67, a. 1.

27. See *ST* II-II, q. 60, a. 4, ad 3.

28. Endicott quotes references to this argument from a group of authors so diverse (Endicott's word is "bizarre") that it includes Frederick Schauer, Ronald Dworkin, Michael Moore, and even Jacques Derrida. See Endicott, *Vagueness in Law*, 11–12. Besides Aquinas, I can also add Kelsen to this list. See Hans Kelsen, *Pure Theory of Law* (University of California Press, 1967), 349.

considerations of various applicable levels of *ius* (to be declared and determined). These activities may be correctly referred to under the heading of the interpretation of law. Since, for Aquinas, the nature of law is broader than the sole reference to positive law, interpreting law in a particular case cannot be reduced to only the activity of the interpretation relative to applicable positive legal norms. What is being interpreted is *ius*, in all its four constitutive causes: the thing itself (i.e., the relevant facts of the case and the order of their relevance), the pertinent relationships of justice, the relevant juridical titles, and the (individual and common) good that is reached in virtue of *ius*.[29] Aquinas does not neglect the importance of interpretation of positive laws within a broader enterprise of the interpretation of *ius*: "He that pronounces judgment, interprets [*interpretatur*], in a way, the letter of the law [*legis dictum*], by applying it to some particular case."[30] But again, a judge's task of interpreting law is not confined to interpreting posited legal sources: "A judge is an interpreter of justice."[31]

29. Aquinas's account of interpretation thus roughly corresponds to Brian Leiter's estimation of the possible aspects of law's indeterminacy, at least by way of analogy, given Leiter's predominantly positivistic account of law's nature: "To say that the law is indeterminate is to say that the class of legal reasons (hereafter 'the Class') is indeterminate. The Class, in turn, consists of four components: 1. Legitimate *sources* of law (e.g., statutes, constitutions, court decisions, social policy, morality); 2. Legitimate *interpretive* operations that can be performed on the *sources* in order to generate rules of law (e.g., proper methods of interpreting statutes or prior cases or of reasoning about moral concepts as these figure in the sources); 3. Legitimate *interpretive* operations that can be performed on the *facts of record* in order to generate facts of legal significance; and 4. Legitimate *rational* operations that can be performed on facts and rules of law to finally yield particular decisions (i.e., deductive reasoning)." See Brian Leiter, "Legal Indeterminacy," *Legal Theory* 1, no. 4 (1995): 481. For Leiter's adherence to legal positivism, see Brian Leiter, "Why Legal Positivism," University of Chicago Public Law and Legal Theory Working Paper No. 298, December 14, 2009, accessed April 8, 2024, https://dx.doi.org/10.2139/ssrn.1521761. See also Brian Leiter, "Why Legal Positivism (Again)," University of Chicago Public Law and Legal Theory Working Paper No. 442, September 10, 2013, accessed April 8, 2024, https://dx.doi.org/10.2139/ssrn.2323013.

30. *ST* II-II, q. 60, a. 6.

31. *ST* II-II, q. 67, a. 3.

Judgment as an Act of Justice and the Problem of an Unjust *Iudicium*

When faced with controversy or uncertainty regarding the relevant facts of the case or the *ius* to be declared or determined by competent authorities, since issues of justice are by definition other-directed and thus between two or more people, Aquinas holds that it is necessary that there be an impartial superior who can issue a *iudicium*.[32] And since a *iudicium* involves the activity of interpreting *ius* with a view to the declaration or determination of what is just in a particular case—that is, since *iudicium* denotes an instantiation of justice—the author of *iudicium* must be vested with particular authority,[33] which is necessary to enable him to be what Aquinas calls (following Aristotle) a "personification of justice [*iustitia animata*]."[34] Given that the *ius positivum* determination of *ius naturale* in virtue of the promulgation of positive laws requires an appropriate public authority, it is also necessary that an *iudicium*, as an act of declaring or determining *ius* in a particular case, be pronounced by public authority.[35] Aquinas speaks of the public authority that pronounces a *iudicium* predominantly in terms of the legal practice of judicial power, but it is possible to extend this authority to include all subjects who authoritatively perform the activity of interpretation with a view to declaring or determining *ius*, and thus also to certain instances of the legal practice of administrative power. Being vested with public authority, Aquinas says, "gives a judgment its coercive force."[36]

However, solely being vested with public authority is insufficient for enabling the subject who ought to declare or determine *ius* in a particular case to be a personification of justice, or for an *iudicium*

32. *ST* II-II, q. 60, a. 1, ad 3.

33. *ST* II-II, q. 60, a. 1, ad 4.

34. *ST* II-II, q. 60, a. 1. See also *Sent. Eth.* V, lect. 1, n. 955. For Aristotle's original argument, see *Nic. Eth.* V.4, 1132a20–1132a25.

35. *ST* II-II, q. 60, a. 6.

36. *ST* II-II, q. 60, a. 6, ad 4.

of that subject to be an instantiation of justice and *ius*. True, one of the requirements for a decision to be an act of justice is that it is issued by the subject "who is in authority."[37] A violation of this requirement is described by Aquinas as "usurpation," and the *iudicium ultra vires* is faulty and illicit for that reason.[38]

But this is not the only requirement necessary for an *iudicium* to be an act of justice. We saw in the previous chapter that in Aquinas's view, an unjust law does not constitute *ius* at all, and that a *lex injusta* may be said to not be a *lex* at all. Following the same pattern, an unjust *iudicium* does not constitute *ius* and is not an *iudicium* at all.[39] It can be called a *ius* only in a "deteriorated [*detorqueantur*]" and improper sense of that term.[40] Aquinas is very clear that the first requisite for a judgment to be an act of justice is that "it proceed from the inclination of justice [*inclinatione iustitiae*],"[41] that is, that it take into consideration all the relevant levels of *ius* (including metapositive levels of *ius*) and be in principle oriented toward declaring or determining what is to be given to the titleholder in justice. To be apt to correctly declare or determine *ius*—that is, to be just—a judgment must relate to an object that has the properties of justice: outwardness,[42] other-directedness,[43] and obligatoriness proper to justice.[44]

Finally, to be an act of justice, an *iudicium* must be pronounced according to the "rule of prudence [*rectam rationem prudentiae*]."[45] In Aquinas's estimation, a judgment respects the necessary standards of prudence when the facts of the case have been established, and the relevant *ius* has been declared or determined by applying the degree of inferential reasoning that yields a sufficient certainty

37. *ST* II-II, q. 60, a. 2.
38. See *ST*, II-II, q. 60, a. 2; II-II, q. 60, a. 6, ad 4.
39. *ST* II-II, q. 70, a. 4, ad 2.
40. See *ST* II-II, q. 57, a. 1, ad 1.
41. *ST* II-II, q. 60, a. 2.
42. *ST* II-II, q. 60, a. 2, ad 1; II-II, q. 60, a. 3, ad 3.
43. *ST* II-II, q. 60, a. 1, ad 3; II-II, q. 67, a. 3.
44. "A judgment is an act of justice, in as much as the judge restores to the equality of justice those things which may cause an opposite inequality" (*ST* II-II, q. 63, a. 4).
45. *ST* II-II, q. 60, a. 2.

attainable in the matters of the particular case in point. Such is the certainty that overcomes mere suspicion, because it is apt to exclude, on solid grounds, the possibility of a substantially different outcome of the *iudicium*.[46] If a judgment is pronounced without this required certainty of inferential reasoning, it is thereby faulty and illicit, and it thus fails to qualify as a suitable basis for an act of justice.[47]

Aquinas and the Stages of the Interpretation of Law

What exactly is the task of the subject vested with appropriate authority when interpreting *ius* in a particular case? What are the sources of *ius* that this subject must consult before and after deciding whether to declare or determine the *ius* on the basis of the facts of a particular case?

For Aquinas, the author of *iudicium* interprets the law (*ius*) in a particular case by reasoning on the basis of the relevant rules of law ("*ex regulis iuris*").[48] But what are the relevant rules of *ius*? Once the facts of the case are sufficiently established, the author of a future *iudicium* must first inquire—that is, interpret—whether that case may be resolved by simply declaring that the matter in hand falls, and is resolvable, within the scope of juridical goods that are established at the level of *ius naturale* and of positive-law based *ius positivum*. If this is the outcome of the interpretation of law, then the *iudicium* declares that the only (or the best) admissible interpretation of the facts in light of the relevant law was secured without having to further determine *ius*. Such is, for example, the case of a car entering a park, or of recreational fishing (or firing up a barbecue) in a national park for reasons of leisure or even malice, disconnected from any emergency whatsoever, against the rules that prohibit these

46. Aquinas speaks of a kind of certainty (*certitudo*) that can be achieved in the realm of human acts that are the object of a *iudicium* to-be-pronounced, that is, the certainty that is "befitting the matter in point," which can be distinguished from "the certainty of a demonstration," namely, a certainty that can be achieved in natural sciences, or absolute certainty. See *ST* II-II, q. 60, a. 3, ad 1. See also *ST* II-II, q. 70, a. 2.

47. *ST* II-II, q. 60, a. 1.

48. *ST* II-II, q. 60, a. 1, ad 1.

behaviors by unequivocally covering such activities and objects in the general classifying terms contained in said rules.

Aquinas approaches the issue of the relevant rules of *ius* by asking "whether we should always judge according to the written law."[49] His answer is that since an *iudicium* is a "declaration or determination of what is just," and since "a thing becomes just in two ways," that is, as an *ius naturale* or as a positive-law based *ius positivum*, it may be said that it is necessary to judge according to positive laws only if these laws appropriately contain *ius naturale*, and only if said laws fittingly determine the core of *ius naturale* for more specific issues by establishing *ius positivum*.[50] Thus, if a legal official authorized to issue an *iudicium* interprets law in a particular case without considering the relevant juridical goods established at the level of *ius naturale* or of positive-law based *ius positivum*, the judgment will be accordingly defunct and unjust.[51] And if positive laws contain something contrary to *ius naturale*, an *iudicium* "should not be delivered according to them."[52]

Having established the necessity to consult the relevant *ius naturale* and *ius positivum*, Aquinas tackles the issue of an *iudicium* that has to not merely declare these already established levels of *ius* but further determine *ius* in a particular case, because both *ius naturale* and *ius positivum* still represent an underdetermined juridical order for identifying *ius* in that case. Interestingly enough, he tackles that issue by formulating versions of the following questions: Is rule-skepticism viable? Would it not be better if all *ius positivum* were determined at the level of *iudicium*? Is all positive law *iudicium*-made law?[53] He answers these questions by highlighting that it is better that positive laws determine *ius* (on the basis of *ius naturale*) as much as possible because these laws seek to capture the order of justice by "taking many instances into consideration ... in the

49. *ST* II-II, q. 60, a. 5.
50. *ST* II-II, q. 60, a. 5.
51. *ST* II-II, q. 60, a. 5.
52. *ST* II-II, q. 60, a. 5, ad 1.
53. See *ST* I-II, q. 95, a. 1, arg. 2 and arg. 3.

abstract and of future events," which is always preferable, in Aquinas's view, to the arrangement wherein *ius* is interpreted exclusively in particular cases arising from present controversies.[54]

Aquinas is aware that it is impossible for positive laws to determine the relevant *ius* in all imaginable cases, and that, accordingly, certain matters will have to be left to the determination in virtue of *iudicium*.[55] In these cases, the *iudicium* further determines law for that particular case, and this *determinatio* has to be consistent with the applicable positive laws that manifest both *ius naturale* and *ius positivum*.[56] Such is the case when, under the relevant rule of "no vehicles in the park," someone drives into a park by using a certain means of transport but the applicable rules of both *ius naturale* and *ius positivum* are insufficient, at the time of application, to establish whether that means of transport qualifies as a vehicle. Consequently, the only way to determine the *ius* in question and decide whether said rule has been violated, is by way of *iudicium*.

Equity as a Stage in the Interpretation of Law

Lawrence B. Solum provides us with a rather efficacious attempt at detecting a general meaning of equity in the present-day legal mentality. In his view, reasoning according to the standards of equity implies that "legal decision makers sometimes ought to depart from the rules in order to do justice in particular cases."[57] Thus defined, the concept of equity may be seen to be locked in a certain tension with the concept of law, depending on how exactly one understands the nature of law. To those who adopt the claim that all law is positive law as the core thesis of law's ontology, equity may turn out to be a problematic concept, because it runs contrary to that claim, unless of course, the positive laws or the social-factual conditions for legal

54. See *ST* I-II, q. 95, a. 1, ad 2.

55. See *ST* I-II, q. 95, a. 1, ad 2 and ad 3.

56. See *ST* II-II, q. 60, a. 5.

57. Lawrence B. Solum, "A Virtue-Centered Account of Equity and the Rule of Law," in *Virtue Jurisprudence*, ed. Colin Farrelly and Lawrence B. Solum (Palgrave Macmillan, 2008), 142.

validity somehow permit recourse to equity in legal practice. On the other hand, to those who claim that there are certain elements of juridicity beyond positive laws or beyond social-factual conditions for legal validity, the concept of equity may be almost entirely absorbed, and may even lose its distinctive features, in the assessment of those nonposited elements of law. This latter account of equity seems to correspond to Dworkin's theory, as Solum suggests: "One could say that Dworkin has simply eliminated the idea of equity altogether, by arguing for an expansive concept of the complete set of legal rules in which every case should be decided according to the rules and principles."[58]

Accordingly, in Anglo-American legal accounts of this concept, equity may be seen to denote a supplemental source of judge-made law, the juridicity of which is explained either according to the above described "all law is positive law" thesis or in a Dworkinian (or other comparable) account of law's nature.[59] In the legal systems steeped in, or somehow influenced by the continental-European tradition, equity seems to be predominantly understood to denote one of the various techniques of interpretation of positive legal norms, wherein the juridical status of that technique seems to be ultimately dependent upon the varieties of an "all law is positive law" thesis.[60]

How does Aquinas envision equity from the viewpoint of his account of the nature of law? An answer to this question should start with the following argument: for Aquinas, equity is a mode of interpreting the facts of a case in light of the relevant *ius*, in those cases which are in principle materially covered by positive-law-based *ius positivum*, but the application of those positive laws, and the abstention from further interpretation and determination of *ius* through *iudicium*, would cause injustice. Thus, in those cases, the

58. Solum, "A Virtue-Centered Account of Equity and the Rule of Law," 152.

59. For more details, see Wesley Newcomb Hohfeld, "The Relations between Equity and Law," *Michigan Law Review* 11, no. 8 (1913): 537–71; Paul B. Miller, "Equity as Supplemental Law," in *Philosophical Foundations of the Law of Equity*, ed. Dennis Klimchuk, Irit Samet, and Henry E. Smith (Oxford University Press, 2020), 92–115.

60. For example, see Giovanni Tarello, *L'interpretazione della legge* (Giuffrè, 1980), 380–82.

iudicium further determines *ius* in accordance with the criterion of equity by introducing an exception from prima facie applicable positive-law-based *ius positivum*, when the latter does not really constitute an *ius* or the just thing to be attained in a particular case. This happens, for example, when under the relevant rule of "no vehicles in the park," an ambulance drives into a park to intervene and provide help in a medical emergency, which could not be efficiently provided in any other way than by violating the aforementioned rule.[61]

Breaking down this line of argument into its constitutive elements, it is necessary to say that, first of all, for Aquinas, equity (*aequitas*, the Latin translation of the term *epikeia* or *epieikeia*, used by Aristotle[62]) is a mode of the interpretation of *ius*. In each particular instance where the facts of the case seem to fall under the scope of a positive law that determines *ius positivum*, the author of a future *iudicium* must verify—that is, interpret—that the application of positive law does not lead to injustice given the facts of the case and the orders of *ius* applicable to these facts. If it does not lead to injustice, then the "letter of *lex* ought to be followed"[63] because it establishes *ius positivum* in those cases where, in the absence of that determination, there were no sufficient criteria to ascertain what is just.[64] In Aquinas's words, when authors of an *iudicium* interpret *ius*, they should always also "interpret" whether "laws that are correctly posited [*leges rectae positae*]" perhaps "fail [*deficiunt*] in some cases" because their application would be unjustly "burdensome" for some interested persons.[65]

61. Aquinas provides an example of a "besieged city" in which it is "established that the gates of the city are to be kept closed, this is good for the public welfare as a general rule: but, if it were to happen that the enemy are in pursuit of certain citizens, who are the defenders of the city, it would be a great loss to the city, if the gates were not opened to them: and so in that case the gates ought to be opened, contrary to the letter of the law, in order to maintain the common good, which the lawgiver had in view" (*ST* I-II, q. 96, a. 6).

62. As Aquinas says, "*epikeia*" denotes that "which we call equity [*aequitas*]" (*ST* II-II, q. 120, a. 1).

63. *ST* II-II, q. 120, a. 1, ad 1.

64. See *ST* II-II, q. 57, a. 2, ad 2; II-II, q. 60, a. 5, ad 1.

65. *ST* II-II, q. 60, a. 5, ad 2.

It should be highlighted that in case of the equitable interpretation of *ius*, the problem is not in the *ius positivum* established by positive laws. Indeed, these laws are, as Aquinas says, correctly posited, and to the extent that they are just, they establish *ius* for many of the cases they cover. For example, the rule "no vehicles in the park" establishes *ius positivum* for several cases. In certain cases, however, the verbatim execution of that rule may prove to be defunct, not on account of its inherent injustice but because an equitable interpretation of *ius* prevents its application "according to the letter of the law"[66] in a particular case for justified reasons.[67] Thus, it is the facts of the case that provide the relevant elements for interpreting an application of positive law to be unjust in that case: "in [some] cases it is bad to follow a positive law, and it is good to set aside the letter of the law and to follow the dictates of justice and the common good."[68]

What is the juridical status of the equitable interpretation and determination of *ius*? Aquinas emphasizes that it is impossible to think of equity as something other than justice and law (*ius*): "*Epikeia* does not set aside that which is just in itself but that which is just as determined by [positive] law."[69] Thus, when authors of an *iudicium* set aside prima facie applicable positive laws, they are reasoning from within the realm of justice. Indeed, as Aquinas repeats over and over, equity is a form of justice and thus a fully juridical mode of interpreting *ius* in a particular case.[70] Equity is not some metalegal criterion for reasoning that invokes nonjuridical or extrajuridical values. Equitable interpretation and determination of *ius*

66. *ST* II-II, q. 60, a. 5, ad 2.

67. "It would be passing judgment on a law to say that it was not well made; but to say that the letter of the law is not to be observed in some particular case is passing judgment not on the law, but on some particular contingency" (*ST* II-II, q. 120, a. 1, ad 2).

68. *ST* II-II, q. 120, a. 1.

69. *ST* II-II, q. 120, a. 1, ad 1.

70. "*Epikeia* is a part of justice" (*ST* II-II, q. 120, a. 2); "*Epikeia* is better than a certain, namely legal justice, which observes the letter of the law; yet since it is itself a kind of justice, it is not better than all justice" (*ST* II-II, q, 120, a. 2, ad 2); "It is true that what is equitable is one kind of just thing" (*Sent. Eth.* V, lect. 16, n. 1081).

may indeed lead to an outcome in which a positive law is deemed inapplicable because it is conducive to injustice in a particular case, but the standards of such interpretation and determination are bound by other relevant orders of *ius*.

In the first place, equitable interpretation and determination of *ius* must take *ius naturale* into consideration and proceed according to its directives, especially if the application of an otherwise just positive law in a particular case would be contrary to *ius naturale*.[71]

In the second place, Aquinas understands equity as a reasoning that exceeds positive-law-based *ius positivum*, which is deemed unjust in a particular case, by performing a *determinatio* of justice at the level of *ius positivum*.[72] Indeed, the object of *aequitas* denotes an *iudicium*-based *ius positivum* because it is "directive of the *lex*, where *lex* is deficient for some particular case."[73] In an equitable *determinatio* of law, the author of an *iudicium* determines *ius positivum* on the bases of *ius naturale*, as well as on the basis of the other potentially applicable elements of positive laws. When determining *ius* in the process of equitable interpretation, the author of a *iudicium* is authorized to create law in a particular case because it is "manifest" and beyond doubt that the intention of a lawgiver was not to apply a general norm of positive law (according to its letter) to that particular case.[74] In Aquinas's estimation, equitable interpretation and determination of *ius* may occur because it can be established that the lawgiver somehow had the recourse to equity ("*recurrendum ad aequitatem*") in view for a particular case.[75] As Aquinas says, in such a case, "even the lawgiver himself would decide otherwise"

71. *ST* II-II, q. 60, a. 5, ad 2. For the argument that the equitable interpretation and determination of law is bounded by *ius naturale* (i.e., "contained *under* the naturally just [*sub iusto naturali*]"), see *Sent. Eth.* V, lect. 16, n. 1081 (emphasis added). See also the following argument: "The equitable [*id quod est epikees*] … is a just thing and it is better than one kind of just thing; not better than what is naturally just that is laid down absolutely, that is, universally, but better than what is legally just" (*Sent. Eth.* V, lect. 16, n. 1087).

72. *ST* II-II, q. 120, a. 2, ad 1.

73. *Sent. Eth.* V, lect. 16, n. 1087.

74. *ST* II-II, q. 120, a. 1, ad 3.

75. *ST* II-II, q. 60, a. 5, ad 2.

than what is established by the relevant positive laws, and "if he had foreseen the case, he might have provided for it by law."[76]

In sum, what is contained in an *iudicium*, pronounced on the basis of equitable interpretation and determination of law, is *ius*, more precisely, it is *iudicium*-based *ius positivum*.[77]

Is Law (*Ius*) an Interpretive Concept According to Aquinas?

In the course of this chapter, it became evident that the determination of *ius* by way of *iudicium* may be said to enter into the nature of law, since not everything regarding *ius* can be established at the level of *ius naturale* or determined at the level of positive-law based *ius positivum*. But does this mean that Aquinas's account of law's nature is essentially interpretive, comparable to Dworkin's core thesis on what law is?

First of all, it must be noted that Aquinas's account of law's nature is certainly more "interpretive" than Hart's position on law's indeterminacy. Hart holds that in an open-texture situation of law, the law-applying organs create law for a particular case by exercising discretion, "instead of merely applying already pre-existing settled law."[78] As seen before, Hartian judicial discretion is not unlimited, and the law-applying organs must make law that is harmonized, to the greatest possible degree, with the standards supplied by the sufficiently determinate rules of the legal system. By contrast, Aquinas holds that in cases where law is partly indeterminate or incomplete, there are usually certain elements of juridicity, whether nonposited or posited, that are relevant for such cases and must be taken into consideration in the process of interpreting and determining law.

76. *ST* II-II, q. 60, a. 5, ad 2.

77. For an excellent account of equity as a part of justice and of the object of equity as ultimately a kind of *ius positivum* in the texts of Thomas Aquinas, see Santiago Vigo Ferrera, *"Apud nos dicitur aequitas": L'equità quale giustizia nella tradizione giuridica realista* (Giuffrè Francis Lefebvre, 2023), 289–397.

78. Hart, *The Concept of Law*, 272.

Where Hart speaks of the judicial "creation" of law and of limited "discretion," Aquinas focuses on the "interpretation" and "determination" of law, whereby all the relevant elements of juridicity are gathered and become operative in a law-applying decision that ultimately establishes the *ius* in a concrete case. Where Hart sees a penumbra of uncertainty and open texture, Aquinas perceives the elements of law in need of completion in a particular case by way of *iudicium*.

Second, it may be said that Aquinas's account of interpretation is perhaps less "interpretive" than Dworkin's position on law's nature. Indeed, it seems that for Dworkin, interpretation is predominantly, if not entirely, about discovering what law is in light of what it ought to be, given the relevant principles of political morality that provide the best interpretation of applicable legal norms and of the relevant facts of a particular case. Dworkin expands the horizon of legal sources to include both posited laws and nonposited elements of juridicity for the purposes of establishing an account of law's nature wherein virtually everything is settled by the relevant law, and the task of law-applying organs is merely to declare what law is (even after Herculean efforts) rather than to further determine it. In other words, his account of law is focused more on interpretation that shows the existing right answer to legal questions than on law's determination. By contrast, for Aquinas, the interpretation of law includes the possibility that law-applying organs may find that law has to be further determined to establish *ius* in the cases when *ius naturale* or positive-law-based *ius positivum* are underdetermined, or when it is necessary to proceed by equitable interpretation that includes determination of *ius*.

In sum, for Aquinas, (1) law-applying organs will certainly arrive at points where law is insufficiently determined in a particular case. In his view, (2) these points are neither necessarily open-texture areas to be resolved by judicial discretion, nor are they necessarily settled law awaiting to be discovered. Instead, (3) if upon interpretation, these points are not resolvable by declaring the pertinent nonposited or posited law, then it is the duty of law-applying organs to settle or determine law by interpreting the facts of a particular case in light of the relevant elements of applicable juridical orders (*ius naturale*, positive-law-based *ius positivum*) that constrain that determination. All three theses may be said to ultimately enter into Aquinas's account of the nature of law.

Chapter 8

Rights and the Nature of Law

Rights and Their Unifying Principle

The main premise of this chapter is the argument that rights are also relevant for understanding law's nature. Of course, to grasp the pertinence of rights to the nature of law, it is first necessary to comprehend what they are. Throughout the chapter, I will understand the term rights to denote so-called "subjective rights," that is, the various instantiations of the advantageous or beneficial faculties that a titleholder has "over" (or regarding) a thing in a relationship of justice. The concept of subjective rights shifts the focus from the thing-based and other-directed account of *ius*, paradigmatic for conceptualizing law in Thomistic juridical realism, to a subject-centered perspective of the titleholder with regard to the things that are his *suum*, his *ius*.

Normally, the titleholder's faculties over a thing that is his *ius* consists of a complex network of entitlements regarding a thing, included in the measure of *ius* and awarded according to the title of attribution. These entitlements correspond to multiple ways in which a certain thing belongs to a titleholder. Wesley Newcomb Hohfeld offered what is still considered to be a useful schema of all these faculties in which he claimed to have broken down complex jural relations into their "lowest common denominators," namely, into claim-rights, liberties, powers, and immunities, together with their correlatives and opposites.[1] Understanding these faculties regarding a particular *ius* is certainly useful for identifying the concrete, nuanced, and often complex ways in which a thing belongs to a titleholder, as well as of the ways according to which a thing should be given to a titleholder by the debtor (or according to which a debtor ought to otherwise respect the attribution of a thing to a titleholder). As Hohfeld correctly says, breaking down complex jural relations (or, as he calls them, "aggregates of jural relations") to the most basic instances of subjective rights contributes to "judicial reasoning" and "to the solution of concrete problems of litigation."[2]

Having established the existence of these singled-out faculties at the lowest level of jural relations, the further question is whether there is a need for some unifying principle that gathers these various typologies of subjective rights into a coherent whole. Nigel Simmonds phrases this question in the following way: "[Do] rights operate on a deeper level of legal and moral coherence, with the Hohfeldian positions merely being various forms in which rights may be established and protected? Can rights be thought of as a coherence-providing organizing ideas located at a more abstract level than the various Hohfeldian bipolarities?"[3] Even Hohfeld himself held that in reference to his account of rights, "the deeper the analysis, the greater becomes one's perception of fundamental unity and harmony in the law."[4]

1. See Wesley Newcomb Hohfeld, *Fundamental Legal Conceptions as Applied in Judicial Reasoning and Other Legal Essays* (Yale University Press, 1919), 35–64. Finnis offers an excellent synthesis of Hohfeldian subjective rights and their correlatives: "(1) A has a *claim-right* that B should φ, if and only if B has a *duty* to A to φ; (2) B has a *liberty* (relative to A) to φ, if and only if A has a *no-claim-right* ('a no-right') that B should not φ; (2′) B has a *liberty* (relative to A) not to φ, if and only if A has a *no-claim-right* ('a no-right') that B should φ; (3) A has a *power* (relative to B) to φ, if and only if B has a *liability* to have his legal position changed by A's φ-ing; (4) B has an *immunity* (relative to A's φ-ing), if and only if A has no power (i.e., a *disability*) to change B's legal position by φ-ing" (Finnis, *Natural Law and Natural Rights*, 199).

2. Hohfeld, *Fundamental Legal Conceptions as Applied in Judicial Reasoning*, 63–64.

3. Nigel Simmonds, "Puzzles of Rights," *The American Journal of Jurisprudence* 65, no. 2 (2020): 189.

4. Hohfeld, *Fundamental Legal Conceptions as Applied in Judicial Reasoning*, 64.

Perhaps the most famous attempts to find such a unifying principle of jural relations in the present-day legal context may be found in the so-called "will" and "interest" theories of rights.[5] The "will" theory of rights is often considered to be championed by Hart, who holds that the "unifying element,"[6] that explains "why these four [Hohfeldian] varieties in spite of differences are referred to as rights"[7] is the idea that the law gives an individual "exclusive control, more or less extensive, over another person's duty so that in the area of conduct covered by that duty the individual who has the right is a small-scale sovereign to whom the duty is owed."[8] In other words, according to the "will" theory of rights, the constitutive core element of the concept of right, and thus of each Hohfeldian type of subjective rights, is the legally designated individual's effective sphere of control over another person's duty, which the titleholder may exercise at his choice or will.

According to the other theory of rights, known as the "interest" theory, which is sometimes emblematically associated with Joseph Raz, the concept of rights becomes intelligible only when the right-holder's well-being, interest, or benefit is directly correlative to the existence of another person's duty: "To assert that an individual has a right is to indicate a ground for a requirement for action of a certain kind, i.e., that an aspect of his well-being is a ground for the duty on another person. The specific role of rights in practical thinking is, therefore, the grounding of duties in the interests of other beings."[9]

5. Jeremy Waldron refers to these two theories in terms of the "ways of presenting the unity or integrity of the cluster" of Hohfeldian elements of jural relations. See Jeremy Waldron, introduction, in *Theories of Rights*, ed. Jeremy Waldron (Oxford University Press, 1984), 11. Similarly, Finnis deems these two theories "the principal competing answers" to the broad question regarding "the underlying principle, unifying the various types of relationships that are reasonably said to concern rights" (Finnis, *Natural Law and Natural Rights*, 203).

6. H. L. A. Hart, "Definition and Theory in Jurisprudence," in *Essays in Jurisprudence and Philosophy*, 35.

7. Hart, "Definition and Theory in Jurisprudence," 35.

8. Hart, *Essays on Bentham*, 183.

9. Joseph Raz, "The Nature of Rights," in *The Morality of Freedom* (Oxford University Press, 1986), 180.

When these concepts of rights are contextualized in their respective positivistic accounts of law's nature, both Hart and Raz may be seen to argue that rights become legally relevant only when they are ultimately grounded in validly posited laws, and thus their existence and legality can be established without any necessary or conceptual reference to their moral merit.[10]

But even when we put aside the positivistic premises embraced by the majority of the proponents of both "will" and "interest" theories of legally relevant rights, one wonders whether the reference to "will" (or choice, or power) and to "interest" (or benefit, or well-being) is really the deepest line of reasoning that provides a framework of rights with optimal evaluative coherence. The same question persists even if one shifts the focus from subject-centered choices and interests to duties, which seems to be the most frequent strategy in the search for an alternative account of the evaluative foundations of rights.[11] Is there another possible unifying principle for rights from the viewpoint of which the references to will, to interest,

10. "So whether the laws are morally good or bad, just or unjust, rights and duties demand attention as focal points in the operations of law which are of supreme importance to human beings and independently of moral merits of the laws" (Hart, *The Concept of Law*, 269); "The truth [of legal right-statements] can be established without using moral argument" (Joseph Raz, "Legal Rights," in *Ethics in the Public Domain: Essays in the Morality of Law and Politics* (Oxford University Press, 1994), 266).

11. For an interesting argument on the importance of duty for understanding the underlying logic and the evaluative foundations of rights, see Rowan Cruft, *Human Rights, Ownership, and the Individual* (Oxford University Press, 2019). Cruft's line of reasoning is quite similar to what I refer to as the obligatoriness of justice. I hold, following Aquinas's insights, that justice originates in a thing-centered duty that is owed to another person, and that, consequently, the juridical phenomenon (*ius*) is essentially other-directed and thus presupposes the centrality of the debtor's viewpoint. Of course, the aspects of this thing-centered duty may be transposed to match the viewpoint of the titleholder and his corresponding thing-centered subjective rights. As will be shown in this chapter, I do think that the various instantiations of subjective rights are important, and may even be seen to be essential, for understanding the nature of law. Cruft does not consider the thing-centered feature of the phenomenon of legal duty, and neither does he ground his analysis on considerations relative to justice. But he does maintain that from some point of view at least, nothing of essential importance would be lost if we were to dispense with the concept of a violable right, since the content of that concept may be seen to be secured and explained by a proper account of duties (Cruft, *Human Rights, Ownership, and the Individual*, 3). In fact, to corroborate his thesis, Cruft even points to the fact that, "according to some, the Ancient Greeks and Romans lacked our rights notion; it is a medieval or

or even to duties may be seen to denote only fragments of a larger whole, rather than the ultimate foundational arguments?

Finnis points to such a unifying principle when he reports on the tendency to speak of rights as "relationships between persons and one subject-matter or (in a broad sense) *thing*,"[12] or, said differently, in terms of "two-term relations between a (class of) persons and a (class of) *subject-matter* (life, body, free speech, property or ownership of property)."[13] In his brief survey of this tendency, he notes that there are cases in which the initial right-duty framework of titleholders and debtors is legally altered, while still maintaining one and the same subsisting objective (e.g., a payment of a certain sum of money under a contract), such as when a debt is either subsequently legally transferred to other persons, or broadened to also include a legally relevant interests of other persons, or altered in other significant ways. In these complex cases, he claims, consistently keeping the "substance of the same subsisting objective" in focus may be possible in virtue of a viewpoint wherein the thing itself should be awarded a greater relevance, since it provides "an intelligible unity to a temporal series of the many and varying sets of Hohfeldian rights."[14]

Anthony Honoré takes this argument even further.[15] In his view, Hohfeld's schema should not obfuscate the fact that there is something about rights that may be thought of in terms of a unifying conceptual center, identifiable as the constant point of reference for various claims, liberties, powers, or immunities that gravitate toward that same point. For example, as he says, the right of bodily security is the aggregate of the claim to not be assaulted (a right *in rem* against an indefinite class of people), of the claim not to be bitten by a dangerous dog (a right *in personam* against a few definite

perhaps specifically Christian creation or discovery" (Cruft, *Human Rights, Ownership, and the Individual*, 1).

12. Finnis, *Natural Law and Natural Rights*, 201.

13. Finnis, *Natural Law and Natural Rights*, 218 (emphasis added).

14. Finnis, *Natural Law and Natural Rights*, 201.

15. See Anthony M. Honoré, "Rights of Exclusion and Immunities Against Divesting," *Tulane Law Review* 34 (1959–1960): 456–57.

persons, namely those who own or are otherwise responsible for a dangerous dog), and of other connected claims. It is more coherent, in Honoré's view, to think of, say, the right of bodily security as a unifying center of these aggregated claims, and thus to think that this right—bodily security (or a payment of a certain sum of money under a contract, from the previous paragraph)—is "protected by certain claims," that it "gives rise to certain liberties," and so forth.[16] In his estimation, to uphold the use of the term "right" primarily for denoting a single conceptual center of various claims, liberties, etc., does not mean "to deny that there may be some cases in which *the right actually consists in a claim or liberty*"; rather, it means to "reject a definition which identifies a right with a claim or liberty, or even with an aggregate of claims or liberties."[17] As he puts it:

> Lawyers feel, justifiably, that there is something to be said of the right itself as opposed to the particular claims by which it may happen to be protected. The right unifies the claims and, very often, outlives them. It existed before some of the claims presently recognized were evolved; it will continue to be the same right, in an intelligible sense, when new modes of protection are evolved.[18]

Both Finnis's and Honoré's reflections are close to what I will propose as the unifying principle of subjective rights, as this principle follows from the main tenets of Thomistic juridical realism. To highlight, as Finnis does, the need for identifying the consistency in the reference to the thing itself (e.g., a payment of a certain sum of money under a contract) across various changes in rights-based faculties regarding this thing, or to emphasize, as Honoré does, the need for maintaining a conceptual center or point of reference (e.g., right of bodily security) for the simultaneous existence of a multitude of subjective rights relative to that thing, is only a short step away from envisioning rights from a thing-centered (or *rei*-centric)

16. Honoré, "Rights of Exclusion and Immunities Against Divesting," 457.

17. Honoré, "Rights of Exclusion and Immunities Against Divesting," 457–58 (emphasis added).

18. Honoré, "Rights of Exclusion and Immunities Against Divesting," 457.

situation of *res clamat domino*—in each moment, a thing "calls out" for its titleholder, on the basis of a relationship of justice.

It is precisely this thing-centered perspective of justice that constitutes the unifying principle of subjective rights in Thomistic juridical realism. Each type of Hohfeldian rights-based position in jural relations—claim, liberty, power, immunity—may be shown to be an aspect, in a broader framework of justice, of "giving" to each titleholder that thing which is his own *ius*, or of otherwise respecting the attribution of a thing to a titleholder on the basis of a title. In fact, subjective rights may be said to reveal the concrete perspective from which a thing ought to be "given" to the titleholder. According to this realistic unifying principle, the jural relations are optimally described by focusing not only on the subjective rights of the titleholder, or on the corresponding duties of the debtor, but by considering the relevant relationships of justice, wherein at the center we find the thing itself (in the broadest possible sense of that term). *Ius*, or the object of justice, is ultimately the thing itself. Subjective rights are then describable as thing-centered faculties of the titleholder: just as the things themselves form part of the nature of law as its material cause, so too they form part of the essence of subjective rights.

Again, the varieties of subjective rights can indeed help us in identifying and understanding the relevant ways in which a thing belongs to the titleholder and in which it should be "given" to him by the debtor. Rights make *ius* more intelligible and nuanced. As Simmonds and Neoh correctly note, what we refer to as a "right" is usually "a complex bundle of [Hohfeldian] claim-rights, liberties, powers, and immunities"; thus, for example, with regard to the right of ownership, an owner of land "typically enjoys (*inter alia*) the claim-right that others should not trespass on his land, the liberty to walk upon his land, the power to transfer title to others, and an immunity against having his title altered or transferred by the act of another."[19] Each subjective right is seen to be particularly pertinent

19. Nigel Simmonds and Joshua Neoh, *Central Issues in Jurisprudence* (Sweet & Maxwell, 2022), 316.

in a determinate jural relation or in the face of a specific juridical controversy. But in approaching these relations and controversies, it is fitting to keep the focus on the thing itself (e.g., land, bodily security, etc.) because the decisive interest or benefit of the titleholder does not primarily reside in a faculty (claim, liberty, power, immunity) that concerns a thing but in the thing itself from the standpoint of a determinate faculty. Thus, it is also true that the thing that is constituted as *ius* makes the corresponding subjective rights more intelligible, content-laden, and realistic.

There are certain rights, such as the right of ownership, which are ideally describable in terms of the aggregate of included subjective rights, wherein it is not easy to point to the subjective right or faculty that defines or is decisive for understanding the right in question. Then, as Honoré says, there may be some cases where the thing itself to which we refer as "right" primarily consists in one of the types of subjective rights. For example, the right to bodily security may be said to primarily consist in a claim that bodily security be respected and not violated by others who are in a position to do so, and religious liberty may be said to primarily consist in a liberty to form, express, and live-out decisions regarding personal assent in matters of faith to the extent that other individuals or group-persons, such as the political community, are in the correlative position of "no-right" regarding aforementioned liberty and thus must refrain from possible ways of interference, etc. In all these cases, subjective rights are, in a way, instrumental to understanding the relevant relationships of justice regarding a thing to which these rights refer.

Rights and the Attainability of *Ius*

Besides their instrumental contribution to the identification and interpretation of *ius*, subjective rights may be seen to have another, perhaps even more important, role, one that is indeed essential for understanding the overall nature of law. It pertains to law's essence that it be attained, realized, fulfilled. For the purposes of justice—that is, of giving to each titleholder his own *ius*—it is not sufficient that *ius* be correctly identified in terms of its being a just thing, including the elucidation of the relevant subjective rights or faculties that the titleholder has over the thing that is his *ius*. The effective attainment of *ius*—the fully actualized giving or respecting relative to that which is just—must also be secured, at least in principle.

Accordingly, the effective attainment of *ius* seems to be premised on, among other things, a discrete, overarching subjective right that consists in the titleholder's *faculty to demand* that the thing, which is his *ius*, be given or respected, so as to be able to fully enjoy the thing from the viewpoint of all the relevant Hohfeldian subjective rights. The titleholder's faculty to demand the thing that is constituted as *ius* is inherent in each relationship of justice and may be seen to be the structural consequence of the framework of justice.

In the second chapter, we already saw that obligatoriness is one of the essential properties of justice. When seen from the perspective of the titleholder of *ius*, obligatoriness of justice corresponds to the necessary emergence of the faculty to demand, on the part of the titleholder, that this obligatoriness be resolved in the effective performance of what is just, that is, in the proper act of justice. Both the obligatoriness of justice, which stands at the basis of *ius*, and the faculty to demand that what is constituted as *ius* be really attained through appropriate human acts, find their rationale in the final cause of *ius*: indeed, what is at stake in the realm of justice and *ius* is a form of human good, the juridical good. The juridical good forms part of law's nature not only as an ideal objective but also as an actualized reality. Between the obligatoriness of *ius*, considered predominantly from the perspective of the debtor, and the juridical good, which constitutes the *telos* of *ius*, we find, on the part of the titleholder, an overarching subjective right structured as a faculty to demand the thing, which cannot be reduced to any single subjective right from the Hohfeldian schema.

In sum, to each thing-centered *ius*, and thus also to each Hohfeldian subjective-right component of *ius*, there corresponds a discrete subjective right that has the structure of a faculty to demand the thing itself that is constituted as *ius*, that is, to demand the Hohfeldian subjective-right "component" of the just thing itself. The demand aims for the debtor to give or respect the *ius* in question. From the viewpoint of the relevant Hohfeldian subjective right, this is done either voluntarily or in a subsidiary way, in virtue of the titleholder's activation of the coercive mechanism supporting the legal practices in a community, which will secure the effective attainment of *ius*.

For these reasons, the subjective-right faculty to demand the *ius* pertains to the very nature of law. In addition, since it is possible that the owed and demanded *ius* is not given voluntarily by the debtor, and since, in that case, it is necessary to support the actualization of *ius* by some form of an institutionalized coercive mechanism backing the practices of legal officials, the institutional coercive support of the faculty to demand the *ius* may also be said to form part of the nature of law, as a subsidiary feature of said faculty.[20]

Once we adopt the thing-centered framework of a relationship of justice, together with the titleholder's faculty to demand the *ius*,

20. The structural field of this argument roughly corresponds to an aspect of Raz's "systemic moral property of law" (already quoted in this book), which concerns law's reliance on the use of force for the actualization of *ius*, or, to use Raz's words, for law-applying. Being a positivist, Raz maintains that the law, by its nature, has an essential task to secure—even through coercive mechanisms—a situation whereby the content of its posited norms is authoritatively actualized, regardless of the moral merit of those norms. In his view, it is unlikely that such a situation could be achieved in a peaceful and coordinated way without the institution of (positive) law. As a "structure of authority," he says, law is "in the business of telling people what they must do" (Raz, "About Morality and the Nature of Law," 180), and where needed (e.g., when people do not voluntarily do what the law tells them to do), this systemic "business" of law includes what Raz considers to be a morally valuable function of coercing people to comply with the law, that is, to actualize whatever the law tells us to do (see Raz, "About Morality and the Nature of Law," 172). Thomistic juridical realism may also be seen to endorse the thesis that law has the essential task of securing the actualization of *ius* in a peaceful and coordinated way. However, from the viewpoint of Thomistic juridical realism, the evaluative dynamism behind actualizing law through institutional means of enforcement is grounded in the very framework of justice and its intrinsic imperative to attain *ius*, its object, rather than in the authoritative features of the institution of law, which, in Raz's view, operates autonomously from the moral merit of posited legal norms.

as the unifying principle for Hohfeldian subjective rights, the core tenets of the "will" and "interest" theories of rights may be seen to denote fragments of a larger whole. The source of a subjective right or of a duty is not reducible to the titleholder's choice or interest. Rather, that source corresponds to the entirety of the underlying structure of justice.

Of course, this does not mean that the elements of interest and will are irrelevant. *Ius* certainly provides the titleholder with an interest that the *ius* be actualized and respected in all the relevant ways. According to the "interest" theory of rights, rights may be said to be intelligible from the viewpoint of the titleholder's advantages or benefits, even without their being entirely dependent on the right-bearer's subjective interpretation of what constitutes her interest. Rather, interests protected by rights seem to correspond to an objective notion of interest. As Raz says, "rights are vested in right-holders because they possess certain general characteristics," and they "serve their interests as persons with those characteristics," even if they, in fact, "may be against their interests overall."[21]

The evaluative dynamisms of (1) the obligatoriness of justice, (2) the concrete interest of the titleholder relative to his rights-based advantage or benefit, and (3) the goods-based final cause of *ius*, together generate on the part of the titleholder a faculty to demand the thing that is his *ius*. To be sure, a titleholder may in principle, and for a variety of motives, choose not to exercise this faculty. But his will or choice not to exercise the faculty to demand *ius* does not mean that the subjective-right faculty to demand is itself necessarily inexistent, or that the *ius* in question (together with the relevant Hohfeldian subjective rights) does not exist. At first sight, it seems that the "will" theory of rights is generally compatible with this line of reasoning. Hart argues that the fullest measure of rights-based

21. Raz, "The Nature of Rights," 180. Raz provides some examples to clarify this aspect of the "interest" theory of rights: "Though rights are based on the interests of the right-holder, an individual may have rights which it is against her interest to have. A person may have a property which is more trouble than it is worth. It may be in a person's interest to be imprisoned, even while he has a right to freedom" (Raz, "The Nature of Rights," 180).

control over another person's duty comprises three distinguishable elements:

> (1) the right holder may waive or extinguish the duty or leave it in existence; (2) after breach or threatened breach of a duty he may leave it "unenforced" or may "enforce" it . . . ; and (3) he may waive and extinguish the obligation to pay compensation to which the breach gives rise.[22]

On closer inspection, however, there is one crucial difference between a Hartian approach to rights and the corresponding arguments of Thomistic juridical realism. For the latter theory, when a titleholder waives a right and thereby loses effective control over the correlative of a Hohfeldian subjective right, what he waives is only the exercise of the subjective-right faculty to demand or enforce the actualization of an *ius*. The thing that is constituted as *ius*, and the relevant Hohfeldian subjective rights, do not lose their juridical status if the titleholder waives the exercise of his faculty to demand them, provided that the relevant *ius* does not tie such a waiver to its extinction. They remain legal rights that were at least in principle demandable, and which the titleholder for some reason chooses not to demand if he has such a choice according to the relevant juridical titles.

Hart is correct to say that "it is hard to think of rights except as capable of exercise."[23] Indeed, the attainability of rights is not only their essential feature but also forms part of the very nature of law. But as I sought to explain in this chapter, there is much more to rights than the sheer subjective-right faculty to demand, and thereby control, the attainment of obligations at the titleholder's will or choice. In Hart's version of the "will" theory of rights, Hohfeldian subjective rights are legally relevant only insofar as validly posited rules recognize or respect the emergence of the titleholder's effective legal power to control and enforce these rights. However, if the faculty to demand the effective actualization of rights is grounded in the framework of justice, as is the case in Thomistic juridical

22. Hart, *Essays on Bentham*, 183–84.
23. Hart, *Essays on Bentham*, 184.

realism, then it is possible to see that the Hohfeldian types of subjective rights are not simply reducible to special cases of legally awarded powers underlying a titleholder's choice.[24] The overarching, subjective-right faculty to demand can then be seen as discrete from but also connected to both (1) the thing itself constituted as *ius* (at the center of the jural relations) and (2) the Hohfeldian types of subjective rights (which explain the various possible positions in jural relations).

Indeed, in Thomistic juridical realism, the subjective-right faculty to demand is in the service of the actualization of both the *ius* and the Hohfeldian subjective rights. And as seen in the previous section, Hohfeldian subjective rights are in the service of the better, more nuanced intelligibility of the thing-centered *ius*. *Ius* remains, as always in Thomistic juridical realism, the conceptual core of the nature of both law and rights.

Accordingly, Thomistic juridical realism offers a distinctive approach to understanding the concept of human rights, ordinarily envisioned as essentially subjective rights. However, based on the previous line of argument, it is possible to establish a conception of human rights that distinguishes three levels of analysis. First, the thing itself (*res*) that is protected as a human right (e.g., life, freedom of movement, free choice of employment, etc.), is already constituted as fully law (*ius*) insofar as it is established as the object of justice by the relevant natural or posited juridical titles. In the case of human rights, the natural-law titles are particularly pertinent to the extent that the protected good in question does not need further positive-law determination to be established as *ius*. In addition, aspects of the human right already constituted as *ius* may be seen from the viewpoint of Hohfeldian subjective rights, that is, as a claim-right, liberty, power, and immunity, while keeping the thing-centered (or good-centered) framework of these subjective rights in mind. Finally, the titleholder of a human right may be seen to

24. This is essentially Hart's position. See Hart, *Essays on Bentham*, 188–92. See also Hart, "Definition and Theory in Jurisprudence," 35–36.

possess a subjective-right faculty to demand the respect of that right from the viewpoint of the relevant Hohfeldian subjective-rights position in jural relations.

A Brief Historical Excursus #4: *Ius* and Subjective Rights

With these presuppositions in mind, we are now equipped to better understand the stages of a complex debate on the history of the concept of subjective rights. For present purposes, it is not necessary to reiterate all the details of the debate. It is sufficient to focus only on certain points of the debate that reveal some important arguments regarding the relevance of subjective rights for elucidating law's nature.

To present the basic question of the debate, I will take as the starting point Aquinas's account of *ius*. Here is the question: Was Aquinas familiar with a meaning of *ius* that is analogous to Hohfeldian subjective rights? There are at least three levels of answers to that question. First, in the textual locus where he defines *ius* and provides a list of the various analogous or derivative meanings of *ius*, there is no mention whatsoever of subjective rights. *Ius* is defined as "the just thing itself,"[25] and everything that Aquinas adds to that definition in this text and in the surrounding textual loci of his treatise on *ius* and justice moves only in the direction of his development of what I refer to in this book as the four causes of *ius*. For some reason, Aquinas does not deem it important to include or reflect upon the concept of subjective rights in his arguments for the definition of *ius*. Second, when he elaborates on his primary, thing-centered, justice-based notion of *ius*, he seems to imply that certain subjective meanings of *ius* depend on this former notion,[26] and I sought to emphasize these implications in the previous two sections of this chapter. Aquinas's framework of the relationships of justice may be seen to fruitfully entail the existence of Hohfeldian subjective rights,

25. *ST* II-II, q. 57, a. 1, ad 1.
26. For this implication, see Finnis, *Aquinas: Moral, Political, and Legal Theory*, 133–38.

as well as of an architectonic faculty to demand the actualization of these rights, provided that the primary meaning of *ius* is secured as central in that analysis. Third, it seems to be sufficiently demonstrated that Aquinas had no intention of eliminating the usage of the term *ius* in a subjective sense, as a faculty of the titleholder, and he occasionally uses this term in that sense.[27] Studies have shown that his occasional usage of a subjective notion of *ius* does not alter his definition of *ius* according to its primary, thing-centered, justice-based meaning in any significant way.[28] In sum, these three lines of argument seem to coexist in Aquinas's legal-philosophical mind without any significant tension between them.

Michel Villey's arguments catalyzed the debate on both the historical origin and the doctrinal importance of subjective rights. He holds that although we can identify certain references to a subjective sense of *ius* before the fourteenth century, it is not possible to encounter a definition or a fully formed conception of *ius* framed in entirely subjectivist terms of individual faculties over things, which would be wholly detached from an "*ius* as *ipsa res iusta*" framework, prior to the writings of William of Ockham, and certainly not in Aquinas's texts.[29]

27. See Dominic Legge, "Do Thomists Have Rights?" *Nova et Vetera (*English edition*)* 17, no. 1 (2019): 133.

28. For example, see Annabel S. Brett, *Liberty, Right and Nature: Individual Rights in Later Scholastic Thought* (Cambridge University Press, 1997), 88–97; Brian Tierney, "Villey, Ockham and the Origin of Individual Rights," in *The Idea of Natural Rights: Studies on Natural Rights, Natural Law and Church Law 1150–1625* (Scholars Press, 1997), 22–25; Brian Tierney, "Natural Law and Natural Rights: Old Problems and Recent Approaches," *The Review of Politics* 64, no. 3 (2002): 391–95; and Brian Tierney, "Author's Rejoinder," *The Review of Politics* 64, no. 3 (2002): 416. I am citing these two authors since neither of them has any particular scholarly interest, for the purposes of some broader thesis on the nature of rights, in proving that Aquinas's usage of subjective-rights language did not alter his *ius*-realist meaning of *ius*. Tierney's findings are particularly interesting in this sense, since his conclusions on Aquinas's *ius*-realist position actually go against his overall project of identifying earlier medieval developments of the doctrine of subjective rights.

29. Michel Villey, "Droit subjectif I (La genèse du droit subjectif chez Guillaume d'Occam)," in *Seize essais de philosophie du droit dont un sur la crise universitaire* (Dalloz, 1969), 140–78. Villey's line of reasoning in defense of this thesis was accompanied by some idiosyncratic arguments, which certainly did not contribute to an easier understanding of his ideas. Thus, for example, (1) he deems the concept of subjective rights to be juridically

Thus, for the purposes of my present analysis, the search for historical occurrences of a subjectivist meaning of *ius*—the traces of which may be found across the entire history of legal philosophy—is too wide and may set us off course. A large part of the debate on the historical origin of subjective rights was dedicated to this broad line of examination. Instead, I am more interested in the results reached by focusing more narrowly on fully developed primary (and analogous) meanings of *ius*. From that viewpoint, Villey's thesis seems to correspond to the actual stages of the historical development of the concept of subjective rights. To my knowledge, besides occasional usages of the term *ius* for denoting certain faculties of the titleholder, before the fourteenth century, there are no definitions or explicit and developed conceptions of the term *ius* comparable to those found from that period onward, such as the following:

> *Ius* is predicated of every human act, power or acquired disposition that issues from an imperative of the human mind, be it internal or external, immanent or transitive upon some external thing or an aspect of it ... in conformity with *ius* so-called in its first signification [i.e., *lex*].... It is in this signification that we are accustomed to say: "this is someone's right," when he wills or handles a particular thing in conformity with *ius* so-called in the first sense.[30]
>
> Every *ius* is either divine or human, and, if human, is *ius* either natural and of heaven or positive and of the forum.... Now, the right of heaven [*ius poli*] is nothing but a power conforming to right reason without a pact; the right of the forum [*ius fori*] is a power resulting from some pact, sometimes conforming with right reason and sometimes not.[31]
>
> According to the latter and strict acceptation of *ius*, this name is properly wont to be bestowed upon a certain moral power [*facultas quaedam moralis*] which every man has, either over his own property

inessential, since it represents nothing more than a degradation of an objective meaning of *ius*, and (2) in his view, all law seems to be ultimately judicially made. See Michel Villey, *La formation de la pensée juridique moderne* (Presses Universitaires de France, 2013), 244, 248, 356.

30. Marsilius of Padua, *The Defender of the Peace*, trans. Annabel Brett (Cambridge University Press, 2005), II, 10.

31. Ockham, *The Work of Ninety Days*, 56–58.

> [*circa rem suam*] or with respect to that which is due to him [*ad rem sibi debitam*]. For it is true that the owner of the thing [*dominus rei*] is said to have a right in that thing [*ius in re*].[32]
>
> *Ius* is a moral quality [*qualitas moralis*] annexed to a person, enabling him to have, or do, something justly.[33]

On the opposite side of the debate, Finnis acknowledges that, indeed, from the viewpoint of the historical analysis of the definitions of *ius*, "somewhere between" Aquinas and the authors of the above cited explanations of *ius*, "we have crossed the watershed."[34] However, in Finnis's view, nothing important was lost with the shift towards a modern vocabulary of subjective rights. As he puts it,

> The modern vocabulary of natural rights is a many-faceted interest for reporting and asserting the requirements or other implications of a relationship of justice from the point of view of the person(s) who benefit(s) from that relationship. It provides a way of talking about "what is just" from a special angle: the viewpoint of the "other(s)" to whom something ... is owed and due, and who would be wronged if denied that something.[35]

Thus, Finnis does not seem to be discordant with my assessment that it is indeed possible and beneficial to identify and explore the notion of subjective rights, understood in terms of the entitlements that the titleholder has over *ius*, including the faculty to demand the thing itself, as well as Hohfeldian subjective rights. I hold that Aquinas was at least implicitly aware of this subjective-rights perspective of the titleholder.

However, I disagree with Finnis's thesis that nothing important was lost after the watershed, that is, after legal theorists started to

32. Suárez, *A Treatise on Laws and God the Lawgiver*, I, 2, 5. For an excellent study of the development of the idea of subjective rights in the Spanish Scholastics, see Alejandro Guzmán Brito, *El Derecho como facultad en la neoescolástica española del siglo XVI* (Iustel, 2009). For an impressive study by the same author on the origin of the term "subjective right," see Alejandro Guzmán Brito, "Historia de la denominación del derecho-facultad como subjetivo," *Revista de Estudios Histórico-Jurídicos* 25 (2003): 407–43.

33. Grotius, *The Rights of War and Peace: Book One*, I, 1, 4.

34. Finnis, *Natural Law and Natural Rights*, 205–10.

35. Finnis, *Natural Law and Natural Rights*, 205.

define *ius* almost exclusively in terms of subjective rights. Finnis maintains that even Aquinas's account of justice and *ius* may be seen to be paradigmatically based on a subjective-rights framework, since that account "entails that—though it does not clearly appear from [Aquinas's] formal account of the senses of *ius*—in his view, *ius* (a right) is something that belongs to the subjects of law or moral relationships, and therefore has the essential characteristic of a subjective right."[36]

Continuing his promising analysis of the tendency to speak of a right as a "relationship between persons and one subject-matter or (in a broad sense) *thing*,"[37] Finnis arrives at the conclusion that this relationship "can be spoken of either as an ensemble (a single *ius*) or by articulating its content in terms of the respective benefits ... which are articulated by statements about the subjective right(s) involved in the relationship."[38] These two ways of speaking about rights are perfectly interchangeable, in his view. It is possible that Finnis simply holds that the alternative framework to that of subjective legal rights can only be based in their Hohfeldian correlatives, and that the content of both rights and duties is sufficiently secured at the level of positive law so as to eliminate any practical need to think of the concept of *ius* in terms of anything other than subjective rights and positive laws.[39] In his *Natural Law and Natural Rights*, he tackles this issue in the section that bears the subtitle "Are Duties Prior to Rights?" and his definitive answer to that question seems to

36. Finnis, *Natural Law and Natural Rights*, 465. Finnis's line of reasoning on this point is practically equivalent to Suárez's assessment of Aquinas's primary meaning of the term *ius*. To my knowledge, Suárez is probably the first author to claim that Aquinas's concept of *ius* does not refer to a thing-centered, justice-based good but to a subjective-rights framework: "Since the word [*ius*] is an ambiguous term, we must distinguish between its different meanings, that we may employ it only in that acceptation which is pertinent to our purposes. For *ius* sometimes refers to the moral right [*morale facultatem*] to acquire or retain something ... and the said right is, as we learn from St. Thomas (II-II, q. 57, a. 1), the true subject matter of justice [*quod est proprium objectum iustitiae*]" (Suárez, *A Treatise on Laws and God the Lawgiver*, II, 17, 2).

37. Finnis, *Natural Law and Natural Rights*, 201.

38. Finnis, "'Natural Law,'" 207.

39. Finnis, *Aquinas: Moral, Political, and Legal Theory*, 134–35. See also Finnis, "Grounding Human Rights in Natural Law," 214.

be in the negative.[40] In his view, the modern vocabulary of rights is entirely explainable in terms of a transposition of the same content that pertained to the perspective of the bearer of Hohfeldian duties, no-rights, liabilities, and disabilities prior to the watershed, to the perspective of the titleholder.[41] If that is really the case, then, really, nothing important was lost in crossing the watershed.

But that is not the case, and something was indeed lost when the prewatershed realistic definitions of *ius*, which may be seen to also include a reference to subjective rights, were substituted with the postwatershed accounts of *ius* explained entirely in terms of subjective rights (where the term *ius* is not meant to denote positive laws). What was lost is the unifying conceptual framework that gathers the existence of plural subjective rights under the conceptual umbrella of *ius*, the nature of which also includes, besides rights, a reference to the duties of the debtor, the relevant relationships of justice, the reliance on the title of *ius* (paradigmatically natural and positive laws), the reference to the thing itself and its ontological features, and the telic horizon of a specific justice-based form of human good—these aspects were all included in a single concept of *ius* before the watershed. After the watershed, and until today, an objective meaning of *ius* is reducible to positive law, while the only other meaning of *ius* seems to be reserved for Hohfeldian subjective legal rights.[42] Speaking in terms of the four causes of *ius*, only

40. Here is the core of his answer to the question of whether duties ought to be considered to be prior to rights: "Let me conclude this review of the shift of meaning in the term 'right' and its linguistic predecessors by repeating that there is no cause to take sides as between the older and the newer usages, as ways of expressing the implications of justice in a given context. Still less is it appropriate to argue that 'as a matter of juristic logic' duty is logically prior to right (or vice versa)" (Finnis, *Natural Law and Natural Rights*, 210).

41. See John Finnis, "On Moyn's Christian Human Rights," *King's Law Journal* 28, no. 1 (2017): 14. See also Finnis's following claim: "To say that *ius* is something people, one by one, have is to say that it is 'subjective' in the sense that it belongs to subjects (persons). And this having (to which others have the duty actively to respond ... extends ... centrally ... to being the proper beneficiary of the duties (negative and positive) of another or others" (Finnis, *Natural Law and Natural Rights*, 423).

42. I do not mention "moral" rights or "moral" *ius*, because these expressions seem to me to present an attempt to connect two contradictory terms. If something is *ius*, then it is already in some way sufficiently specified from within the broader moral domain to

an aspect of the efficient cause (i.e., the juridical title of *ius*) survived the watershed and was included in the (objective) meaning of *ius*—positive law. In addition, Hohfeldian subjective rights also survived and formed part of the concept of *ius*. However, these rights cannot be considered to constitute a cause of *ius*, but only aspects of its measure and obligatoriness—or, when we speak of the faculty to demand *ius*, its structural consequence—seen from the viewpoint of the titleholder. Everything else was eliminated from the nature of *ius* after the watershed.

The range of the debate on the significance of the historical meanings of subjective rights may be narrowed, for the purposes of this book, to include the following disagreement. On one side, Villey highlights the importance of an objective meaning of *ius* but denies any viability to the concept of subjective rights. Moreover, it is far from clear whether he intended this "objective" meaning of *ius* to denote the very nature of law, in a way comparable to the essence of *ius* described in this book, rather than proposing an upgrade in conceptualizing rights. On the other hand, Finnis holds that in an account of law's nature, the legally relevant concept of *ius* may be successfully reduced to the framework of subjective rights, without any remainder, besides the reference to positive law (and the reference to natural law, but only within the limits of law's evaluative life).

This chapter has shown that there is another way to conceptualize both *ius* and subjective rights, a way that takes into consideration both Villey's and Finnis's contentions but which also seeks to transcend what I believe to be certain limits in the approaches of both authors.

---

be distinctly juridical. If something is moral, then it is still insufficiently specified to be referred to as *ius* or as a right in any juridical sense. It is of course possible, from the viewpoint of the broad moral realm, to speak of moral faculties, powers, etc., but a reference to a "moral right" or "moral *ius*" seems to me to denote only an analogous and imprecise usage of the terms "right" or *ius*.

Chapter 9

Conclusion

What Law Is "In": A Summary

Gathering the core arguments developed throughout the book, the main question may be best answered by taking into consideration all four causes of *ius*. For Thomistic juridical realism, the nature of law (*ius*) is complex and it cannot be fully expressed by focusing on only one phenomenon through which law is essentially manifested; law's ontology embraces more than one such phenomenon. Therefore, I will answer the core question of this book from the viewpoint of each of the four causes of *ius*, while also considering all the other causes. I believe this is the best approach to understanding the entirety of what law is.

Law (*ius*) is "in" all those things (*res*) that are caught in the relationships of justice on account of being brought within the range of the essential properties of that virtue by certain juridical titles (such as natural and positive laws). The effective attainment of justice regarding those things denotes a specific form of human good.

Law (*ius*) is "in" all those relationships that have the structure of the virtue of justice, and which regard the things that are brought within the reach of that virtue by the relevant juridical titles, the end of those relationships corresponding to the attainment of a specific form of human good.

Law (*ius*) is "in" all those legal rules (*leges*), whether natural or positive—as well as "in" other juridical titles—the content of which brings certain things within the range of the evaluative reach circumscribed by the properties of the virtue of justice, in such a way that the attainment of the content of these rules represents a specific justice-based form of human good.

Law (*ius*) is "in" all those human goods that have been rendered juridical on account of their being constituted as the objects of the virtue of justice by having been brought within the reach of that virtue by the relevant juridical titles. In addition, these human goods always correspond to certain, broadly speaking, things, realities, acts, or states of affairs, that is, they always fall on the level of *res*.

What Is "In" Law?

Exploring the answer to the question of what law is "in" paves the way for a better understanding of the response to a parallel question: which phenomena ordinarily studied by legal philosophy may be said to form part of the nature of law?

Even if they are not in any way posited by valid legal norms or included in the validity conditions for the identification of posited law, the precepts of *natural law* may be said to be fully juridical when they are seen as forming part of the cumulative activation of the four causes of *ius*. As a result of that activation, the precepts of natural law, together with the other corresponding aspects of *ius* (things, relationships, goods), constitute the nonposited elements of juridicity.

Validly *posited legal rules*, which declare or determine these nonposited elements of juridicity, also form an essential part of law's nature (together with the things, relationships, and goods to which these rules refer). The positive-law declarations of the nonposited elements of juridicity contribute to the intelligibility (1) of these elements and (2) of the ways according to which these nonposited elements of law figure as the core content in the totality of the rules of the legal system and of the juridical goods in a community. In addition, the fabric of law needs the positive-law determinations of nonposited elements of juridicity because the range of these elements is not sufficient to cover all the issues of social coordination that are imperative to settle what is just. In fact, the largest part of the juridical goods in a community are the result of positive-law determinations. To be law, such determinations must take into consideration and be harmonized with *ius naturale.*

The nonposited elements of juridicity, together with the positive-law determinations of these elements, still do not cover all the community's needs for identifying what is just. Apart from the *juridically relevant acts* that establish *ius* as a result of the *will of private individuals* (such as contracts and wills), the fabric of law also includes the *legal officials' authoritative declarations and determinations of what is just,* which are arrived at in the course of established legal practices, wherein law is interpreted by these officials for particular cases. To constitute law (i.e., to constitute *iudicium*-based *ius positivum*), the interpretation of law by the legal officials must be performed in accordance with both the relevant aspects of *ius naturale* and the positive-law based *ius positivum.*

Questions of *authority* relative to the creation of positive laws, as well as those relative to the law-creating and law-applying practices of legal officials, may be seen to enter the fabric of law as a part of the necessary conditions for the existence of these juridical titles of *ius positivum,* and thus as a part of the efficient cause of *ius.*

Finally, since the very structure of *ius* as the object of justice requires its own sufficient intelligibility and attainability, *subjective rights* may be seen to form part of the nature of law. In this sense, Hohfeldian subjective rights contribute to a better intelligibility of the ways according to which a thing (*res*) is owed to the titleholder in the relevant relationships of justice based on the relevant juridical titles. In addition, the framework of the relationships of justice presupposes the effective attainment of *ius,* and this presupposition points to the necessary existence of the titleholder's subjective-right faculty to demand the *ius* from the debtor(s).

Furthermore, if the duty of justice and the corresponding titleholder's faculty to demand the attainment of *ius* have not been properly met by the debtor in a voluntary fashion, the effective attainment of *ius* must be made possible and secured in some way by the *coercive mechanism supporting the legal practices in a community*. To that extent, the coercive enforcement of law may be said to form part of law's nature as a subsidiary feature of a titleholder's subjective-right faculty to demand the *ius*, with a view to the effective attainment of what is just.

All these phenomena may be said to be "in" law (i.e., to form part of law's nature) for the reasons summarized here and developed throughout the book.

The Payoffs of Thomistic Juridical Realism

Since the account of law's nature proposed by Thomistic juridical realism may strike some, or even most, readers as quite peculiar in comparison to the standard accounts of the essence of law, it could be useful to briefly reflect on some of the payoffs of this approach. As seen throughout the book, Thomistic juridical realism is a version of a natural-law theory of law, deeply marked by its affinity to the legal-philosophical family of theories gathered under the name "virtue jurisprudence." What are the benefits that this approach offers in comparison to other theories? In what follows, I identify at least five payoffs. In their brief enumeration, I will offer my evaluation of the extent to which it is realistic for supporters of other legal-philosophical approaches to recognize these features of Thomistic juridical realism as indeed payoffs.

First, Thomistic juridical realism is an account of virtue jurisprudence that conceptualizes law as something essentially other-directed, and thus in principle altruistic. Whatever law is, it is approached, understood, and lived-out as something that paradigmatically belongs to another person. Of course, this does not mean that the acting person in law is deprived of the importance of her perspective on the jural relations she is involved in. Other-directedness presupposes the perspective of the acting person. In addition, as seen in the previous chapter, there is more than one way in which the subjective rights of the titleholder form part of the nature of law. Nonetheless, it seems to me that it is beneficial to conceptualize law in an other-directed framework (which does not cancel out the jural perspective of the acting person) instead of envisioning law purely from the perspective of the individual acting subject and of his potential conflicts with others. It seems to me that the supporters of other theories of law's nature should not find difficulties in perceiving (and hopefully even developing) the legal-theoretical appeal of the feature of other-directedness.

Second, for Thomistic juridical realism, the nature of law is profoundly goods-based. One of the causes of *ius*, its final cause, consists in a specific form of human good that is brought about by each attainment of *ius*. In this sense, law is seen as something good in its very essence, and it is possible to refer to the concrete thing that constitutes *ius* as the juridical good, while keeping in mind the cumulative activation of all four causes of *ius*. The goodness of law, as proposed by Thomistic juridical realism, transcends the purely formalistic account of juridical goodness promoted by Kelsen, according to which the goodness of law is constituted by whatever the content of posited legal norms (including deeply immoral and unjust acts and states of affairs).[1]

In addition, the goodness of law proposed here is not dependent upon law's positivity, and the book makes the case that law is good even when it is not posited and even in abstraction from the question of whether it is posited or not. This latter argument seems to me to upgrade Finnis's account of law as a positivized reason for action, and thus his own line of argument on law's goodness. In Finnis's theory, it is possible to say that what law demands, on account of its positivity, is really not at all something good because it is to a

1. See Kelsen's claim that "The concept of law is [not] outside the concept of the good. For the concept of the 'good' cannot be defined otherwise than as that which ought to be: that which conforms to a social norm; and if law is defined as a norm, then this implies that what is lawful is 'good'" (Kelsen, *Pure Theory of Law*, 66).

certain extent unjust; it is also possible to say that something is good in a legally relevant way, but only to the extent that this good is validly posited. There is no place in his theory for the possibility that something is law because it is good in some juridically relevant way, even if it is not posited. There is nothing juridical about basic human goods unless they are somehow posited, claims Finnis. Thomistic juridical realism takes the law's goodness even more seriously than a Finnisian version of a natural-law theory of law. It is precisely for this reason (i.e., for taking the law's goodness very seriously) that supporters of other approaches to law's nature may find this feature of Thomistic juridical realism to be something less than a payoff. At the same time, however, it is possible that some of these readers will be sympathetic to any theory that reflects on the goodness of law on a higher level than Kelsenian formalism.

The previous payoff is logically followed by another: Thomistic juridical realism provides the tools to make the case for the existence of certain nonposited elements of juridicity. I am aware that for a broad range of readers, this will not be seen as a payoff because it challenges all legal-philosophical approaches that endorse the thesis that all law is positive law; hence, it challenges virtually all legal positivists and a significant number of today's natural lawyers and nonpositivists. I continue to believe that my thesis on the existence of nonposited law may find supporters not only among Thomists and Dworkinians, although I would much appreciate seeing it further developed by those who hold Aquinas's and Dworkin's legal theories in high esteem. It seems to me that at least among natural lawyers, and perhaps even among nonpositivists who are not natural lawyers, there should still be, at least in principle, an openness for some workable consensus on this thesis.

With regard to legal positivists, a possible acceptance of the thesis that not all law is posited would have to be premised on a different conception of a rule of recognition of what counts as law that would not rely on social-factual criteria, such as the unanimous practice of legal officials, but would somehow leave room for at least some elements of nonposited law. There must be some way for legal positivists to concede that not all law is posited, without thereby endorsing the entirety of Dworkin's critique of positivism or endorsing a maximalist natural-law theory of law. Would positivism really be subject to a mutational jump if its proponents held that some, even a very limited set of values similar to Hart's minimum content of natural law, could be thought of as nonposited law or as a necessary (instead of merely contingent) connection between law and morality? Would that really be the defeat of all that legal positivism stands for? Considerable ground would still remain available for being covered by the typically positivist analysis, such as the inquiry into the question of why some law, or almost all law, is indeed necessarily posited. Why is it that the debate between positivists and natural lawyers cannot profitably shift toward questions regarding the extent to which law must be posited, instead of insisting on positivity as the *conditio sine qua non* of all law?

Fourth, Thomistic juridical realism highlights the importance of reintroducing the things themselves into the nature of law. Things (in the broad Thomistic meaning of *res*) constitute the content of our laws and the object of our legal rights. They are largely what law is really about, what it seeks to protect or achieve. Law is always in some way meant to fall on the level of things. This line of reasoning does not seem to compromise the central tenets of legal positivism,[2] and we have already seen that law was explicitly and, arguably, unanimously envisioned according to a thing-centered framework at least until the fourteenth century. Would it not be better to admit that our legal reasoning is so thing-centered as to warrant the inclusion of things into the very nature of law? As shown in this book, such inclusion is not to the detriment of other phenomena that may also be seen to form part of law's nature, such as rules and subjective rights.

2. See, for example, Julie Dickson's continuous usage of the term "things" in her claim that the role of the rule of recognition is to identify certain "things as constituting valid law" or to recognize certain "things as sources of law" (Dickson, "Is the Rule of Recognition Really a Conventional Rule?" 375–76, 378–79, 381, 383–85, 393, 395–96, 398, 400–402).

It seems to me that this payoff is available to supporters of various approaches to the essence of law.

Finally, the fifth payoff concerns the more structured way of interconnecting law and justice. It is one thing to make a general claim on some important ways of relating law to justice, which most legal philosophers and legal practitioners seem to share, and it is quite another thing to make that interrelatedness more specific. One of the main ideas of this book is that justice constitutes a point of entry into the inquiry of what law is, and the case was made in the book that the idea of justice may be shown to provide the unity for certain experiential facets that strike us as constitutive of what law is: the facets regarding the state of affairs in which things are attributed and in which it is possible and fitting to understand that these things are also somehow owed. The book then makes the argument that justice enters the very idea of juridicity and constitutes one of the causes of *ius*. Perhaps certain readers will find some of the arguments that the book makes about justice more relatable than others, depending upon their own idea of what law is and how its interconnectedness with justice should be envisioned. But I believe that most readers will share the book's general direction of conceptualizing legally relevant justice as something more substantive than purely formal justice with its limited scope of treating like cases alike (and different cases differently) according to the criteria established by posited legal rules.

Transcending the Dichotomies in Legal Philosophy

Understanding the complex nature of law according to its four causes contributes to a novel way of approaching certain arguments that usually constitute points of legal-philosophical debate. Thomistic juridical realism shows at least some of the ways in which these debates may be englobed into a broader account of what law is.

One of the points of the debate between legal positivists and natural lawyers concerns the issue of whether law is a natural kind or an artifactual kind. According to the core thesis of the artifactual theory of law, which largely overlaps with the central tenets of legal positivism, in a bifurcation between natural kinds and artifactual kinds, law is describable only as a complex institutional artifact humanly created for determinate purposes, and there is no way of conceptualizing law in terms of a natural kind, such as water, silver, the law of gravity, or the DNA structure.[3] In what is arguably the most authoritative response to that claim on behalf of the natural-law theory of law, Finnis suggests that for understanding what law is, we "need a better inventory of kinds"[4] than the reduction of all that can (or cannot) be said about law into a bifurcation between natural and artifactual kinds. It is not my intention to engage all the complexities of this particular debate. I wish only to highlight that an account of law's nature that embraces its four causes, as presented in this book, leaves enough room for conceptualizing aspects of law as something that pertains to a natural kind (since the things themselves enter the fabric of law as its material cause), as well as to an artifactual kind (given the pertinence of the artifactual aspects of positive laws and of the practice of legal officials to the efficient cause of law). In addition, Thomistic juridical realism reflects on further causes of law that are not reducible to natural or artifactual kinds. The essential reference to justice and to a justice-based form of human good points to certain evaluative features, which remain lost from view if we limit our metaphysical range of inquiry only to things such as water and the decisions of the constitutional courts.[5]

Next, the account of law's nature presented in this book rethinks the debates on the typologies of the possible or necessary connections between law and morality. Since the authors on each side of

3. For the core claims of the artifactual theory of law, see Luka Burazin, Kenneth Einar Himma, and Corrado Roversi, eds., *Law as an Artifact* (Oxford University Press, 2018).

4. Finnis, "Aquinas and Natural Law Jurisprudence," 49.

5. For further details on the points of debate between the artifactual theory of law and Thomistic natural-law theories of law, see Petar Popović, "Both Directions at Once? A Thomistic Response to the Artifactual Theory of Law," in *The Artifactual Nature of Law*, ed. Luka Burazin, Kenneth Einar Himma, Corrado Roversi, and Paweł Banaś (Edward Elgar, 2022), 89–110.

these debates seem to hold that there are at least some possible, as well as some necessary, law-morality connections, Thomistic juridical realism focuses on the question of how law may be said to be "in" (or part of) the broader sphere of morality but without being undistinguishably identified with the whole range of moral values. In this book, I have to some degree followed Hart's general line of argument that justice is particularly suitable to provide the legally relevant standard for exploring the connections between law and morality.[6] Throughout the text, and following Aquinas's insights, I explored the extent to which justice may indeed assist us in understanding the interconnectedness between law and morality, whether from the viewpoint of the presence of morality in law or from the complementary viewpoint of the conditions for establishing a presence of law in morality. I am aware that the book does not resolve all the issues of the law-morality connection, and that it may in some ways complicate things even further. However, the book does dispel at least some of the common intellectual prejudices against the natural-law argument for a necessary connection between law and substantive morality, such as the claim that law is so intertwined with morality that the role of law is to basically enforce or juridicize the entirety of the moral realm.

Then, Thomistic juridical realism presents its own position relative to the present-day reading of the famous Hobbes's dictum *auctoritas non veritas facit legem*.[7] Indeed, legal positivism claims that authority is an ultimate ground for justification of law-creation and law-application,[8] and not the moral merits (or the moral *ver-*

6. Hart, *The Concept of Law*, 7, 157–58.

7. It seems that the earliest version of the dictum, in its complete formulation, may be found in the 1668 Latin edition of Hobbes's *Leviathan*. See Thomas Hobbes, *Leviathan, sive De Materia, Forma, et Potestate Civitatis Ecclesiasticae et Civilis* (Apud Joannem Blaeu, 1668), XXVI, 22.

8. See, for example, Raz's thesis: "In as much as the law consists of the standards of political communities it claims to have authority over its subjects. Put in a different way: It is part of the ideal of law that it should have such authority, though it often fails to live up to that ideal. This point ... follows from the fact that the law consists of those standards which become the standards of a political community by being enacted, endorsed, or enforced by the organs of that community, as it is plain that those organs claim legitimate

itas) of the acts of law-creation and law-application. Perhaps some nonpositivists and natural lawyers who endorse the "all law is positive law" thesis could offer a more nuanced reading of that dictum, but in the ultimate analysis, they will have to defend the claim that without authoritative positing there is no law. Thomistic juridical realism, in my opinion, offers further nuance by advocating for the existence of nonposited law, that is, law not justifiable by invoking intentional acts pertaining to human authority. At the same time, however, this approach highlights that appropriate authority does, indeed, constitute a foundational aspect of positive-law based and *iudicium*-based *ius positivum*. To the extent that this authority is lacking altogether, or that it is in some essential sense deficient, positive laws and the law-making or law-applying decisions of legal officials will be precluded from establishing *ius*. Furthermore, as seen throughout the course of this book, even those parts of *ius* established by human authority cannot justify their obligatoriness exclusively by arguments concerning authority—they also need to appeal to the activation of the deontic and virtuous dynamism that is inherent to justice. The ultimate justification of all law, however, is that part of moral *veritas* that concerns the evaluative standard of justice across all the relevant levels of *ius*, especially regarding the highest level, *ius naturale*, which is outside of the reach of human authority in those aspects that do not need further determination.

Finally, it seems to me that Thomistic juridical realism, at least to some degree, transcends the discussions relative to the question of how many "lives" law may be said to have, and the further question of how these "lives" are interrelated. There seems to be considerable common ground between legal positivists, natural lawyers, and nonpositivists on the thesis that law has at least two "lives"—one social-factual and the other evaluative—provided that law is never envisioned without due emphasis on its social-factual "life." I can see the benefits in arguing that there is something more to law than

moral authority, and in claiming that they are authoritative they claim that the standards that they lay down or endorse are so as well" (Joseph Raz, "On the Nature of Law," in *Between Authority and Interpretation*, 104).

its social-factual "life," a line of analysis that is intriguing, in different but not incompatible ways, to both legal positivists and natural lawyers, as well as to nonpositivists. It is highly likely that the whole discussion on law's "lives" originated in the need for such an analysis, but it seems to me that this analysis may occasionally lead to somewhat awkward results, such as in the case of unjust laws where the "two-lives" framework of law enters a schizophrenic situation of "lives" turning against one another, or where it is possible to hold, within a single framework of what law is, that there are central cases of law (just laws) and borderline cases of law (unjust laws). Of course, it is not impossible to envision the "two-lives" framework of law, even in such extreme situations.[9] But this is certainly not the only framework capable of explaining the multiple aspects of what law is. For example, we could say, as this book does, that law has a single life but multiple causes, each of which contributes in its own way to understanding what law is, without the practical possibility that one of law's causes turns against the other(s).

Transcending the Dichotomies in Thomistic Juridical Realism

The theses advanced in this book may prove to be helpful for addressing some of the debates that take place among the authors who support Thomistic juridical realism. Although these authors share the same, or at least a similar, legal-philosophical platform, they do not form a unified doctrinal front on all the relevant arguments. As is common in legal philosophy, sometimes the effort of these authors to better understand the aspects of the shared platform involves scholarly exchanges or debates.

One such exchange took place with regard to the question of

9. It is quite interesting that in the legal positivist camp endorsing the "dual nature of law" approach, John Gardner embraces Finnis's thesis on the central case and borderline cases of law without any problems (see Gardner, "Hart on Legality, Justice, and Morality," 228), while Julie Dickson remains unconvinced by that thesis (see Dickson, *Elucidating Law*, 92–94).

whether the essence of *ius* in Thomistic juridical realism is best describable in terms of a substance (i.e., thingness) or in terms of a relationship.[10] The attentiveness to all four causes of *ius* resolves the debate regarding this question, since from the four-causes perspective, the nature of law may be seen to embrace both its thingness (the material cause of law) and its relational character (the formal cause of law, that is, justice, and the final cause of law, namely, the other-directed juridical goodness). As seen in the first section of this final chapter, law can be defined by showing how it can be found, from different perspectives, "in all those *things*" and "in all those *relationships*" provided that all the causes of law are properly referenced, even while we focus on just one of these causes.

Next, since Thomistic juridical realism may be seen to be primarily interested in exploring the features inherent in the semantics of the concept of *ius*, in some cases it is possible that the phenomenon of *lex*, especially humanly posited *lex*, ends up being studied only as an inessential appendix to the analysis of *ius*. The prevalent focus on the identification of the juridical phenomenon primarily in those things or realities (*res*) that constitute the objects of the virtue of justice may contribute to the formation of a flawed mindset, according to which it is possible to dispense with positive (or even natural) legal norms almost entirely in an explanation of the nature of law. According to that mindset, the primary ontological carriers of the juridical phenomenon are the things themselves and not legal norms, be they natural or positive. Michel Villey is an example of an author who seems to have endorsed such a position.[11] The difficulty

10. For the terms of this debate, see Jean-Pierre Schouppe, *Le réalisme juridique* (E. Story-Scientia, 1987), 136–37; Jean-Pierre Schouppe, "Réflexions sur la conception du droit de M. Villey: une alternative à son rejet des droits de l'homme," *Persona y Derecho* 25 (1991): 151–69; and Thierry Sol, "La notion de droit subjectif chez Villey et Hervada," *Ius Ecclesiae* 28, no. 2 (2016): 323–44.

11. It seems that Villey understands each instantiation of *lex* to primarily denote a moral rule regulating human conduct, and he has certain difficulties in both (1) grasping the juridical value of legal rules and (2) comprehending why we should give importance to grasping the juridical value of *lex*. See Michel Villey, *Philosophie du droit: I. Définitions et fins du droit* (Dalloz, 1978), 103–4; 126–27. Another proponent of Thomistic juridical realism, Javier Hervada, criticizes Villey on this point. See Javier Hervada, *Lecciones*

of some proponents of Thomistic juridical realism in thinking of legal rules (be they natural or positive) as the foundational cause of law (*ius*) originates in the following chain of arguments: if there is only one foundational cause of *ius* available, then that cause is certainly not *lex*; rather, this single cause must be sought in a combination of other foundational elements, namely, the things themselves and the idea of justice—*res iusta*. However, if the nature of law is seen according to the simultaneous activation of its four causes, the aforementioned difficulty disappears, and it becomes possible to define law by saying that it can, indeed, be found "in all those *legal rules*," provided that this definition properly implements the other causes of law. To say that legal rules, whether natural or positive, form part of the efficient cause of law means that the need for the existence of these rules pertains to the very nature of law for the various reasons explored in chapters 4 and 5 of this book.

Finally, among the jurists who support a version of Thomistic juridical realism, it is possible to hear an argument that the juridical phenomenon can easily be found in the reality of things, that the reality itself reveals what law is, and that if one is interested in identifying law, it is sufficient to simply consult reality and find it there. Formulated in this way, the argument is an oversimplification (and hardly a useful one) of the realistic emphasis on the material cause of law, namely, its thingness. Since one of the peculiarities of Thomistic juridical realism is the inclusion of the things themselves in the nature of law, some proponents of this legal-philosophical approach may overstate that inclusion by claiming that it is sufficient to carefully observe reality as it is—that is, the things themselves as they really are—and the juridical phenomenon will sooner or later somehow emerge and reveal itself to the careful observer.

---

propedéuticas de filosofía del derecho (EUNSA, 2008), 314–15. It is quite possible that Villey arrived at these somewhat idiosyncratic conclusions by following his equally peculiar thesis that all law is (or at least ought to be) ultimately judicially made, and thus what law is should not be seen as primarily dependent on the content of positive laws: "The just apportionment of goods, duties, or powers (*suum cuique*) must be defined by the judge's decision or by the work of the jurist." See Michel Villey, "Sur les essais d'application de la logique déontique au droit," *Archives de philosophie du droit* 17 (1972): 408.

For example, it is possible to find versions of these arguments in Villey's texts.[12] In a direct exchange with Villey that took place in 1972, Finnis correctly notes that this argument "leaves the reader puzzled."[13] Returning to the same critique of Villey on a later occasion, Finnis, again correctly, highlights that "the claim that juridical science, law-making, or legal interpretation can be grounded on *observation of facts* must be judged a flight from the rational requirement of pointing to reasons,"[14] that is, to reasons for action (i.e., to evaluative arguments).

Indeed, as seen previously in this book, the mere observation of things as they are will not get us very far in identifying law, because things do not of themselves possess juridicity as a part of their ontological identity. Rather, things become juridicized, so to speak, and their ontological identity is introduced into the realm of law, not by the sheer self-explanatory reference to the argument that they constitute the material cause of law but only when these things are seen from the viewpoint of other causes of law (justice, juridical titles, juridical goods). It is indeed possible to hold that law is thing-centered, from the viewpoint of the material cause of law, only on the basis of the reasons for action that are provided by the other causes of law (*ius*).

12. See, for example, the following argument: "The only path that [Aquinas] points us to, regarding the discovery of what is right according to nature [*droit naturel*] ... is that of observing the things, the nature of the things: *consideratio rei*, [which can be] translated as the observation of reality." See Michel Villey, "Si la théorie générale du droit, pour Saint Thomas, est une théorie de la loi," *Archives de philosophie du droit* 17 (1972): 430.

13. John Finnis, "Un ouvrage récent sur Bentham," *Archives de philosophie du droit* 17 (1972): 425.

14. Finnis, "'Natural Law,'" 206–7.

Bibliography

Primary Sources

Aquinas, Thomas. *Summa Theologiae: First Complete American Edition in Three Volumes*. Translated by Fathers of the English Dominican Province. Benziger Brothers, 1947–1948.

———. *Commentary on Aristotle's Nicomachean Ethics*. Translated by C. I. Litzinger, OP. Dumb Ox Books, 1993.

———. *Commentary on Aristotle's Metaphysics*. Translated by John P. Rowan. Dumb Ox Books, 1995.

———. *Commentary on Aristotle's Physics*. Translated by Richard J. Blackwell, Richard J. Spath, and W. Edmund Thirkel. Dumb Ox Books, 1999.

———. *Commentary on Aristotle's Politics*. Translated by Richard J. Regan. Hackett Publishing Company, 2007.

Aristotle. *Physics: Books I and II*. Edited by William Charlton. Oxford University Press, 1992.

———. *Politics*. Translated by Ernest Barker. Oxford: Oxford University Press, 1995.

———. *Nicomachean Ethics*. Translated by Terence Irvin. 2nd ed. Hackett Publishing Company, 1999.

Augustine. *The City of God: Books XVII–XXII*. Translated by Gerard G. Walsh. The Catholic University of America Press, 1954.

———. *On the Free Choice of the Will*. In *On the Free Choice of the Will, On Grace, and Other Writings*, translated by Peter King. Cambridge University Press, 2010.

Austin, John. *The Province of Jurisprudence Determined*. Cambridge University Press, 1995.

Blackstone, William. *Commentaries on the Laws of England—Book 1: Of the Rights of Persons*. Oxford University Press, 2016.

Cicero. *On the Laws*. In *On the Commonwealth and On the Laws*, translated by James E. G. Zetzel. Cambridge University Press, 1999.

Grotius, Hugo. *The Rights of War and Peace: Book One*. Edited by Richard Tuck. Liberty Fund, 2005.

Hobbes, Thomas. *Leviathan, sive De Materia, Forma, et Potestate Civitatis Ecclesiasticae et Civilis*. Apud Joannem Blaueu, 1668.

———. *Leviathan*. Edited by John C. A. Gaskin. Oxford University Press, 1996.

———. *De Cive*. In *Three-Text Edition of Thomas Hobbes's Political Theory: The Elements of Law, De Cive, and Leviathan*, edited by Deborah Baumgold. Cambridge University Press, 2017.

Marsilius of Padua. *The Defender of the Peace*. Translated by Annabel Brett. Cambridge University Press, 2005.

Ockham, William. *The Work of Ninety Days*. In *A Letter to the Friars Minor and Other Writings*, translated by John Kilcullen. Cambridge University Press, 1995.

Plato. *Laws: Books 1–6*. Translated by Robert G. Bury. Harvard University Press, 1961.

———. *Republic*. Translated by C. D. C. Reeve. Hackett Publishing Company, 2004.

Suárez, Francisco. *A Treatise on Laws and God the Lawgiver*. In *Selections from Three Works*, translated by Gwladys L. Williams, Ammi Brown, and John Waldron. Clarendon Press, 1944.

Vitoria, Francisco de. *Comentarios a la Secunda Secundae de Santo Tomás*. Vol. 3, *De Iustitia (qq. 57–66)*. Edited by R. P. V. Beltrán de Heredia. Salamanca, 1934.

Watson, Alan, ed. *The Digest of Justinian*. Vols. 1–4. University of Pennsylvania Press, 1998.

Secondary Sources

Alexy, Robert. *The Argument from Injustice: A Reply to Legal Positivism*. Oxford University Press, 2002.

———. "Some Reflections on the Ideal Dimension of Law and on the Legal Philosophy of John Finnis." *The American Journal of Jurisprudence* 58, no. 2 (2013): 97–110.

———. "The Dual Nature of Law." In *Law's Ideal Dimension*. Oxford University Press, 2021.

———. "Law, Morality, and the Existence of Human Rights." In *Law's Ideal Dimension*. Oxford University Press, 2021.

Arnaud, André-Jean. "Fact as Law." In *Semiotics, Law and Social Science*, edited by Domenico Cardozo and Bernard S. Jackson. Gangemi Editore, 1985.

———. "Juridicité." In *Dictionnaire encyclopédique de théorie et de sociologie du droit*, edited by André-Jean Arnaud. Librairie Générale de Droit et de Jurisprudence, 1993.

Baur, Michael. "Law and Natural Law." In *The Oxford Handbook of Aquinas*, edited by Brian Davies and Eleonore Stump. Oxford University Press, 2012.

Bertea, Stefano. "The Dual Nature Thesis as a Cornerstone of Jurisprudence." *The American Journal of Jurisprudence* 67, no. 1 (2022): 57–82.

Bix, Brian H. "Joseph Raz and Conceptual Analysis." *APA Newsletter on Philosophy of Law* 6, no. 2 (2007): 1–7.

Brett, Annabel S. *Liberty, Right, and Nature: Individual Rights in Later Scholastic Thought*. Cambridge University Press, 1997.

Brock, Stephen L. *The Light That Binds: A Study in Thomas Aquinas's Metaphysics of Natural Law*. Pickwick Publications 2020.

Budziszewski, J. *Companion to the Commentary on Thomas Aquinas's Treatise on Law*. Cambridge University Press, 2014. https://www.cambridge.org/gb/files/1814/0898 /2129/ 9781107029392online.pdf.

Burazin, Luka, Kenneth Einar Himma, and Corrado Roversi, eds. *Law as an Artifact*. Oxford University Press, 2018.

Butchvarov, Panayot. "Metaphysics." In *The Cambridge Dictionary of Philosophy*, edited by Robert Audi. 3rd ed. Cambridge University Press, 2015.

Casey, Conor. "Continuity and Evolution in Vermeule on Legal Interpretation." *The American Journal of Jurisprudence* 69, no. 1 (2024): 29–43.

Casey, Conor, and Adrian Vermeule. "Myths of Common Good Constitutionalism." *Harvard Journal of Law & Public Policy* 45, no. 1 (2022): 103–44.

Coyle, Sean. *Natural Law and Modern Society*. Oxford University Press, 2023.

Cruft, Rowan. *Human Rights, Ownership, and the Individual*. Oxford University Press, 2019.

Dickson, Julie. "Is the Rule of Recognition Really a Conventional Rule?" *Oxford Journal of Legal Studies* 27, no. 3 (2007): 373–402.

———. "Legal Positivism: Contemporary Debates." In *The Routledge Companion to Philosophy of Law*, edited by Andrei Marmor. Routledge, 2012.

———. "Law and Its Theory: A Question of Priorities." In *Reason, Morality and Law: The Philosophy of John Finnis*, edited by John Keown and Robert P. George. Oxford University Press, 2013.

———. *Elucidating Law*. Oxford University Press, 2022.

Duxbury, Neil. "Juridicity as a Theme in French Legal Philosophy." *International Journal for the Semiotics of Law* 2, no. 1 (1989): 85–95.

Dworkin, Ronald. *Taking Rights Seriously*. 2nd ed. Harvard University Press, 1978.

———. "'Natural Law' Revisited." *University of Florida Law Review* 34, no. 2 (1982): 165–88.

———. "A Reply by Ronald Dworkin." In *Ronald Dworkin and Contemporary Jurisprudence*, edited by Marshall Cohen. Duckworth, 1984.

———. *Law's Empire*. The Belknap Press of Harvard University Press, 1986.

———. "On Gaps in the Law." In *Controversies about Law's Ontology*, edited by Neil MacCormick and Paul Amselek. Edinburgh University Press, 1991.

———. *Justice in Robes*. The Belknap Press of Harvard University Press, 2006.

———. *Justice for Hedgehogs*. The Belknap Press of Harvard University Press, 2011.

Dyzenhaus, David. "Dworkin and Unjust Law." In *The Legacy of Ronald Dworkin*, edited by Wil Waluchow and Stefan Sciaraffa. Oxford University Press, 2016.

Endicott, Timothy A. O. *Vagueness in Law*. Oxford University Press, 2000.

Errázuriz, Carlos José. *Il diritto come bene giuridico: Un'introduzione alla filosofia del diritto*. EDUSC, 2021.

———. *Cos'è il diritto divino nella Chiesa? Essenza e rilevanza pratica*. EDUSC, 2025.

Ezcurdia, Maite. "The Concept—Content Distinction." *Philosophical Issues* 9 (1998): 187–92.

Finnis, John. "Un ouvrage récent sur Bentham." *Archives de philosophie du droit* 17 (1972): 423–27.

———. *Moral Absolutes: Tradition, Revision, and Truth*. The Catholic University of America Press, 1991.

———. *Aquinas: Moral, Political, and Legal Theory*. Oxford University Press, 1998.

———. "Aquinas on Ius and Hart on Rights: A Response to Tierney." *The Review of Politics* 64, no. 3 (2002): 407–10.

———. *Natural Law and Natural Rights*. 2nd ed. Oxford University Press, 2011.

———. "'Natural Law.'" In *Collected Essays*. Vol. 1, *Reason in Action*. Oxford University Press, 2011.

———. "Reason, Authority, and Friendship." In *Collected Essays*. Vol. 1, *Reason in Action*. Oxford University Press, 2011.

———. "Describing Law Normatively." In *Collected Essays*. Vol. 4, *Philosophy of Law*. Oxford University Press, 2011.

———. "A Grand Tour of Legal Theory." In *Collected Essays*. Vol. 4, *Philosophy of Law*. Oxford University Press, 2011.

———. "Legal Philosophy: Roots and Recent Themes." In *Collected Essays*. Vol. 4, *Philosophy of Law*. Oxford University Press, 2011.

———. "The Truth in Legal Positivism." In *Collected Essays*. Vol. 4, *Philosophy of Law*. Oxford University Press, 2011.

———. "On Hart's Ways: Law as Reason and as Fact." In *Collected Essays*. Vol. 4, *Philosophy of Law*. Oxford University Press, 2011.

———. "Natural Law Theory: Its Past and Its Present." *The American Journal of Jurisprudence* 57, no. 1 (2012): 81–101.

———. "Coexisting Normative Orders? Yes, but No." *The American Journal of Jurisprudence* 57, no. 1 (2012): 111–17.

———. "Reflections and Responses." In *Reason, Morality and Law: The Philosophy of John Finnis*, edited by John Keown and Robert P. George. Oxford University Press, 2013.

———. "What Is the Philosophy of Law?" *The American Journal of Jurisprudence* 59, no. 2 (2014): 133–42.

———. "Law as Fact and as Reason for Action: A Response to Robert Alexy on Law's Ideal Dimension." *The American Journal of Jurisprudence* 59, no. 1 (2014): 85–109.

———. "Grounding Human Rights in Natural Law." *The American Journal of Jurisprudence* 60, no. 2 (2015): 199–225.

———. "Aquinas and Natural Law Jurisprudence." In *The Cambridge Companion to Natural Law Jurisprudence*, edited by George Duke and Robert P. George. Cambridge University Press, 2017.

———. "On Moyn's Christian Human Rights." *King's Law Journal* 28, no. 1 (2017): 12–20.

———. "Natural Law Theories." In *The Stanford Encyclopedia of Philosophy* (Summer 2020 ed.), edited by Edward N. Zalta. https://plato.stanford.edu/archives/sum2020/ entries/natural-law-theories/.

———. "Aquinas's Moral, Political, and Legal Philosophy." In *The Stanford Encyclopedia of Philosophy* (Spring 2021 ed.), edited by Edward N. Zalta. https://plato.stanford.edu/entries/aquinas-moral-political/.

Flores, Imer B. "The Problem about the Nature of Law vis-à-vis Legal Rationality Revisited: Towards an Integrative Jurisprudence." In *Philosophical Foundations of the Nature of Law*, edited by Wil Waluchow and Stefan Sciaraffa. Oxford University Press, 2013.

Froelich, Gregory. "The Equivocal Status of *Bonum Commune*." *The New Scholasticism* 63, no. 1 (1989): 38–57.

Gardner, John. "Legal Positivism: 5½ Myths." In *Law as a Leap of Faith*. Oxford University Press, 2012.

———. "Some Types of Law." In *Law as a Leap of Faith*. Oxford University Press, 2012.

———. "Hart on Legality, Justice, and Morality." In *Law as a Leap of Faith*. Oxford University Press, 2012.

———. "The Virtue of Justice and the Character of Law." In *Law as a Leap of Faith*. Oxford University Press, 2012.

Geach, Peter. *The Virtues*. Cambridge University Press, 1979.

George, Robert P. Introduction. In *Reason, Morality and Law: The Philosophy of John Finnis*, edited by John Keown and Robert P. George. Oxford University Press, 2013.

Giudice, Michael. *Understanding the Nature of Law: A Case for Constructive Conceptual Explanation*. Edward Elgar, 2015.

Gorsuch, Neil M. "Intention and the Allocation of Risk." In *Reason, Morality and Law: The Philosophy of John Finnis*, edited by John Keown and Robert P. George. Oxford University Press, 2013.

Green, Leslie. "General Jurisprudence: A 25th Anniversary Essay." *Oxford Journal of Legal Studies* 25, no. 4 (2005): 565–80.

———. "Positivism, Realism and Sources of Law." In *The Cambridge Companion to Legal Positivism*, edited by Torben Spaak and Patricia Mindus. Cambridge University Press, 2021.

———. Introduction. In *The Germ of Justice: Essays in General Jurisprudence*. Oxford University Press, 2023.

———. "The Inseparability of Law and Morals." In *The Germ of Justice: Essays in General Jurisprudence*. Oxford University Press, 2023.

Guzmán Brito, Alejandro. "Historia de la denominación del derecho-facultad como subjetivo." *Revista de Estudios Histórico-Jurídicos* 25 (2003): 407–43.

———. *El Derecho como facultad en la neoescolástica española del siglo XVI*. Iustel, 2009.

Hart, H. L. A. "Are There Any Natural Rights?" *The Philosophical Review* 64, no. 2 (1955): 175–91.

———. *Essays on Bentham: Studies in Jurisprudence and Political Theory*. Oxford University Press, 1982.

———. Introduction. In *Essays in Jurisprudence and Philosophy*. Oxford University Press, 1983.

———. "Definition and Theory in Jurisprudence." In *Essays in Jurisprudence and Philosophy*. Oxford University Press, 1983.

———. *The Concept of Law*. 3rd ed. Oxford University Press, 2012.

Hennig, Boris. *Aristotle's Four Causes*. Peter Lang, 2019.

Hervada, Javier. *Lecciones propedéuticas de filosofía del derecho*. 4th ed. EUNSA, 2008.

———. *Critical Introduction to Natural Right*. Translated by Mindy Emmons. 2nd ed. Wilson & Lafleur Ltée, 2020.

Hittinger, Russell. *A Critique of the New Natural Law Theory*. University of Notre Dame Press, 1987.

———. "Varieties of Minimalist Natural Law Theory." *The American Journal of Jurisprudence* 34, no. 1 (1989): 133–70.

———. "Liberalism and the American Natural Law Tradition." *Wake Forest Law Review* 25 (1990): 429–99.

———. "The Coherence of the Four Basic Principles of Catholic Social Doctrine: An Interpretation." In *On the Dignity of Society: Catholic Social Teaching and Natural Law*. The Catholic University of America Press, 2024.

Hohfeld, Wesley Newcomb. "The Relations between Equity and Law." *Michigan Law Review* 11, no. 8 (1913): 537–71.

———. *Fundamental Legal Conceptions as Applied in Judicial Reasoning and Other Legal Essays*. Yale University Press, 1919.

Honoré, Anthony M. "Rights of Exclusion and Immunities Against Divesting." *Tulane Law Review* 34 (1959–1960): 453–68.

———. *Making Law Bind: Essays Legal and Philosophical*. Oxford University Press, 1987.

Jensen, Steven J. *Knowing the Natural Law: From Precepts and Inclinations to Deriving Oughts*. The Catholic University of America Press, 2015.

Kelsen, Hans. "The Natural-Law Doctrine before the Tribunal of Science." In *What Is Justice? Justice, Law, and Politics in the Mirror of Science: Collected Essays by Hans Kelsen*. University of California Press, 1971.

———. "Law, State, and Justice in the Pure Theory of Law." In *What Is Justice? Justice, Law, and Politics in the Mirror of Science: Collected Essays by Hans Kelsen*. University of California Press, 1971.

———. *Pure Theory of Law*. Translated by M. Knight. University of California Press, 2005.

———. *General Theory of Law & State*. Transaction Publishers, 2006.

Kempshall, Matthew S. *The Common Good in Late Medieval Political Thought*. Clarendon Press, 1999.

Köpcke, Maris. "Finnis on Legal and Moral Obligation." In *Reason, Morality and Law: The Philosophy of John Finnis*, edited by John Keown and Robert P. George. Oxford University Press, 2013.

———. *Legal Validity: The Fabric of Justice*. Hart Publishing, 2019.

Kretzmann, Norman. "Lex Iniusta Non Est Lex: Laws on Trial in Aquinas's Court of Conscience." *The American Journal of Jurisprudence* 33, no. 1 (1988): 99–122.

Legge, Dominic. "Do Thomists Have Rights?" *Nova et Vetera* (English edition) 17, no. 1 (2019): 127–47.

Leiter, Brian. "Legal Indeterminacy." *Legal Theory* 1, no. 4 (1995): 481–92.

———. "Why Legal Positivism." University of Chicago Public Law and Legal Theory Working Paper No. 298, December 14, 2009. https://dx.doi.org/10.2139/ssrn.1521761.

———. “Why Legal Positivism (Again).” University of Chicago Public Law and Legal Theory Working Paper No. 442, September 10, 2013. https://dx.doi.org/10.2139/ssrn.2323013.

———. “The Demarcation Problem in Jurisprudence: A New Case for Scepticism.” *Oxford Journal of Legal Studies* 31, no. 4 (2011): 663–77.

Lewis, V. Bradley. “Catholic Social Teaching on the Common Good.” In *Catholic Social Teaching: A Volume of Scholarly Essays*, edited by Gerard V. Bradley and E. Christian Brugger, 235–66. Cambridge University Press, 2019.

MacCormick, Neil. Foreword. In *Controversies about Law's Ontology*, edited by Neil MacCormick and Paul Amselek. Edinburgh University Press, 1991.

Mackie, John L. *Ethics: Inventing Right and Wrong*. Penguin Books, 1977.

McCall, Brian M. *The Architecture of Law: Rebuilding Law in the Classical Tradition*. University of Notre Dame Press, 2018.

Miller, Paul B. “Equity as Supplemental Law.” In *Philosophical Foundations of the Law of Equity*, edited by Dennis Klimchuk, Irit Samet, and Henry E. Smith. Oxford University Press, 2020.

Moreland, Michael P. “Friendship as the Primary Purpose of Law.” *The American Journal of Jurisprudence* 67, no. 2 (2022): 279–92.

Padovani, Andrea. “Birth of a Legal Category: Subjective Rights.” *Divus Thomas* 116, no. 3 (2013): 37–53.

Popović, Petar. “Natural Juridical Goods: The Juridical Status of Basic Human Goods in Aquinas's Jusnaturalist Philosophy.” In *The Goodness of Rights and the Juridical Domain of the Good: Essays in Thomistic Juridical Realism*. EDUSC, 2021.

———. “Rawls's Juridical Constructivism Revisited: Priority of law and Rights over Ideas of the Good.” *Revus: Journal for Constitutional Theory and Philosophy of Law* 43 (2021): 113–34.

———. *Natural Law & Thomistic Juridical Realism: Prospects for a Dialogue with Contemporary Legal Theory*. The Catholic University of America Press, 2022.

———. “And Then There Were Two: Further Remarks on Identifying the Core Question in the Hart-Dworkin Debate.” *Rivista di filosofia del diritto* 11, no. 2 (2022): 415–34.

———. “Hart on the Role of Justice in the Concept of Law: Some Further Remarks.” *Jurisprudence* 13, no. 4 (2022): 489–515.

———. “Both Directions at Once? A Thomistic Response to the Artifactual Theory of Law.” In *The Artifactual Nature of Law*, edited by Luka Burazin, Kenneth Einar Himma, Corrado Roversi, and Paweł Banaś. Edward Elgar, 2022.

———. “Reading Finnis and Aquinas on Justice as the Evaluative Standard for Positive Law.” *The American Journal of Jurisprudence* 68, no. 1 (2023): 63–75.

———. "Le norme prese sul serio nel giusnaturalismo neoclassico: La necessità della legge positive secondo John Finnis e il giusrealismo tomista." *Ius Ecclesiae* 35, no. 1 (2023): 83–108.

———. "Are There Any Elements of Juridicity beyond Positive Law in Robert Alexy's Non-Positivism?" *Revus: Journal for Constitutional Theory and Philosophy of Law* 49, no. 1 (2023): 87–105.

———. "The Concept of *Ius* in Thomas Aquinas: Analysis of Central Texts and Sources." In *The Concept of Ius and the Nature of Law in Thomas Aquinas*, edited by Loïc-Marie Le Bot and Petar Popović. The Catholic University of America Press, 2025.

Priel, Dan. "The Misguided Search for the Nature of Law." Osgoode Legal Studies Research Paper No. 34, August 13, 2015. https://dx.doi.org/10.2139/ssrn.2642461.

Radbruch, Gustav. "Statutory Lawlessness and Supra-Statutory Law (1946)." *Oxford Journal of Legal Studies* 26, no. 1 (2006): 1–11.

———. "Five Minutes of Legal Philosophy (1945)." *Oxford Journal of Legal Studies* 26, no. 1 (2006): 13–15.

Raz, Joseph. "The Nature of Rights." In *The Morality of Freedom*. Oxford University Press, 1986.

———. "Legal Rights." In *Ethics in the Public Domain: Essays in the Morality of Law and Politics*. Oxford University Press, 1994.

———. "Can There Be a Theory of Law?" In *Between Authority and Interpretation: On the Theory of Law and Practical Reason*. Oxford University Press, 2009.

———. "Two Views of the Nature of the Theory of Law: A Partial Comparison." In *Between Authority and Interpretation: On the Theory of Law and Practical Reason*. Oxford University Press, 2009.

———. "On the Nature of Law." In *Between Authority and Interpretation: On the Theory of Law and Practical Reason*. Oxford University Press, 2009.

———. "About Morality and the Nature of Law." In *Between Authority and Interpretation: On the Theory of Law and Practical Reason*. Oxford University Press, 2009.

———. "Kelsen's Theory of the Basic Norm." In *The Authority of Law: Essays on Law and Morality*. 2nd ed. Oxford University Press, 2011.

———. "The Argument from Justice, or How Not to Reply to Legal Positivism." In *The Authority of Law: Essays on Law and Morality*. 2nd ed. Oxford University Press, 2011.

Roniger, Scott. "Natural Law and Friendship with God." *The Thomist* 83, no. 2 (2019): 237–76.

Roversi, Corrado. "Ontology of Law." In *Encyclopedia of the Philosophy of Law and Social Philosophy*, edited by Mortimer Sellers and Stephan Kirste. Springer, 2018. https://doi.org/10.1007/978-94-007-6730-0_59-1.

Russell, J. S. "Trial by Slogan: Natural Law and Lex Iniusta Non Est Lex." *Law and Philosophy* 19, no. 4 (2000): 433–49.

Schauer, Frederick. "On the Nature of the Nature of Law." *Archiv für Rechts- und Sozialphilosophie* 98, no. 4 (2012): 457–67.

———. "Law's Boundaries." *Harvard Law Review* 130, no. 9 (2017): 2434–62.

Schouppe, Jean-Pierre. *Le réalisme juridique*. E. Story-Scientia, 1987.

———. "Réflexions sur la conception du droit de M. Villey: une alternative à son rejet des droits de l'homme." *Persona y Derecho* 25 (1991): 151–69.

Sériaux, Alain. "Res clamat domino." In *Un droit en perpétuel mouvement: Mélanges offerts à Geneviève Pignarre*, edited by Christophe Albiges et al. LGDJ, 2018.

Simmonds, Nigel. "Puzzles of Rights." *The American Journal of Jurisprudence* 65, no. 2 (2020): 181–201.

Simmonds, Nigel, and Joshua Neoh. *Central Issues in Jurisprudence*. Sweet & Maxwell, 2022.

Simon, Yves-René. *The Tradition of Natural Law: A Philosopher's Reflection*. Fordham University Press, 1992.

Sol, Thierry. "La notion de droit subjectif chez Villey et Hervada." *Ius Ecclesiae* 28, no. 2 (2016): 323–44.

Solum, Lawrence B. "On the Indeterminacy Crisis: Critiquing Critical Dogma." *The University of Chicago Law Review* 54, no. 2 (1987): 462–503.

———. "A Virtue-Centered Account of Equity and the Rule of Law." In *Virtue Jurisprudence*, edited by Colin Farrelly and Lawrence B. Solum. Palgrave Macmillan, 2008.

———. "Virtue as the End of Law: An Aretaic Theory of Legislation." *Jurisprudence* 9, no. 1 (2018): 6–18.

Stavropoulos, Nicos. "The Debate That Never Was." *Harvard Law Review* 130, no. 8 (2017): 2082–95.

Stoljar, Natalie. "What Do We Want Law to Be? Philosophical Analysis and the Concept of Law." In *Philosophical Foundations of the Nature of Law*, edited by Wil Waluchow and Stefan Sciaraffa. Oxford University Press, 2013.

Tamanaha, Brian. "What Is 'General' Jurisprudence? A Critique of Universalistic Claims by Philosophical Concepts of Law." *Transnational Legal Theory* 2, no. 3 (2011): 287–308.

Tan, Seow Hon. *Justice as Friendship: A Theory of Law*. Routledge, 2016.

Tarello, Giovanni. *L'interpretazione della legge*. Giuffrè, 1980.

Tasioulas, John. "'Law as the Art of Justice': On Vermeule's *Common Good*

Constitutionalism." *The American Journal of Jurisprudence* 69, no. 1 (2024): 61–76.

Tierney, Brian. "Villey, Ockham and the Origin of Individual Rights." In *The Idea of Natural Rights: Studies on Natural Rights, Natural Law and Church Law 1150–1625*. Scholars Press, 1997.

———. "Natural Law and Natural Rights: Old Problems and Recent Approaches." *The Review of Politics* 64, no. 3 (2002): 389–406.

———. "Author's Rejoinder." *The Review of Politics* 64, no. 3 (2002): 416–20.

Treggiari, Ferdinando. "Il lessico giuridico della povertà: Ideale minoritico e diritto nel primo secolo dopo Francesco." *Ius Ecclesiae* 32, no. 2 (2020): 549–78.

Veech, Max L., and Charles R. Moon. "De Minimis Non Curat Lex." *Michigan Law Review* 45, no. 5 (1947): 537–70.

Vermeule, Adrian. *Common Good Constitutionalism: Recovering the Classical Legal Tradition*. Polity, 2022.

———. "The Bourbons of Jurisprudence." Harvard Public Law Working Paper No. 22-31, August 22, 2022. https://papers.ssrn.com/sol3/papers.cfm?abstract_id=4192796.

———. "Common Good as a Legal Concept." *Ius & Iustitium* (blog). November 16, 2022. https://iusetiustitium.com/the-common-good-as-a-legal-concept.

Vigo Ferrera, Santiago. *"Apud nos dicitur aequitas": L'equità quale giustizia nella tradizione giuridica realista*. Giuffrè Francis Lefebvre, 2023.

Villey, Michel. "Droit subjectif I (La genèse du droit subjectif chez Guillaume d'Occam)." In *Seize Essais de philosophie du droit dont un sur la crise universitaire*. Dalloz, 1969.

———. "Si la théorie générale du droit, pour Saint Thomas, est une théorie de la loi." *Archives de philosophie du droit* 17 (1972): 427–31.

———. "Sur les essais d'application de la logique déontique au droit." *Archives de philosophie du droit* 17 (1972): 407–12.

———. *Philosophie du droit*. Vol. 1, *Définitions et fins du droit*. 2nd ed. Dalloz, 1978.

———. *La formation de la pensée juridique moderne*. Presses Universitaires de France, 2013.

Viola, Francesco. *Il diritto come pratica sociale*. Jaca Book, 1990.

———. "Introduction: Natural Law Theories in the 20th Century." In *A Treatise of Legal Philosophy and General Jurisprudence Legal Philosophy in the Twentieth Century*, vol. 12, *Legal Philosophy in the Twentieth Century—The Civil Law World (Tome 2: Main Orientations and Topics)*, edited by Enrico Pattaro and Corrado Roversi. Springer, 2016.

———. "Positivizzazione del diritto tra immanenza e trascendenza." In *Verità e prassi tra immanenza e trascendenza: Prospettive di etica, politica e diritto*, edited by Tommaso Allodi, Elvio Ancona, and Shaban Zanelli. Perugia Stranieri University Press, 2020.

Waldron, Jeremy. "What Is Natural Law Like?" In *Reason, Morality and Law: The Philosophy of John Finnis*, edited by John Keown and Robert P. George. Oxford University Press, 2013.

Webber, Grégoire. "Asking Why in the Study of Human Affairs." *The American Journal of Jurisprudence* 60, no. 1 (2015): 51–78.

Index

Exploring the Nature of Law: Thomistic Juridical Realism and the Elements of Law's Ontology was designed in Minion with Open Sans display type and composed by Reflective Book Design of Durham, North Carolina.